My Billion Year Contract

My Billion Year Contract

MEMOIR OF A FORMER SCIENTOLOGIST

Nancy Many

Library of Congress Control Number: 2009908640
ISBN: Softcover   978-0-578-03922-0

Cover Design by Jefferson Hawkins

To order additional copies of this book, contact:
www.MyBillionYearContract.com

CNM Publishing
1-818-885-9921

Contents

This book is dedicated to my husband and love of my life, Christopher

In Memory of
Lisa McPherson
1959-1995
and
Greg Bashaw
1954-2001

Preface

IN 2005, THANKS to Tom Cruise, Scientology was part of the daily news. Whether it was his romance with Katie Holmes, his couch jumping, or his attacks on Matt Lauer regarding psychiatry, the subject of Scientology seemed to be everywhere. My twenty-year involvement with Scientology involved overseeing the international expansion of the group, years of espionage for them, and well over seven years working with their celebrities and celebrities they wanted to make into Scientologists. I also spent time in their Rehabilitation Project Force. The constant chatter about Scientology dredged up many memories for me. A person who is sent for rehabilitation is there until one gets one's mind back on track with Scientology. This project force is an experience that only the most dedicated members, only those of us who had signed a one billion year contract, are allowed to receive. I suspected that Tom was not aware of all that Scientology feels about psychiatry (that it is the sole cause of the decline in this part of the universe) and that these evil people (psychiatrists) have simply been reincarnating over and over with the prime purpose of wreaking havoc on our otherwise lovely planet, Earth.

I was hesitant to attempt to write my memoir. At the time, I expressed in my journal, "There is currently so much press about Scientology and Tom Cruise. It brings up for me this entire other side of what Scientology is, and I just want to fling the story out there. I want to write about the Rehabilitation Project Forces where people are guarded constantly until their thinking 'comes right.' I want to call the press and let them know that Katie Holmes is being baby sat to make sure that no negativity about Scientology reaches her ears. She is at a delicate point in her Scientology indoctrination and could easily be swayed away. Tom is spouting these attacks on psychiatry, Brooke Shields, and others. I just want to let the people know that Scientology has driven people crazy, that Scientology carries some responsibility in the deaths of Lisa McPherson and Greg Bashaw." I continued, "I want to let it be known that Scientology has a multi-year plan for world domination and for the adulation of L. Ron Hubbard as the next messiah for planet Earth.

"I want to spit it all out in a rush of truth. The desire to speak comes in a garbled mishmash of emotions and memories. I find myself with an urge to throw up and recognize it as the day I had hours and hours of dry heaves while being interrogated, locked away in a 'counseling' room at Scientology's international headquarters. My spirit is enveloped with a wave of fear of things they can do, things they have done to others, things they have already done to me, and things that can come to me.

"My mind is racing a million miles a minute and I fear I could not clearly get what happened to me out. Then it would be worse. I would have tried to communicate and failed. I want to speak the truth as I have seen it and uncover the areas of truth that Tom Cruise and others have been so carefully shielded from."

Despite my reservations, I actually wrote my memoir at that time. It sat on a shelf for a few years until one night, several months ago, I received a phone call from a woman I had known. She had read the story I have posted on the

Internet under the pseudonym of Kathryn. She was driving around my block, working up the courage to call me and felt she had nowhere else to go. She had been a member of Scientology for thirty-six years and had given them hundreds of thousands of dollars. She was supposed to go back into one of their higher-level centers in a day or two. She had reached the highest level of Scientology counseling available today (called Operating Thetan [OT] Level 8). She was suicidal and felt that if she reported in she would have an experience similar to mine and end up losing her mind.

We spoke for hours, and she eventually made her decision to leave the group and move to another city. The relief she felt in making that decision was palpable. She went to work on changing her life.

I took my memoir off the shelf.

Chapter 1

Opposite Day

IT WAS AFTER midnight when I carefully sat up in bed and slowly untied the sash my husband had tied around my ankle. I knew he had connected our ankles so he would be awakened if I got up in the middle of the night, but I also knew he didn't understand the truth of what was going on. If he woke, he would only try to stop me from the work I had to do, the planning and preparation I had to do this night. I was now certain that Captain Bill had been right in his theories and views. The alien race, the Marcabians, had indeed taken over the management of Scientology. Captain Bill was once a high-ranking, long-standing member of Scientology, and he told me that the Marcabians had placed invisible "tepaphones" on top of the big blue Scientology complex in Los Angeles. It was through their use that the aliens practiced mind control of human beings, especially the members of Scientology who had reached the higher OT levels. It all made sense now. It had been the intention of Scientology all along that I lose my mind. This also explained why the staff of the upper level Scientology center the International Office of Special Affairs (OSA) were so coldhearted to my pain these past weeks. They were either aliens themselves or controlled by the aliens.

It was clear to me that OSA had no intention of helping me; in fact, they were hoping I would completely drown in my anguish and confusion.

I quietly made my way to the kitchen to make a cup of tea. It was 3 AM, and I had a lot to do. I knew tomorrow was the most important day of my life. A battle would be fought. Win or lose, it would be over by two in the afternoon. I wanted to win and felt I had enough allies and support to achieve the victory I desperately needed.

I took the cup of lemon tea to my desk and turned on the computer and small desk lamp. The hum from my space heater and my curled-up dog kept me company. I knew I needed to list my resources before I could have a solid plan. This was a clash between the damned and the faithful

I made a general plan of how I would survive the large spiritual attack I felt was coming with the dawn of the next day. For some reason, the time of 2:00 PM stuck in my mind as the cutoff time. If I could last until two, all would be well and I would have won this pivotal battle. I did not understand why this Wednesday was the deadline; I just knew it was. I didn't know exactly the form the conflict would take, but I knew it would start in the morning and if I could last until two P.M. the major danger would pass.

I listed the people I felt could give me helpful energy, either directly or indirectly through prayers. This would give me the good energy I would need to go into battle against these alien demons. I placed my allies in order of phone calls and planned the sequence of actions as best I could. I knew some things would unfold in ways I couldn't predict; I had to be ready for however they would develop.

I was not certain upon which side Mick Wenlock fell on. We had worked together years earlier in Scientology, and he was a friend of mine. Through our recent email conversations, he had made it clear that he had left Scientology. During the intense interrogations that Scientology subjected me to for several weeks prior to my mental breakdown, his name had come up often and I questioned just what side he was on. Part of my plan was an e-mail that I wrote and sent to him that night. The intent was to shake Mick up if he was working in concert with Scientology's intelligence unit and the Marcabian aliens.

After a few hours' work, I quietly crawled back into bed and retied my ankle to my husband's. I did not want him questioning me in the morning. It was going to be a busy day.

I woke up as usual and got the kids off to school. Chris left for work. I attempted to act as normally as I could in front of my family. I didn't want concern to get in the way of my master plan. This was as much for their survival as for my own, although they were unaware of the danger.

One of the first calls I made was to Chris's parents, who were born-again Christians from upstate New York. My father-in-law had spoken to his minister and read me a quote from the Bible, something about the *sons*. Things began to click; I realized they were after *my* sons. This was it. *This* was the part I hadn't predicted or seen the night before. I hung up the phone, frantic over how I could protect them. My stepson was older and had not lived with us for several years. He now lived on the other side of town; I didn't feel any danger surrounding him. My oldest son was at a Catholic high school, and I knew it had so much daily prayer that there was a protective bubble. The principal, Sister Lucille, had strong faith and that faith would be protecting my son Carey.

As I paced our small living room, balloons from a weekend party began to burst on their own. I could feel the negative electric energy building and knew I was close to deciphering their plan by the sound of the balloons popping.

OK, so Carey and Corey are safe, I said to myself, calming down about them. My pacing continued, and suddenly more balloons exploded when I started to think of my youngest son, Taylor. He was nine years old and in a public elementary school down the street; he was not safe, not at all.

My mind raced. I had to get him out of that school *now* and under some sort of protection. I realized I could not go myself: that would bring the evil ones right to him. Already the energy in the room was darkening and rustling with intensity. I knew it was not my imagination because balloons continued to pop, balloons that neither my dogs nor I were near.

The school was only a block from our recording studio; I could call the studio manager, Regina! I dialed the phone; and while keeping my voice very calm, I told her Taylor needed to be picked up and brought home right away and could she please go to the school, sign Taylor out, and drive him home for me. It was close, and she promised to do it.

I hung up, relieved but still frantic. What if Regina didn't get there in time? What if the school wouldn't release him to her?

During the last two weeks, I had seen my three Siberian huskies fend off the evil energy; I knew they could offer some protection. I felt such urgency I couldn't wait any longer. I put two of them on their leashes and hurried outside, hoping to meet Regina and Taylor.

As I raced down the street, my two Siberians pulling me, I spotted Regina at a halfway point. She didn't mention my running toward them or judge me. I just *knew* she was on our side (whether she was aware of it or not). I hugged her and thanked her for picking up my son. Then Taylor, the dogs, and I went quickly back to our home.

We needed a distraction. I did not want Taylor to be upset; I wanted him to think it was a fun time. We started to play a game we named opposite day, doing things the opposite of how we would normally do them.

Suddenly I felt a dark energy swirling through the house. I knew at once we had to get out. I heard the *pop pop pop* of exploding balloons, and I knew the energy was growing. Our two black dogs were yelping wildly. We had to move quickly. This time we took Sasha, our red husky, and some Magic: The Gathering cards to play with. I brought the house's portable phone with me, just in case I needed to contact someone else on my list. Since it was opposite day, we climbed out the window instead of using the door.

As my young son and I walked through the streets of Burbank, I could see *them* circling the streets around our house; their cars had a different feel to them. Sometimes as we sat on the curb to play cards, a slow moving car would pass by. The driver would look at us sitting with our red dog. I would notice the driver's spark of recognition before his car moved on to turn the corner. Trying not to spread my fear, I simply told Taylor we needed to get up and keep walking.

We soon arrived at a large intersection; and some people, two women and a man, happened to park their car right where we were standing on the sidewalk. They came around to speak with us and admire the dog. I knew they were pawns. I could actually see the aliens moving in and out of control of their simple bodies and see them focusing on Taylor. I looked down at my portable phone and realized *that* was how they had tracked us; I quickly threw the phone into the bushes.

I was frightened and panicky. My thoughts were racing, but I had to calm them in order to get a fast plan to save my son. I realized that if they could switch bodies, so could I. The best thing for me to do was to act like my nine-year-old son and they would come after me instead of him.

I grabbed the dog's leash and ran into the street wildly, like a kid would. I completely expected to be hit by a car. If they bought the idea that we had switched bodies and my body got hit, then my son would be safe.

I was surprised to arrive safe and sound on the other side. Nothing had happened; no car had hit me. I stood there confused for a moment or two. I saw that Taylor was still on the other side of the busy intersection with those scary people. He was still in danger. They were looking at me, but I could see they had him surrounded. Taylor was standing motionless, silently staring at me. *What to do? What to do?* My mind raced, scanning the streets for an answer.

I noticed I was near a McDonald's restaurant with a kid's fun room in the front and ran toward it. I had to keep them thinking I or my body was Taylor. I ran into the McDonald's and crawled into the round entrance of the ball room. I had forgotten the dog was still with me, still connected by a leash. She crawled in with me.

I sat in the center of the balls with my dog attached to my arm. I felt the surprised energy in the restaurant. I could see through plastic walls the blurry faces of ordinary patrons staring at me in stunned silence. There were a couple of kids who had been playing in the ball room; they did not come near me. Suddenly the McDonald's manager's head broke into the small entrance of the ball room. He was on all fours kneeling outside, and only his head was inside the cramped space where I was sitting with my dog.

"Ma'am, you can't be in here . . . No adults are allowed in the play area and no dogs in the restaurant." He barely blurted it out, his face turning red.

That's when I noticed I still had our dog Sasha with me. I had no idea what my next move should be; my mind was empty.

Taylor's head poked through the small round exit hole on the right.

"Come on, Mom, let's go!"

I looked from the manager's face poking in the left entrance hole to my nine-year-olds in the right exit hole. The manager's face was so red I thought it would explode. My son's was white and pained.

My son put out his hand to me. *"Mom, you have to get out of there."*

I could see through the blurry plastic that Taylor was alone; the three people who had been after him were gone.

I was elated. It had worked. He was safe and he was alone, and since I had ditched the phone, I knew they couldn't track us any farther.

"C'mon, Mom." Taylor motioned his hand toward me.

I crawled out of the ball room, my dog following on her leash. I was about to push the alarm on the emergency exit when Taylor took my arm and guided me out the front door.

I scanned the streets and parking lots and no longer saw

the aliens. I had some sense of safety, but it was nowhere near 2:00 PM so I knew the danger wasn't over.

Taylor and I walked behind the 7-Eleven located next door, and I fell to the ground. I simply could not hold my body up. Taylor pulled on my arm.

"Mom, get up, please, Mom."

I could see he was really getting upset. His face was now flushed, and his eyes darted around to see if this embarrassing situation was being witnessed. I pulled on all the strength I had to get up. We walked in front of the 7-Eleven and around to the other side. I wasn't thinking anything; I was just following my young son's lead when I collapsed again. Try as I might, I could not stand up.

I had fallen partly on the walkway and partly in the street. Taylor pulled my arm, trying to get my body fully on the sidewalk.

Several bystanders came to help. I wasn't certain if they were the same three from across the street, but it didn't matter. I saw the alien/evil control beginning to move in and once again knew I had to take the attention off my son. I tried to get up but kept falling down. I truly had no physical strength. I yelled to my son, *"Call the king. Call the king!"* It was part of a game we had been playing earlier, and the king was in reference to his father at work. I noticed people standing above me, and I could hear whispering among them; their intentions were not good. The energy was dark. A man moved close to Taylor, and I knew he was from the dark. I started to thrash and make any motion I could.

From my position lying on the sidewalk, I noticed large tires and the red side of a fire engine. Men in blue were now around me, touching me, speaking to me. I tried to push them away.

"Ma'am, we're only trying to help you."

And then "You'll have to lie still, or we'll have to put you in restraints."

Restraints, I thought, *who cares about restraints! I'm trying to save my son!*

I heard the firefighters talking among themselves about me, but the energy was very different from the bystanders. I looked over to my right, and I saw my son's tears streaming down his face. I was heartbroken; he was so upset and didn't know what was happening. I could only imagine what was going through his mind. As I looked at him, I noticed that he was now with a policeman and, with tremendous relief, knew the policeman was one of the safe ones. He was a good soul, and Taylor was now protected.

I lay back down but felt an evil energy move through the bystander crowd and flow forward to get involved. I used all my strength to jump up and yell. I didn't understand when all I heard was noise and gibberish coming from my mouth.

"Are you on drugs? Ma'am, are you on drugs?"

I looked at the firefighter blankly. *He thinks I'm stoned.*

"Have you been drinking? Ma'am, have you been drinking?"

Well, of course, I thought, *he can't see the aliens. He has to think I'm hurting my son when the truth is I am saving his very being.*

One of the firemen said to another, "We're going to have to use the restraints."

I could tell by the sound of his voice that he was very sorry about it and I felt bad for him because he thought he was doing something bad to me. I actually was beyond caring about restraints. What difference would restraints make? I had no control over my body, and my mind was a swirling funnel of chaos.

The ambulance came, and I was lifted into it with one firefighter at my side. The door slammed close. The firefighter was angry and yelled at me, "How do you like it now?"

I blacked out.

When I came to, I was being wheeled into a hospital room, and there were doctors and nurses around my head and body.

"Ma'am, what's your name?"

"What day is it?"

"Do you know where you are?"

I just looked at them blankly. I could see a clock and knew it wasn't two yet, so I had to be very careful.

There were people in and out of the room, and I caught snippets of conversation but I was afraid to say anything. I was not certain where I was, but I was certain I was not safe.

I noticed a man at the door. The nurse said, "Your husband is here."

Husband? My husband, Chris? I don't know, is that really him? I don't know. I just looked at him.

"Nancy, it's me, Chris."

Chris. He looked like Chris. He did sound like Chris, but what if this was another trick? I beat them out at the McDonald's, who knows what they were going to do next.

Chris held my hand and said to the nurse who had noticed that I hadn't recognized him, "She wears glasses, she can't see without her glasses."

Glasses? Chris knew I wear contact lenses, why was he telling her I wear glasses?

I pulled him down so I could whisper in his ear.

"Is it safe?"

He brushed my cheek with his hand. "Yes, honey, it is safe, it's safe now."

I saw the clock just behind his head. It's only one o'clock; I knew it's not safe yet.

Regina appeared at the doorway. Chris talked briefly with her, returned to me with my glasses, and put them on my face. It looked like he also handed a bottle of prescription drugs to the two nurses standing in the corner. Now I really couldn't see. I did have my contacts on, and the addition of the strong prescription glasses made everything blurry. Chris left the room, and I could see the two nurses looking at the medicine bottle the Scientology doctor had prescribed me to "help" me the week before.

"*This* is what they gave her to help her sleep!" They laughed with each other as if it was the most ridiculous thing in the world. I had originally thought that the Scientology doctor was in on the plan, but now I knew it for sure.

Chris came back in the room to tell me that an old friend of mine and Kirsten from the intelligence department of Scientology International were in the hospital lobby.

"Don't let them come back here, please," I pled.

"Don't worry, they are not going to see you. They say they are only here to help."

I later found out that as a matter of policy, the prescribing physician (the Scientology doctor) had been notified about my collapse and mental state. She immediately alerted Scientology's Office of Special Affairs who sent people from their intelligence division to the hospital to prevent any psychiatric help or admission. At the time, I only knew that the people in the lobby were not there to help me no matter what they said to Chris.

It was getting closer to two and I now believed that Chris probably was Chris, and he had told me that our son Taylor and our red Siberian husky, Sasha, were safe. But I still heard the aliens using the hospital intercom, passing messages about me; I wondered why Chris couldn't hear them.

The nice nurse came over to the side of my bed.

"Don't you want the restraints taken off?"

I honestly didn't care about the restraints. I could barely feel them, but I could tell that she would like me to want to have them taken off.

"Sure," I answer.

"OK, now I just want to make sure you don't become combative again or we will have to put them back on." She had been such a wonderful nurse.

I looked at Chris standing next to me and I was 90 percent certain it's really him and I was safe.

"I'll be good."

The nurse moved to my side with a clipboard and pen. "Now I have to ask you a few questions, just answer as best you can."

With a little bit of prompting from Chris, I was able to answer the key questions to prevent a mandatory seventy-two-hour psychiatric hold. They included things like "Who are you?" "Where are you?" "What day is it?" "What did you eat for breakfast?" and the all-important "Do you know what happened?"

I must have passed because she had a smile on her face as she unbuckled the restraints.

Chris told me that the doctor wanted me to stay overnight at the hospital but that he's going to get me out of there by signing a paper saying that he was taking me out against medical advice.

"The doctor just wants to get you an MRI to make sure you don't have a brain tumor or something like that."

"Brain tumor?"

"They just need to check it out and then I'll take you home."

"OK."

I noticed that there was an older woman standing directly outside the door to my room. She never spoke nor entered the room. She would make eye contact with me, but I couldn't feel any negativity from her. I wondered who she was and what she was doing there. Perhaps she had been sent for protection.

As they wheeled me out of my small room to go to radiology, I sat up in my hospital bed and stared at her. She simply looked back, no bad energy, no good energy, simply a calming energy.

They wouldn't let Chris into the radiology room. I was very suspicious of the two male technicians. They shifted my body from the bed to the MRI platform. The platform moved my body so that my head entered what appeared to be a large white helmet. The two technicians went behind a screen, leaving me alone on the platform with my head inside this strange white machine. Suddenly I smelled chemicals. *Oh my god, it's gas.* The aliens were trying to get me to breathe in through the machine as a final effort to control me. But I knew at this point it was almost two o'clock and that if I could just hold my breath, this would be the last hurdle I would have to overcome.

I was wheeled back to the room I had been in. Chris signed the papers, and we finally left the hospital to head home. On the way, we made a short stop at the supermarket for milk and something for supper.

Chris parked the car and turned to me. "Will you be OK in there?"

I thought for a bit. Taylor and Chris were with me, the initial drug they had given me when I arrived at the hospital and they thought I had had a seizure had calmed me down somewhat, plus we were now past 2:00 PM, the critical hour.

"Yeah, I'll be fine, just stay close to me." Taylor sat in the cart as I pushed it with Chris standing next to me. Two elderly women came over to admire Taylor.

"What a nice-looking boy he is."

I felt my protective panic rising and was about to shoo them away but they turned and smiled at me. They had brilliant warm smiles, and I knew these two women were from the side of good. I also noticed something else: they both had dark ashes rubbed on their foreheads. I smiled back and pushed the cart forward. *Ash Wednesday, no wonder this happened today.* This had been such an intensely spiritual battle, and since I'd been so out of it these past couple of weeks, I had not realized that today was Ash Wednesday. Somehow, that calmed me and made the events more meaningful. I noticed several other people in the supermarket with ashes on their foreheads and felt much safer.

We paid for our groceries and went home. Chris got me safely to bed and then he called the Scientology doctor from the next room. I only heard the mumbles of the conversation, but after Chris hung up the phone, he came in and sat on the bed with me. He held my hands and looked deep into my eyes.

"The doctor says that the only help for you now is psychiatric drugs, and she is not allowed, as a Scientologist, to prescribe them."

I looked at him with a mix of emotions. I didn't want to go back to the Scientology doctor anyway. I had always felt that she was a tool for the alien Marcabians, only wanting harm to come my way.

"We are on our own, Nancy. There is no help coming from Scientology. There is no help coming from anywhere. We are in this together, and we are going to get through this together."

Chris was talking to me so slowly and deliberately, with him holding my hand and looking deep inside me, it got to *me*—the *me* that had been fighting this war alone for the past two weeks. It didn't matter if we had no more help from Scientology; they were the ones who pushed me over the brink in the first place. I felt they had been actively working to make me worse since my mind cracked two weeks ago. What mattered was that I was no longer alone. Chris was in this with me. I remembered what the nurses had said as they laughed about the chloral hydrate and herbs the Scientology doctor had prescribed me.

I realized exactly what we needed to do. "Let's do the opposite of everything they told us. Let's stop all the drugs, the megavitamins, the herbs, the calcium magnesium drinks, all that stuff."

"OK. We'll get through this, Nancy."

I felt my first bit of hope in two weeks as we embraced.

Chapter 2

Entering the Scientology World

I FIRST ENCOUNTERED Scientology in the early 1970s while attending a small college north of Boston. Things in my life as well as the world around me were unstable. Society seemed in a state of constant flux and turmoil. I had participated in marches for peace, protested the Vietnam War, was involved in taking over a college building, and dabbled in the "sex, drugs, and rock-and-roll" lifestyle that permeated our national youth culture in those years. I was a member of a women's consciousness group and a lapsed member of the Catholic Church.

My departure from Catholicism did not come dramatically; it simply came from distaste for all organized religions. I found my connection to God in nature and in the people around me. I loved the Bible and the interpretive writings of Thoreau and Emerson. I felt closer to God while hiking than I did in a church or at a Catholic Mass. I didn't understand why women could not become priests or why priests couldn't marry. My favorite nun and priest during my high school years were forced to leave their vocations of service simply to get married, although not to each other.

My dream had always been to become a social worker, to counsel and help people. I had already spent two summers with the Paul A. Dever School for the Retarded. I worked with both adults and children and people with many different levels of disability. I knew that my life's passion was helping others and was certain that this was my future career. The college I chose offered a pilot project, sponsored by the state of Massachusetts, where a person could begin working as an apprentice social worker after only four years of college. I was thrilled that I would be able to make some money doing what I loved while I got my master of social work degree.

Unfortunately, that program failed and was being shut down by the school I attended, my dreams along with it. I had just broken up with my long-term boyfriend. I noticed that the friends I was hanging out with wanted to do everything while stoned on marijuana. The only other set of students I saw or knew on the campus were the students who loved to drink and get drunk. I fit in with neither group and felt displaced, floating without an anchor. It was during this time that I got involved in Scientology.

The Scientology center I first noticed was on Beacon Street in Boston, near Fenway Park and Kenmore Square. It looked more like a regular office building than anything else. One very cold October day, I found myself stoned and standing in front of the building with four friends. A large bright poster in the front window caught my attention: *A civilization without insanity, without criminals, and without war, where the able can prosper and honest beings can have rights, and where man is free to rise to greater heights, are the aims of Scientology.* I read the words, but my mind wasn't taking it all in. I began reading again from the top. My friends were anxious to keep moving and get out of the freezing cold, but I had to keep reading.

"Wait," I said. These words struck a chord in me: *nonpolitical in nature, Scientology welcomes any individual of any creed, race, or nation.*

"Come on, Nancy, it's cold out here." Bob tugged at my jacket.

"One more minute," I begged as I scanned the poster again. *The combined truths of fifty thousand years of thinking men, distilled and amplified by new discoveries about man, have made for this success.*

"Nancy!" Marty and Jill yelled sharply. I tore myself away, vowing privately that I would find out more or at least come back without friends and read the entire sign when I wasn't high.

We made it to the next couple of blocks to Jill's apartment and warmed up with hot tea. When we were settled, Jill said, "Stay away from them, Nancy, I have some friends who got really screwed over by those people."

"How?", I asked.

"Money, that's all they're about, all they want is your money." Even though my other friends agreed with that sentiment, something in that poster touched me. I wanted those aims. How could anything be wrong with a group that wanted those aims?

Within the month, a friend of mine at college, Sue, got a letter from a friend of hers who had moved to California. In it, she raved about a new group she encountered called Scientology. I told Sue of the poster I had seen, and we agreed to go to Boston and check it out together.

We attended an open house. The building was clean and businesslike, with two large course rooms filled with tables and chairs. Some smaller rooms, we were told, were for private counseling and a few offices for the staff that worked there full-time. All the people were so friendly and seemed so happy. But nothing really captured me as very different until the end of our tour. We were told to maintain our silence as we were going to witness an actual private counseling session on a small stage in the back classroom. The audience was asked to be as quiet as possible while the counselor (which we were told was called an *auditor*) and the client (which they called a *preclear*) took their chairs. The auditor was operating a machine I had already seen called an E-Meter. The preclear was holding a tin can in each hand that was connected by a wire to the machine itself.

I listened as the preclear was questioned about an area of her life she had difficulty with and she spoke freely about it. She spoke of some injury she'd experienced a couple of weeks ago, and soon the auditor was asking if there was an earlier similar time she had felt a pain like this. They continued in this way, and after three or four earlier incidents were discussed, I realized that she was now speaking about memories from a previous lifetime. The preclear was talking about things that she felt had happened to her in a lifetime before this one!

I turned to one of the staff giving us our tour and whispered, "Is she talking about her past life?"

"Yes," he whispered back matter-of-factly.

I felt such elation, a sense of being in the right place. I could not *believe* that no one had mentioned this to me before! I had been ready to write Scientology off as just another interesting group prior to witnessing this amazing auditing session onstage. Here was a group that actually helped people recover memories of past lives. Memories that were buried, but still affected the person in the present. It resonated with me.

I was practically floating out of the room despite the late hour. My girlfriend Sue did not share my enthusiasm; she was tired, and we had a long way to go to get back to school. We took some literature, bought some books, and left. I left that night feeling a sense of peace and euphoria that I had found something I had been searching for.

When I was fifteen, I had read books about the possibility that we may have lived before. Even at a young age, it moved something within me, and I searched for any information that I could find on it. My father, a devout Catholic, told me if I really wanted to learn about reincarnation, I should read the writings of St. Thomas Aquinas. I soon discovered that in the early Catholic Church, a belief in past lives had been held but then was dropped. I learned that there were many practices that exhibited the belief in the possibility, even a high probability, of the return of one's soul to this world. For me, this theory of past lives was something that simply made sense. It explained why I could sometimes meet people and have a feeling of instant recognition. It was why when I traveled to places I had never been before, I sometimes felt something familiar, even predicting at times what was around the corner.

The notion that we returned after death to live again did not contradict any of my Catholic beliefs or other personal beliefs. It was something that was simply a belief of mine.

Prior to my visit to the Scientology open house, I had never found or seen a way of accessing or actually remembering who or what I was. I was so excited that night as Sue and I took the subway and then hitchhiked back to school.

That first paperback book, *Scientology: A New Slant on Life*, got put aside due to the demands of my college classes. I also heard more negativity about Scientology from several other people.

"They play with dark forces."

"They hurt people."

"They are very greedy and only care about the money."

The book languished on my shelf in my college dorm for a couple of months.

Shortly after Christmas break, I was involved in a heavy study period, cramming for finals. I was having an especially difficult time with my biology class. Methamphetamines were common "study aids" in those days, used to help us pull all-nighters. That night I took a black beauty and was wide-awake but just couldn't get into my biology materials. As I looked around my room, the book *Scientology: A New Slant on Life* caught my eye. I picked it up and decided to read it.

At this point, my mind was filled with criticism and attitude against Scientology. I had heard so much negativity about it that I found myself looking for things to challenge. It was not a very big book, perhaps 150 pages. I found myself initially seeing many things to either disagree with or think, *So what? That's no big deal.*

However, midway through the book, I noticed I was actually nodding my head, especially while reading the chapter on the "Death of Consciousness." Hubbard said, *"Have you watched the high alertness of a young man breasting the forces which oppose life, and then watched another in old age?"* Hubbard went on to say, *"Suppose we had a man who had retained all his ability to reason and yet had a great deal of experience. Suppose our graybeards could think with all the enthusiasm and vitality of youth and yet had all their experience as well. Age says to youth, 'You have no experience!' Youth says to age, 'You have no vision; you will not accept or even examine new ideas!' Obviously, an ideal arrangement would be for one to have the experience of age and the vitality and vision of youth."*

Wow, I thought, *that's exactly how I feel,* coming from an era that felt like the largest generation gap ever. I looked forward into the lives of those much older than me and saw the burdens of paying the mortgage and working a nine-to-five job while losing the joy of taking a hike or just sticking one's thumb out and experiencing life as it unfolded. I agreed with most of my generation in that I wanted something different.

I stopped, put the book down, and had a serious conversation with myself. Even though I had liked the "Aims of Scientology" and found their form of counseling, which included past lives, to be personally attractive, I had since not found one person who had anything good to say about the subject. I reminded myself that my purpose here was to read the book critically and not to lap it up mindlessly. I put myself back in a critical frame of mind and went back to reading the book. I found a few comments on the place of women in society, which I disagreed with and which confirmed to me that this was not a group that had all the answers. I kept reading.

After another fifty pages or so, I slowly realized that Hubbard was making sense. There was just no way around it; he was making sense *to me.*

"When you start to introduce order into anything, disorder shows up and blows off. Therefore, efforts to bring order in the society or any part of it will be productive of disorder for a while every time.

"The trick is to keep on bringing order; and soon the disorder is gone, and you have orderly activity remaining. But if you HATE disorder and fight disorder only, don't ever try to bring order to anything for the resulting disorder will drive you half mad.

"Only if you can ignore disorder and can understand this principle, can you have a working world."

I recalled the times I had decided to reorganize a part of my room. I remembered that there would come a point when I would look around at the chaos that my room had become, wondering why I had even started. Hubbard was right; if I just kept at it for a few more minutes, the corner would be turned. The order I originally wanted would soon appear.

I decided this was something I could work with and I should stop trying to find fault and simply read the book.

Upon finishing it, I realized a couple of things: First off, there was not much in the book that didn't resonate with me. I also noticed that most of it was simple common sense that on some level I already knew. There was nothing new here; no brilliant or earth-shattering shift came from reading it. However, I also recognized that I had never found a book where the writer had reached me so easily, had written these concepts in simple terms, and communicated to me in such clear language.

This was not a bad thing. Why were all these other people saying bad things about it?

It was well past dawn by this time, and I felt refreshed and energized and ran down the two flights of stairs to burst into my friend Sue's room.

"Sue, you have got to read this book!"

Sue was getting ready for her first class, barely awake and ironing a blouse.

"What book?"

"The Scientology book, remember the one that we got from the center in Boston?"

Sue looked at me blankly. "Oh. no, I haven't read it."

"You have to. I just finished reading it, and it's a really simple book but has a lot of usefulness in it."

Sue and her roommate looked at me.

I realized I was too chipper for them in this early morning hour and backed off.

"Are you going to breakfast?" I asked.

"In about five minutes."

"OK," I said. "I'll be back."

I realized that I had to contain my excitement because others were not feeling what I felt. They just didn't understand. We went to breakfast and talked of classes and boyfriends and the upcoming party over the weekend.

I had no one to share this with, this newfound sense of peace and something to hold on to. I already knew that there weren't that many people who felt as I did about past lives and had yet to find a person with good things to say about Scientology, so I shut up about it.

Several days later, I had finished my morning classes and was sitting in the coffee house in the student union. I took an inventory of my life and realized that I was starting to think in a different direction than my friends. I was tired of getting stoned every day; in fact, the last couple of times weren't even fun. I had just completed a semester wherein I had made the dean's list, but my hopes for the special social work program were dying. I had to acknowledge that it was something that might not even work out for me.

I had no more classes that day. I was caught up on my schoolwork, and I had nothing else going on. I decided to call the people at the Boston Scientology center and see if there was someone I could see today. I wanted to know more about them, on my own and for myself.

That day was a major turning point for me. I went to the organization in Boston and spoke to several people. Soon it got too late for me to make my way back to the dorm, and one of my newfound Scientology friends offered me a couch at their apartment. I was entering a new world.

The people I spoke to that day about Scientology promised everything I wanted to hear. I could begin counseling and helping people in a short amount of time, months as opposed to the years I was looking at through college. Several local Boston Scientologists offered me a place in their lives. I really liked these people and wanted to know them better. The living quarters were communal with several apartments scattered near the main office or Org as they called it (short for organization), and rent was cheap. I had never lived communally, but in the late '60s and early '70s, it wasn't unusual. The thought of sharing living quarters with others who felt as I did was appealing. There was no drug use within the group, yet there was a very hopeful and electric energy that made the highs from drugs seem tame. I was drawn to it on many levels.

Many of my friends and peers were experimenting with different ways of living than their parents had expected them to. While I loved to watch the Hare Krishna's chant and dance on the Boston Common, I couldn't see changing my life in that direction. But still . . .

I was concerned about the religious aspect of Scientology. I had left not only the Roman Catholic Church but also all organized religions. The staff members speaking with me about joining were adept at handling my concerns. One of the staff comforted me by showing me a policy letter by L. Ron Hubbard wherein he said essentially supported what she was saying. Hubbard wrote in Hubbard Communications Office Policy Letter (HCOPL) 29 October 1962 entitled "Religion," "Scientology 1970 is being planned on a religious basis throughout the world. This will not upset in any way the usual activities of any organization. It is entirely a matter for accountants and solicitors [attorneys]."

Personally, I found it to be a prospering business rather than a religious congregation. There were no church services ever; none of the members I was talking to even called it a church. They called their place of business the Org. Other staff members helped me with my decision not to get involved with any organized religion by explaining that Scientology was a practical philosophy. Not some "pie in the sky" thinking, but actual tools that people could use to better their lives. It was nondenominational, meaning it contained nothing in it that would conflict with the person's religion they walked in with. They could still be practicing Jews, Catholics, Buddhists, or whatever and still be a Scientologist. This gave me answers to my questions, and over the years when introducing new people to the organization, I would call upon these descriptions and others I had read from Hubbard to show that joining this organization presented no threat to whatever religion they called their own. It was a practical philosophy, nondenominational in context.

I received a lot of benefit out of the first course I took, the communications course. It cost $25, and at that time, it felt like a fortune. But I was given a lot of encouragement from all my new Scientology friends, and I soon got the money.

The course broke down the various components of communication into much smaller parts. Students would practice these smaller segments, gaining confidence and clarity as time went on. Hubbard taught that the very first step to communication was that the person had to be in the present moment. Sometimes, instead of simply being there with the person with whom we are speaking, we might still be upset about an emotional conversation from the previous day with someone else entirely. Or we're worried about something that might happen in the future. This takes energy from the conversation we're attempting to have in the present. The purpose of practicing this communication fundamental (the idea of simply being present) was to move us into the present moment.

The communication course contained two drills a person practiced repeatedly to increase his or her ability to "be there" and to do nothing else *but* be there. In many ways, they were very similar to meditation and the Christian practice of contemplative prayer, which I would study years later. I would find that when I first sat down to "just be there," my mind would be a swirl of thoughts. Over time and with practice, I found my center, a place of peace without all the raucous thoughts that had previously been clouding my mind. I could simply sit in front of another person and just *be*.

I could not see anything but positive in a person learning how to quiet his or her mind and simply arrive in the present moment. I gained from this and wanted to share this with others. I wanted others to share the experience I had.

The organization in Boston in 1972 was small enough (approximately fifty staff) that I was on a first-name basis with everyone who worked there. L. Ron Hubbard (the founder of Scientology) personally had sent several of his top executives to Boston as part of what was called a command team. This select group contained personnel who had run many of the top Scientology organizations in the United States. They had been sent to Boston to expand Scientology's presence, increase enrollment, and send a large percentage of the income generated to advanced organizations and management. The executives who were part of this command team all personally knew and had worked directly with L. Ron Hubbard. Through them, I heard many personal stories of not only Hubbard's never-ending drive for greater and greater production, but also his sense of humor and compassion. Watching this small group of people who had worked so closely with Hubbard seemed to give me a better measure of the man himself. Their stories personalized him for me. They gave me a unique sense of him as a real person, a man who sometimes made mistakes, got upset, and was not always right. He was human, and while I respected Hubbard and admired his work, I never expected perfection. I did find that many of his materials had the ability to take already-existing complex philosophies and distill them for me into simple, understandable, and useful concepts. Not only could I finally understand these concepts, I found that I could put them into use in my life.

One day, I arrived at the organization in the early afternoon. I was attempting to juggle my college classes along with my Scientology course work and the work I had begun to do with Scientology. Bill Franks, a tall, handsome member of the command team, asked me to come to his office. He didn't say another word till we arrived there and he offered me a seat.

"Have you heard about the Sea Org?" he asked.

I knew that all the members of the command team were called officers in the Sea Organization. They always wore uniforms similar to those of naval officers and could be a striking sight when seen walking in a group along the streets of Boston. Gold braid, service ribbons, naval caps, and a smart military bearing defined this elite group of Hubbard's personal representatives.

"Yes," I answered.

"Would you like to join?"

Join. I hadn't even known that it was possible, and I felt honored that he was even asking me. I knew that Sea Org members devoted their lives to the forwarding of the purpose and the aims of Scientology. I had learned that they even had a small fleet of ships and traveled the world, bringing the sunshine of Scientology with them wherever they went.

"I still would like to finish this semester at college."

"Not a problem. That is only two more months, and we'll work that schedule out." He reached into a drawer, pulled out a manila folder, and placed a document in front of me.

I noticed the distinct wreath-and-star symbol of the Sea Organization at the top of the page and read the short contract.

> I, _____ DO HEREBY AGREE to enter into employment with the SEA ORGANIZATION and, being of sound mind, do fully realize and agree to abide by its purpose which is to get **ETHICS IN** on this PLANET AND UNIVERSE and, fully and without reservation, subscribe to the discipline, mores and conditions of this group and pledge to abide by them.
>
> THEREFORE, I CONTRACT MYSELF TO THE SEA ORGANIZATION FOR THE NEXT BILLION YEARS.
>
> Signed_____
> Date_____

Wow. A billion years.

That's a long time, or at least this entire lifetime for sure. Do I really want to only do this for the rest of my life?

As I thought this over, I remembered a briefing another member of the command team had given only last week; Hubbard had a plan to Clear the planet within five years. "Clearing the planet" was a rallying cry for Scientologists throughout the world, the end result being a complete achievement of the aims of Scientology. The expectation and goal was that within five years, everyone would be a Scientologist. Everyone!

Can I contribute five years of my life to help achieve a civilization without insanity, without criminals, and without war? Do I want to help create a world where the able can prosper and honest beings can have rights? A place where man is free to rise to greater heights? Is this what I want? Are those aims of Scientology that I had read in the storefront window last fall my goals too? Yes *yes, they are.*

"All right," I said as I picked up the pen to sign.

Bill was obviously happy about my choice, and we left his office sharing my new status with the staff we met along the way back to my course room. I was greeted with great smiles and big hugs. I was thrilled to be a full-time member of the group. I had signed my billion year contract; I was a Sea Org member.

Much to the unhappiness of my family, I dropped out of college and fully entered the world of Scientology. I agreed with the stated Scientology goals of "making the world a better place" and "helping mankind." I knew Scientology was not a mainstream-established group and at that time of my life and with the transitional state of the world in the early '70s, that was just fine with me.

Now that I had officially signed my contract and become a member of the staff, I was allowed to attend staff meetings. On a wall in the back of the organization was a large chart called the Seven-Division Organizing Board. Every Scientology organization in the world has the exact, same layout. This huge chart contains the function of every position in the organization, laid out in colored tape. The job titles and names of the responsible personnel are placed on this board. The board covers every duty in the entire organization, which, if all done correctly, would bring about a better world. The Org Board, as it's known, breaks down into seven divisions, each one delineated by a different color: (1) Communications Division, (2) Dissemination Division, (3) Treasury Division, (4) Technical Division, (5) Qualifications Division (Quality Control), (6) Public Division (Marketing), and (7) Executive Division.

Each of the seven divisions is broken down into three departments, and within each of these departments, there are sections and units all adding up to the final product of each department.

Each one of the twenty-one departments had a clear and concise valuable final product they were responsible for as did each of the seven divisions. The sum total of the seven divisions would be the product of the organization as a whole. This was quite a structured organization with everyone having his or her job well defined within the framework of the whole.

Each and every morning, the entire staff met in front of the board for a group muster and Chinese school. Chinese school is a repetitive and effective means of robotically learning through a call-and-response method. A leader would call out job titles, duties, and products of each division and department within the organization and the staff would repeat them back in unison. These drills were done every day without fail as a mandatory group activity. Such constant repetition tends to speed its saturation into a person's mental thought processes. As a result, I learned the Org Board very quickly.

This daily drilling of the layout of the organization's structure was important. It was felt that the more each individual member of the organization understood about the functions in other departments and divisions, the stronger the group as a whole would be. If everyone knew where to send each person or piece of paper and he knew which job handled what duty and who specifically was responsible for any given product, it would make for a highly efficient organization. I didn't find much wrong with the premise that an educated staff would be a more efficient staff. Such regimentation and order was a direct result of Hubbard's experience as a naval officer in WWII as the Sea Org was modeled on a similar command hierarchy.

The first position I held at the Boston Org was in sales, and I was assigned as a public registrar. I was soon enrolled in Scientology's sales course, which was based on sales methods developed by Les Dane. Mr. Dane had been a top car salesman and had written several best-selling books, which codified his successes. A course centered on the book *Big League Sales Closing Techniques* had been specifically developed to train registrars how to sell Scientology books and services instead of cars. It was a well-written, simple, and effective book about how to maximize sales, expand your contacts and prospects, and close any sale quickly. Along with exercises and practice drills that L. Ron Hubbard developed to align with the book, it utilized the sales tools employed by Les Dane in the selling of cars to the selling of Scientology's Bridge to Total Freedom.

I was good with people, enjoyed speaking with them, and the executives of the organization thought that I would make a great registrar. As a public registrar for Scientology, I sold courses like the communications course I had taken and from which I had gained so much. I would also be selling personal counseling called auditing that were sold in blocks of twelve and a half hours. Registrars always tried to sell at least twenty-five hours because that was the minimum amount recommended for a beginning person to receive the most benefit. A twenty-five-hour block of personal auditing cost $4,000. This counseling was usually delivered to the person within two weeks. There were many other books, courses, and services available, costing anywhere from hundreds to thousands and even tens of thousands of dollars. The hours of personal counseling someone could buy and receive at the Boston Org could easily run up to two or three hundred, not to mention the recommended courses, books, and tapes. A person could easily spend thousands on Scientology services.

Unfortunately, I had some issues about the amount of money being charged for these courses and counseling. I felt that even the $25 that was charged for the very first class was steep, especially for college students who lived hand to mouth in the Boston area. I could not even fathom asking someone for the thousands of dollars it would cost to receive just a few hours of personal Scientology counseling.

That started to shift for me as I did some of the exercises and drills that were part of the Big League Sales Course. The special drills that were developed did indeed improve my ability to ask for increasingly larger sums of money. For example, I was told to sit silently in front of an upside-down $100 bill until I could confront it and it had no meaning to me other than a piece of paper. The organization's financial officer, Pat Broeker, would get stacks of hundred-dollar bills and let those of us in sales play with them. We would throw them in the air, crumple them up, and throw them at each other, the purpose being to desensitize us to the thought that there were no large sums of money in the world. It was green and black ink on paper, that's all. We were walked to freeway overpasses by our trainers and were reminded that each car passing under us had cost at least $2,000 (this was the early '70s after all). We were asked to count the cars until the concept of "there's no money" would disappear.

After these and many other drills, I began to feel confident that there was indeed quite a lot of money in the world and that my asking someone for five or ten thousand dollars for Scientology services was no big deal, especially when it was their eternal personal and spiritual freedom at stake. My job was to simply locate the people that had that money and match them to the courses or counseling that would do them the most good. Simple.

Hubbard believed that monitoring statistics were a vital component in any organization. Giving each person a numerical reference would represent and measure their production on their job. The numbers would offer each staff member some protection when doing well and serve as a lightning rod for correction when they were not.

Scientology organizations measured these statistics on a weekly basis that would cut off at 2:00 PM on Thursday afternoons. This marked the end of the past weeks work and began the new week with a fresh start. This time was originally set for Thursday to allow all the organizations around the world to send by telex their weekly statistics to the management office headquartered in England. With the time differences and given the time it took to relay this information, this would give international management time to digest the week's production and coordinate new orders or changes for the coming week. By the '70s, Scientology's international organization management was no longer based in England and the telex and communication system was much faster, but this arbitrary cutoff time of two o'clock on Thursday afternoons continued.

If you walked into any organization on a Friday morning, you would find that many of the staff members were not there. They had been pushed to meet and exceed production quotas based on a Thursday deadline, and the reality was they usually needed a little time to recover. As Fridays progressed, the org came back to life, plans were made to increase production, and projects intended to expand the influence of Scientology.

Through the weekend, the production engines would kick in, slowly building in energy until Wednesday nights, wherein virtually any Scientology organization around the world were filled with a veritable frenzy of activity. public people were often asked to stay past the usual 10:00 PM closing, sometimes long into the night, as sales deals were hammered out. Phone calls were made to help track down funds to purchase large packages of services. If a student was anywhere near the end of the course he or she was taking, the student would be asked to remain well into the wee hours of the morning in order to reach their quota before the two o'clock deadline the next day. All organizations continued this hotbed of activity right up till the stroke of 2:00 PM. New and unsuspecting public, who walked into the building thinking this was an ordinary Thursday morning, would soon become swept up in this maelstrom of activity. Executives would be seen flying about from workstation to desk. These executives stood out because they usually had a trail of assistants busily taking notes and gathering steam as they traversed the halls of the building.

The director of the organization had two main areas that he was judged by: the gross income and the paid course or level a person completed. Depending on where these numbers were as of Wednesday night would determine where you would find the director on a Thursday morning.

The understanding was, in no uncertain terms, that every statistic was expected to rise each and every week. Measuring personal and organizational production on a statistical basis week after week became incredibly stressful, and it permeated the organization from top to bottom. The black-and-white reality was either your stats were up or your stats were down, period.

This affected me as an ordinary staff member in several ways. I very quickly learned that my rate of pay and ability to take any time off was directly connected to my statistic. Working for Scientology as a Sea Org member was a 24-7 commitment. This was no nine-to-five Monday-through-Friday job with sick days or two weeks of annual paid vacation. The Sea Org does not subscribe to a forty-hour workweek ethos. Eighty hours, pshaw . . . One hundred twenty hours is nothing. This was commitment with a capital C. A job in Scientology's Sea Organization involves full-time dedication to saving the world.

If my statistic was up, meaning a higher number than the week before, I would be allowed to take some personal time and be treated with a modicum of respect. When my statistic was down, especially if it was down several weeks in a row, not only was I forbidden any time off, but I also had cuts made in my minimal allowance of $20 a week and my very job was in jeopardy.

Chapter 3

My First Scientology Sales Job

MY FIRST JOB was that of a public registrar. The public registrar is the person who interviews individuals new to Scientology and sells them books and basic introductory courses and services. In the Boston Org at that time, there had been just one public registrar, and I became the second assigned to that post to increase production in that area. The statistic we were given was called the Number of New Names to Central Files in a Week. This meant we got credit anytime we sold a book, a course, or a service to someone who had never bought anything from the organization before, a *new* name. His or her name and address was added to the master mailing list in central files where all the names and addresses of people who have ever bought something are kept up-to-date. The direct mail and marketing sections of the organization would then continually mail letters, flyers, and Scientology magazines also tracked by a weekly statistic.

In the early '70s, the Boston Organization seemed fairly disorganized despite the command team sent by Hubbard. I had multiple bosses, three to be exact, and many times they would each give me conflicting priorities. On one particularly frustrating day, I had a blinding series of thoughts that led me to realize that I did not have to be sitting at the desk, hounded by executives to "get my statistic"; in fact, I didn't even have to be in the building. I packed up my materials and a backpack full of books, leaving the building to start selling books around the city. I sold books wherever I could: bus stops, colleges, restaurants, really any place there were people. I began selling books in volume and soon realized the week was over; no one was harassing me, and my statistics were up.

I got very good at selling books on the street, but it didn't generate very much income for the organization. So after three or four weeks of this, the director of the Org decided to forbid the sales of inexpensive paperback books. Now I had to sell only hardback copies, which were priced three or four times the paperback versions. I still sold and sold. I was very good at this, and as long as I sold more than the week before, I was protected. I had learned to keep my stats up.

During these months, I continued to study the course on sales techniques. Every night I would practice and drill scores of sales methods with other students. The next morning and throughout the day, I would go out into the world at large and put into practice what I had learned. I discovered that honesty was very important in sales as well as developing an ability *not* to pressure a person but simply listen and fill a need.

I learned that sales was a game of numbers and that the more no's I collected, the closer I was to finding a person who would say yes. I cultivated persistence as a winning course. It was sales, pure and simple, and I became quite good at it.

As the days and weeks passed, Boston got hotter and muggy. Finally the sticky summer weather got to me. I decided to go where there was air-conditioning and lots of people looking for something to read—the airport! It had people with free time on their hands and anxious for some form of entertainment to make the time go faster. I found, quite by accident, that I sold the most books when I wasn't trying to sell. I would take a break seated next to a person, and we would strike up a conversation and the usual question of "What are you doing?" would elicit my response of "Oh, I'm just out here selling books." I found that I sold more books when I was on break than when I was directly confronting people.

This was an important lesson. There was more communication, more openness, and more fluidity when I had no pressure and was sitting next to the person. Confrontations have a way of closing people up.

During this time, I learned sales skills that have stood by me in the years that followed. The classes and practice drills that I completed during this summer of 1972 were helpful, but it was the actual process of selling the books outside of the organization where I gained the expertise.

I was having a wonderful summer; my statistics were up, and my life was unfettered by executive harassment. I should have known that it was too good to last. One morning just before I was leaving on my daily book route, I was told about the other statistic assigned to the public registrar: income.

Income in volume could not be gathered out on the street selling books, so I found myself back inside the organization, behind a desk selling courses and other services. Using what I had learned over the last three to four months, I soon was regularly making more and more money for the organization, thousands of dollars, week after week. The director and his executive council quickly noticed it, and I was promoted.

My new job was something called gross income expeditor for the foundation organization (night and weekend hours). There was a separate income expeditor for the daytime hours. The position was created by the executive director as a solution to his having to chase up the ten or more separate individuals involved in earning money. Now he only had to deal with one during the day, a friend named David, and myself for the evening and weekend hours. David and I soon became the income-whipping boys.

I was now required to attend the daily executive meetings, which were held in the office of the executive director. The executive director was Alex Sibiersky, a very tall and imposing administrator. He held the rank of lieutenant commander within the Sea Organization; he had worked directly under LRH for years, and the success of the Boston Command Team lay squarely on his shoulders. He had a large laugh but could also yell with piercing energy like no one I had ever met. One afternoon, I was present with the other executives, including my counterpart, David. The executive director was late, and someone had noticed the daily numbers posted on the wall. They made a comment to me that my stats were down as were David's. At that point, David did something remarkable; he got up and just changed his numbers so they were reported as being up. One of the other execs in the room questioned this; and David simply said, "Well, it *will* be up there later this afternoon." Everyone in the room knew that he had just plucked those figures out of thin air. When the director arrived, he noticed David's numbers were up and lavished him with praise. I was so naive; I was stunned to notice that everyone else in the room was silent though everyone knew that David had lied. Then Commander Sibiersky turned to me.

It was then that I found the fatal flaw in living by the numbers. Figures themselves are not the actual things and can be easily manipulated and changed. I was berated in front of the group for not being productive and was then ordered to leave the conference room and get to work rather than stay for the meeting. I felt crushed and betrayed.

Overall, I did well at my job. Income was always a major push in the Org, so executives were constantly working with me and the other registrars to see from whom we were going to get this week's money and how we were going to do it.

Each Thursday morning, the Boston Org would be a buzzing hive of activity. In the registrar's area, this would involve arranging cars and people to pick up checks or going to people's homes or places of businesses to meet with them to close the sale and get the money collected before the 2:00 PM deadline.

I remember sometimes being in an interview with a prospect at Thursday lunchtime. I would do what I could to act as if there was no pressure and no undue attention, just he and I discussing what his next course or counseling purchase should be. Yet I knew I had the attention of at least seven executives out in the hallway, wondering what the result of my interview would be. If I stepped out to go to the bathroom, at least one, if not more of these executives, would want to know the status of the sale and would corner me. As a registrar, I had a supply of blank *counter checks* in my desk. These banking instruments were kept on hand so that they could be used if the prospect had forgotten his checkbook.

Some weeks we made a lot of money, and the sales force and related executives were rewarded with special Friday night dinners at luxurious restaurants. There was definitely a downside to being considered a good registrar; you had to keep your stats up every single week. If my sales and income statistics dropped the following week, then it was understood that there was something within *me* that was wrong and that I had dropped the ball. I had just made a certain amount of money the week prior, so there should be no reason I couldn't do it again this week, plus a little bit more. After all, we were clearing the planet and everyone needed Scientology counseling and training. There was no lack of prospects in a world where everyone needed Scientology.

It was drilled into us that each of us was responsible for our own statistic. If I was not performing up to the expected level, then there was something wrong with me as an individual. A routine solution to such underperformance was to do some MEST work. MEST is an acronym for matter, energy, space, and time: the physical universe. Sometimes, I was not working all that well and needed some additional inspiration; spending time doing MEST work might help me gain some more control over my own universe. MEST work was anything that involved working with the physical universe—items and things, not people. Things did not talk back. If you placed a thing in a certain place, it would not move unless you moved it. There was a strong feeling that if I, as a registrar, could not deal with the challenges inherent in dealing with people, I should spend some time simply working with MEST. This translated into projects like spending the night scrubbing the walls and floors, thoroughly cleaning a large area of the Org, or filing backlogged papers and documents. If I could simply see that I could be in control of physical things, this would supposedly increase my abilities to be in control of people and thus get them to write a check for whatever services they so desperately needed.

Scientology runs on the business model that growth is a weekly measurement, comparing each seven-day period to the previous one. Every post or job in a Scientology organization is expected and required to generate a greater production level than each preceding week. For example, if you sold $5,000 one week and the following week's statistic was $5,010, then your "stats were up" and you were considered "golden." But if instead that second week's production was only $4,990, you were "down stat." You could be accused of stopping the forward progress of the world. Making the world a better place and clearing the planet were very real things, and they took a lot of time and money. We all had to do our part.

On the positive side, the sales personnel were given more attention and help than just about any other staff member. We got courses and counseling in greater volume. Money was the lifeblood of the organization, and it was felt that if we were doing well personally, then we would find it easier to make more money. It was a simple formula.

I always felt the pressure and wished for more time to create and effectively do my job. In the non-Scientology world, most people in sales tended to operate on statistics of a monthly or quarterly basis. There was simply not enough time to build up prospects and close them all within seven days. I remember clearly one Friday night getting dressed up with several other top income producers to go out to a nice dinner and celebrate a high-income week. Unfortunately, I knew that during this past week, I had used up all of my prospects and available possible sales. The odds of my being able to top the dollar amount I had just met were slim to none. So while dressing for this lovely night out, I knew that the very next Friday night I would be in my work clothes spending these same extra hours and part of the night scrubbing walls and floors. It got to the point where I was unable to enjoy the good times because I could anticipate what was soon to follow.

There was a bright side however. I absolutely loved the Scientology personal counseling I received. I would go into a small quiet, safe room with someone trained as a Scientology counselor: an auditor. This trained person would ask specific questions and listen attentively while writing down my responses. He (or she) would help guide me through what I felt was a confused maze of jumbled thoughts to end up at a point of clarity. The purpose of these counseling sessions was to help me uncover forgotten memories that may have been blocking me from enjoying the world, the people, or myself. I believed some of these memories could have been from a previous lifetime.

I remember coming out of one auditing session where we dug into personal areas that had deep meaning to me. I left the session feeling like I was walking on clouds. I was speaking to a person and felt that I could truly see him and his infinite spiritual energy. As I uncovered and cleared away the confusions and pains in my personal life, I gained confidence, both in myself and in the people around me. I felt I could see things much more clearly than ever before. I felt that the troubles of the past no longer interfered with my actions and the creation of my present and future life.

The courses I took covered specific things, like how to improve my communication, how to use planning to accomplish things in my life, or how to really be honest with myself about what my intentions truly were. I found them helpful and felt strongly that they would be helpful for others as well.

One class especially had tremendous impact on me. It was similar to the drills I had done on the communications course except these drills involved groups of people and how one individual can get another person to do something, either directly or through a middleman, and how a person can get a group of people to follow their lead.

My first contact with the class was not as a student but as an extra for the final drill the student needed to pass. This final drill involved two tables of at least four or five people each seated. The student was only allowed to speak with the people at the first table. The student had a coach to help him through the process and to coordinate the level of difficulty so that the student was always improving in some way. I was asked to be one of the people at the second table. The student was instructed to give a command to the people at table number 1: "Give that book to those people and have them place it on their table." Those were the only words the student was allowed to use. The groups at the tables, on the other hand, could say and do just about anything. The idea was to give the student resistance to his orders until he had a breakthrough. It was one of the most entertaining drills I got to work with because we could laugh and joke among ourselves. We could and would talk back to the student as he continued to repeat his command. This would go on for hours and hours with ever-increasing levels of resistance from the groups.

The final point, though, was the most amazing to me. There came a change in the student that was palpable. There was no more effort, strain, or force in his command. It simply came across as pure intention. Even I, as one of the students at the second table (who felt it was my job to create resistance), could not think of any resistance to put up. I didn't even want to. The student willed that book from one table to the other.

When I enrolled in the course myself, I learned that it began at much simpler levels. I would be speaking to one person and try to get him to get the person next to him to put the book on the table. I could not speak to the third person, only the second. I spent hours and hours on this drill, most of the time spent laughing because it was so much like life. I would ask the person I had contact with to ask the third person to place the book on the table, and the responses would be things like "He can't 'cause he's upset from a fight with his girlfriend" or "He doesn't think his mother loves him" or any other ridiculous reason why they couldn't do what I was asking.

My goal was to persist. My job was to really listen and help fix any valid problems but ultimately persist in getting my intention across and move that book. In the process, I went through periods of personal frustration, anger, and wanting to just give up. When I finally finished the drill, I found myself in a place of centeredness just like in the original communications course. I found myself simply "being there," but now I had the additional ability of being able to get things accomplished while remaining centered. No matter how many times I was told no or "It can't be done," I could still hold my center and persist to a point where I would achieve what I set out to do.

When the level of training got to the point where I was the student in front of the two tables of people, it was the same, only on a much more intense level. I discovered that place of intention within me, a place that would allow me to accomplish things and persist through the many roadblocks that life and other people could put in front of me. Just as with the first student I worked with, when I reached that point, not one person at either table could put up any resistance and the book practically floated from one table to the other. It was moments like these that I experienced for myself that drove me to attempt to share Scientology with others. It gave me the ability to sell Scientology without feeling like a used-car salesman because I really had experienced some very magical things.

In retrospect, the clarity and smoothness of intention that I learned while doing those drills was hardly ever in use in the day-to-day activity of the organization. Instead of calm, steady, and positive intention, the executives yelled, screamed, and pressured the staff to increase production. It was the exact opposite of what I had learned in doing those drills. It wasn't an angry force that caused people to move a book from one table to the other. It was respect and a clear intention. That's what I learned when I perfected those drills but was not what I experienced in the day-to-day life of a working staff member within the organization. It was usually kept from the eyes and ears of the paying public; but all the while I worked for the organization, I experienced a lot of anger, threats, and incessant pressure for more and more of whatever my particular product was.

Many years later, I discovered a concept called *cognitive dissonance*. It is the feeling of uncomfortable tension, which comes from holding two conflicting thoughts in the mind at the same time. This can cause an individual to fight within their minds to somehow make it make sense. For me, the wonderful snippets and moments I experienced during courses and counseling, added to the camaraderie with fellow staff members, were what kept me there. These islands of goodness that were all too few and far between kept me involved despite a constant harassment from organization execs along with other forms of degradation. Instead of seeing the reality of the chaos and harassment of people for what it was, I saw the hope of what could be. I felt that the bad times were only temporary and that soon our group would be filled with the kindness and compassion that I had glimpsed in some of my courses and interactions with fellow members in earlier times.

Days turned into weeks and weeks to months, and before I knew it, a year had passed. I quietly married one of the members of the command team, more for the reason of my still being under age and, once married, I would no longer need the permission of my parents. The promise of making the world a better place is what I thought we were doing and was the hope I held on to.

Chapter 4

New England Espionage

ONE NIGHT, MY then-husband Bill was late getting out of a meeting with some others of his command team group. He came to me and said that we had to quietly go home and pack up our stuff. We had to leave the Boston Organization and get information to some higher ups of what was going on there. We packed up our things and went to my parents' home outside of Boston. From there, Bill got in touch with Bob Ramer who was in charge of the Guardian's Office of the Boston Organization. L. Ron Hubbard had two great and separate arms of his organization: one was the Sea Org with the people who have signed their billion year contracts, and the other was the Guardian's Office. Even though it was supervised by L. Ron Hubbard, it was run day to day by his wife, Mary Sue Hubbard. Bob took down all the information and said he would get it off as soon as he could to Bill's superiors, but while we waited, we were to work for JW, the head of his intelligence branch. The Guardian's Office had the ultimate responsibility of taking care of finances, legal, public relations, and intelligence of each organization.

This was my unexpected entrance into a previously unknown region of Scientology. Bill got a job at a private investigator firm so he could learn how PIs operated. I got a job at a mental health facility and gathered personnel information on the psychiatrists who worked in Massachusetts. We kept asking but heard nothing back from our write-up on our situation with the Sea Org. So Bill and I grew where we were planted, working day to day with JW. L. Ron Hubbard had advised a program to be drawn up containing all the agencies that were a danger to him and his incorporation and that may be holding on to information that was untrue about him and the group as a whole. This program was called Snow White. It was not only being implemented in Boston, but was also being implemented in every major city in America, especially where we had Organizations and also at the federal level. We set about getting personnel placed as spies in all the organizations listed in Snow White as well as handling local situations with suppressive persons as needed.

We soon had recruited and placed agents in most of the government or individual corporations named as potential threats to Scientology. Some of the Organizations, to this day, I don't know how they got on the list—like the American Red Cross, the American Cancer Society, and even the YMCA.

We also had people placed in jobs of companies that made sense to me—the Better Business Bureau, the Massachusetts attorney general's office, the division of complaints, and the consumer council of Massachusetts. From these offices, we collected information about who was complaining about Scientology so we could handle the situation before it became too big. For example, a parent would complain to the Better Business Bureau that they felt their youth was spending too much money. The name of the parent and his child's name would be relayed in the agents' daily report. Staff in the org would not divulge how it was found out (most staff didn't know anyway), but they would meet with the youth and make sure that the person got things back in order with his parents. In the ideal situation this would work out and the complaint would be marked as taken care of in the files of the Better Business Bureau. The complaint would be resolved. The consumer's council was one of the places I worked at. They were doing an investigation on Scientology, and I would take home or copy the different versions as the investigation was ongoing. One of the investigators was investigating bait and switch at some local businesses. He asked me to come with him to pretend I was his wife and to spy on them. He told me how this company had advertised that they were selling leather couches for $300, and we were to pretend to be a married couple shopping for a couch. That way, we could see if they really did have several $300 leather couches or were just using that in their ads as a bait to get the customers into the stores to then switch the couches with a more expensive model. He was very concerned as to how I would work out as a spy, and we practiced it several times in his office before we went out to the store. That was a bit surreal. I was there spying on him and his company, and he was teaching me how to spy on these outside organizations.

During those years, we knew that the newspaper the *Boston Globe* was doing an exposé on Scientologists. We wanted to get it stopped, but if we couldn't do that, then we wanted to know who was talking to the reporters and what they were saying. We attempted several times to get a person with a job in there. We even sent a woman up to the ski resort where we knew the reporter was taking a vacation, hoping to get a connection from that avenue. None of those attempts worked, but we did get a janitor placed with a job to clean the *Boston Globe*'s attorneys' offices. Every night, he would go to the offices, pull out the file the attorneys were keeping on the Scientology exposé, and copy any and all new information.

At that time, one of the most well-known suppressive persons was a writer named Paulette Cooper. She lived in New York. One afternoon, we received information that she was coming to Boston to meet with her attorney, F. Lee Bailey, the next morning. We knew which train she was going to be riding in and exactly what she was going to be wearing. I could never understand how they knew what she was going to be wearing the next day; it was only 3:00 PM the day before. I never knew what I was going to wear until I got up in the morning. We were told we were supposed to follow her from when she got off the train till she got to F. Lee Bailey's office near the government center. There were two train stops she could disembark from: one was the Back Bay Station near my home, and the other more likely one was the main South Station due to it being closer to F. Lee Bailey's offices. I was given the Back Bay Station because I had never done a "tail" before and they were pretty certain she would not get off there. Well, that's where she got off, wearing exactly what someone knew yesterday afternoon. I noticed she was very petite and beautiful and did my best to unobtrusively follow her. After a few blocks, I lost her. No wonder they hadn't trusted me. I went into the lobby of the closest hotel and sat at a bank of sit-down glass pay phones. I closed the door so I could phone in my failure. While I was talking, I noticed that the person in the booth directly in front of me was her! Now I wasn't certain what to do. I noticed her outfit, which I was very jealous of, and her petite body and perfect hair. I could hear some of what she was saying but not enough to make anything out. I waited for her to leave the phone booth and then did a slow walk through the busy lunchtime sidewalks. There were enough people that I doubt I was seen. I remember following her, still wondering how they knew her outfit the day before in New York, and now seeing her and how lovely and petite she looked I couldn't imagine how this could be the biggest suppressive person Scientology had. If I got too close to her, I would stop and window-shop, but I never again let her out of my sight and I didn't think she saw me following her. She went straight to where they expected her to go— the law offices of F. Lee Bailey. I still don't understand the importance of that exercise. "They" already knew everything.

More detail can be found on Paulette Cooper and the many atrocities Scientology committed on her on the Internet. They, the higher ups in Scientology intelligence, wanted her to either

to the intelligence team in Boston from L. Ron Hubbard. There was no doubt in my mind as to where the heat to do something like that had come from.

Soon we made a few basic intelligence mistakes, we moved the individuals involved in covert to one home outside the city, and JW moved his file cabinets of confidential information to this house.

The head of the Boston Guardian's Office finally revealed that the reason why we had not heard anything back from my husband Bill's international bosses was that Bob had never relayed the letter, wanting instead to have the free use of Bill and I as undercover staff for JW.

The FBI got a hold of bits of information and interviewed George—the agent we had in the Massachusetts attorney general's office. By then the intelligence bureau from the United States level had already come to Boston and gotten the intelligence files back into the Organization and had scattered the agents both near and far. Bill and I returned to the Sea Organization management level located in New York. I worked there for a year in the division 6 area again though this time it was from a management point of view of all the celebrity centers, orgs and franchises east of the Mississippi.

I did surveys for marketing from our place of the world, including some of the messianic surveys, which I always found more interesting. It was a bit like overt data collection—I would spend hours in libraries.

After a year, I was promoted to the international management level of Scientology. When I arrived, the international management had just left their former base of operations—Hubbard's yacht that the Sea Org called *Flag* (as in the flagship of a naval fleet)—and had opened their new headquarters in Clearwater, Florida.

Chapter 5

International Management

IT WAS IN the summer of 1976 that I came to work at the International Headquarters of Scientology, the Flag Service Organization in Clearwater, Florida.

My first job was in the international marketing area. The sixth division in Scientology's organizational structure, it was the area responsible for the expansion of Scientology by increasing membership throughout the world. On an international level, it was not just selling someone a few courses or counseling: it was getting Scientology groups, franchises, and organizations opened in cities and often countries where they had not existed.

My duties included helping the Division 6 personnel at organizations around the world to increase the numbers of Scientology members and income. Division 6 did contain sales personnel, but as this division mainly dealt with newcomers, the expectations for income were not as high as the sales personnel that dealt with committed members.

The management level supervised the work of the local division 6s throughout the world. Our unit would help create programs and promotion, which would help division 6 staff in their work to expand Scientology internationally.

I was shown to my working space and discovered that part of my position involved answering many letters from Scientology staff all over the world. I was told that all my communications had to go through AVU (the Authorization and Verification Unit) to ensure they were correct before they were mailed. I was very proud of myself as I dropped my first pile of letters off on my way to lunch. I returned an hour or so later only to find my entire morning's work back on my desk, rejected by Phoebe in AVU. Since I had not referenced a single specific L. Ron Hubbard quote or policy letter in all my responses, they were unacceptable as a communication from Scientology management. I quickly realized that I could not simply write something from myself to a staff member; it had to be part of the larger body of policy that made up the organization. Communicating any of my own thoughts was not allowed unless they were specifically referenced to materials written by L. Ron Hubbard. Despite the steep learning curve, I had an excellent memory and could find a Hubbard quote to cover most anything I wanted to say.

It left me with an entanglement of my thoughts with those of L. Ron Hubbard. It has taken me years to untangle those commingled thoughts and separate my own from his. I must acknowledge that there were things he wrote I agreed with, but there were also policies I did not. But that was later; in 1976, I was becoming a higher-level robot.

The first thing that struck me living and working at the international base was how much better the living conditions were. Especially when compared to the New York outer office I had just left. Not only was there good food each day, but we also even had servers who would come around the tables and give us drinks and extras as asked for. This was for regular international staff like me; the senior international executives got an even higher level of service. The international center was located in what was once a large and plush hotel in the heart of Clearwater, Florida. The rooms had that large hotel feel with matching curtains and beddings, each with its own television and private bath. In those first months, the Flag Land Base, as it came to be known, was not crowded and I only had one or two roommates assigned to live with me. This was a vast improvement over the triple-decker bunks crowded into small rooms I had slept in. The food was a daily feast compared to the beans and rice we were lucky to eat in New York. That past winter, New York literally had no money for simple amenities like heat. A coworker and friend, Arnie Lerma, actually broke up furniture, stuffing and burning it in the furnace so we could get warm. I did not understand how such a difference in lifestyle could occur by simply moving up one level in an organization, but it seemed to be the consistent case wherever my travels took me. The Flag management level of the organization got a percentage of all the money made by the lower orgs in the world. This gave them a vast base of income to live and support their staff and buildings. The outer orgs struggled with their weekly and monthly bills while always providing the management level with percentages required off the top.

It was at the Flag Land Base that I remember first learning about the RPF (Rehabilitation Project Force). Members of the RPF wore a navy blue or black boilersuit as a uniform. It was a one-piece jumpsuit with snaps up the front commonly found for sale at hardware stores. The uniform was intended to make it known at a glance that these individuals were being rehabilitated and not currently normal members of the group. They were not to be trusted.

I cannot recall the very first RPF member I saw. I remember that they were just a part of day-to-day life. During my first year or so in Clearwater, I personally knew no one in the RPF program, so there was no connection or recognition as I saw numbers of blue-suited people moving around the base doing chores.

I never did see an RPF member alone. They always seemed to have their heads down, in a rush, literally running from place to place. I remember one early morning I entered the women's bathroom near the auditorium to find a group of four female RPF members cleaning it. I was surprised and about to turn around and find another bathroom when the apparent leader barked for the women to leave. They scooped up their cleaning supplies and quickly left, passing me silently with their heads down.

"Sorry, sir," the leader said as she backed out of the bathroom herself. I imagined they were running off to whatever their next job was. Personnel of higher rank were always called "sir" whether male or female.

When I stepped out of the bathroom, I was surprised to see them all there waiting for me to come out. I realized they did not have another job; they simply were not allowed to be in the same room with me. There they were, three women silently standing in a line with their metal buckets of cleaning supplies and with heads down. I nodded to the leader as I passed, and she opened the door and guided the women back to their toilet-cleaning jobs.

As time went on, I knew a few people who were ordered to the RPF. I could not easily pick them out of a crowd of blue suits, but I knew they were there somewhere. One of the regular duties of the RPF was to set up the chairs for large auditorium events and then restack them when the event was over. They'd arrive as a group without any talk whatsoever; the chairs were quickly set up in straight lines. During the event, they sat on the floor silently in the back while the rest of us, the normal staff, sat in chairs and laughed and socialized.

They were a presence in the daily maintenance of the hotel grounds, but for the most part, they kept to themselves in the back corridors of the large Fort Harrison Hotel. They were forbidden to ride elevators or use the public toilets, having specific facilities that were assigned to them. The bulk of the maintenance of public spaces occurred when the staff and others who were there for advanced services slept. Sometimes if I entered the hotel from a late work night or an early plane arrival, I could see them rushing around doing their daily cleaning chores. The eerie point I remember most clearly was that they made no noise or eye contact.

Once people I personally knew became members of this group, I began to see the RPF a bit differently. I would think about that person, perhaps looking a bit more closely at the dark blue uniforms. I felt somewhat uncomfortable and knew it would be an embarrassment on both our parts to see each other in that changed form.

It was around 1977 that something called the List One Era began. List One was the title of a series of important Scientology people and words, like L. Ron Hubbard, his wife Mary Sue, Scientology, Dianetics, etc. Hubbard had traced back a variety of major problems occurring within Scientology and management, at that time, to personnel who had a specific reaction to the words and items on this List One when questioned on the E-Meter about them. A program was instituted at his direction where every Sea Org executive at the Flag Land Base was questioned about the items on List One. This was done by trained auditors, well schooled in the use of the E-Meter. Individual people were asked the List One words while holding the metal cans attached to the E-Meter. The E-Meter is Scientology's tool developed by Hubbard to help a trained auditor guide a person through an area of problems, pain, and emotion. A small trickle of electricity is passed through a pair of metal cans, which, when held by an individual, will measure a resistance or the amount of charge existing in that area of the person's emotions and thoughts. It cannot tell specifically if the person is lying or not, only that there is some negativity there in the area being discussed. These measurements are fed back through an active needle on the faceplate of the E-Meter in direct reaction to questions asked by an auditor, much like a lie detector will react in different ways when used by a skilled practitioner. There are many needle reactions and manifestations that have been codified over many years of experience, and every auditor is trained and thoroughly drilled to recognize each and every one and know precisely what each one means.

Officers and executives were each required to be checked by specially trained auditors on the entirety of List One. Each item was read off, and these auditors noted on sheets of foolscap paper the reactions of the E-Meter's needle to each of these words and phrases. There was no counseling or discussion. The list was read, and any needle response was written down next to each word. If the auditor noted that a "rock slam" occurred (which is a specific motion of the E-Meter's needle irregularly slamming back and forth across the dial) that meant the person had hidden evil thoughts and had committed evil acts against the group, an individual, or word on the list. If a person rock slammed on a List One item, they were to be immediately quarantined from the group and sent to the RPF for their own rehabilitation. Supposedly, the discovery of such a hidden evil person in the midst of hard-working and honest personnel would bring great relief to those left behind. The difficulties they had been having on their jobs were explained by their close connection to someone who was secretly working against the common good, knowingly or unknowingly evil. These secretly evil people were called suppressive because that is what they were thought to be doing—suppressing the group and individuals around them through action or inaction.

Scores of executives and personnel at the Flag Land Base were found to be in severe and immediate need of rehabilitation. As each one was discovered, they were removed from their current job or post and taken to the RPF. Soon it was determined that if the many trusted leaders that had been in charge of Scientology on an international level had hidden such suppressive tendencies, it was likely that others existed in the smaller organizations across the world.

I flew from Clearwater to Los Angeles on the very first List One mission. Along with my assigned partner, Chris Rightsman, we were sent to find out why the organizations in Los Angeles were not doing as well as expected. Hubbard had telexed management and suggested that perhaps we would find some of these same List One rock slammers in Los Angeles. Chris was sent with me because he was trained in technical matters and was an expert in the use of an E-Meter.

We arrived in LA and began our investigation by going through the local area executive's PC (preclear) folders. We immediately found evidence of List One needle reactions in quite a few of them and realized many of the staff members, especially those that had been around for a while, contained List

One RSs in their folders. This was not going to be as simple as originally thought. In the mid to late 1960s, rock slams were a well-documented needle phenomenon denoting an area in an individual that could be addressed and, once handled, provide spiritual relief. As a result, many of the longer-term Sea Org members had List One RSs in their preclear folders. The problem was that many of these reads had been noted in years past and might have been noted in error.

We returned overnight to Flag management with that information. New programs and future missions were established to search through people's preclear folders, culling them for rock slams. Once a person's folders were searched through and potential List One RSs had been listed, the individual was scheduled for a special session that would verify the reported needle phenomenon.

This project took on a life of its own and grew exponentially. It became a very large part of our lives during this time. There was not a single person in the Sea Org it did not touch in some way, directly or indirectly. From my international view from Flag management, I witnessed the effects of this witch hunt throughout the advanced Scientology organizations across the world.

During this period, I did an evaluation (a full administrative review) of the Org in St. Louis and felt that the executive director just *must* be a List One RSer. Those of us working in management at the time had become cocky, feeling we had gotten so good at discovering these types of personalities that we could even spot them at a distance with no E-Meter verification at all. The result was that the executive director of the St. Louis Org was immediately removed from his position and sent to the RPF in Los Angeles.

The first person I was close to who was found to be a List One RSer was Tom Atlee, the survey officer at Flag. He did many surveys for LRH and helped define the direction that the international marketing was going. His being a List One RSer certainly explained many poor results on the lack of our international expansion. The problem for me was that I knew him personally and found him to be a very nice man. I simply could not reconcile his mild, easygoing personality with his supposed needle phenomenon and reaction to the areas of List One. Tom had been one of the first people to welcome me from New York to the new and larger world of international management. He was always kind to me, never making me feel stupid when I asked questions that clearly showed my inexperience. I never saw him engage in office gossip of any kind. He worked long and hard hours and always had a great attention to detail. When I made errors in my work and he would correct me, there was never any ridicule; I simply needed to learn more.

He had a wife and a new daughter he doted on. He was the type of coworker that I loved to collaborate with—never shirking work but at the same time when things got too serious, he could always be counted on for a dry comment that would break the ice and make us laugh. I kept these contrary thoughts to myself because at that time, there was no questioning the verification of a rock slammer. Once a person had the label of List One RSer, everything they had done contained a double meaning with an evil undercurrent.

Meanwhile, the number of blue boiler suits grew, not only in Florida but also in the lower-level Sea Org units in Los Angeles and in Denmark. Culling and auditing teams were established and sent throughout the world to locate and isolate these potentially evil personnel. It was done in a specific sequence, beginning with the top positions of the organizations and working downward. No day passed when at least one person was found to be a suppressive person and reassigned to the rehabilitation workforce. More and more of these were people I personally knew.

There was a period of a week during which the American Saint Hill Organization in Los Angeles (one of the most advanced Scientology centers in the United States) sent its commanding officer (the Sea Org's title for an executive director) to the RPF, having been found to be suppressive with many List One RSs. Several days later, his replacement was also found to be a List One RSer and she also was removed from her position to be sent to the rehabilitation force. I believe it was a series of four executives within that senior organization who were promoted to replace the commanding officer position only to be found to be suppressive themselves and sent to the RPF within a short period.

A sense of gallows humor began creeping in. It got so bad that it was the kiss of death if you happened to be promoted or assigned to that job and no one wanted it. My two roommates and I had our sneakers at the ready in our closet in preparation for our own rehabilitation future.

A couple of times I woke up at dawn and looked out the window next to my bed. I had a clear view to the top floor of the attached five-story garage. The RPF would be having its morning roll call, and it had grown to well over a hundred staff in there.

Finally, the List One verification unit came for me. It was time for my very own List One rock slam check. I had been receiving daily counseling, and I'd grown increasingly nervous with each passing day. Then in the middle of one session, I suddenly realized that this was it; this was my List One session. I was petrified. What if I was evil and didn't even know it?

The session ended with no verdict one way or the other. I spent several agonizing days waiting nervously for the results, but I slowly came to realize I must have passed. No one in a blue boiler suit had come to take me away; instead, I was sent to attest that the List One security check was complete. I couldn't believe the relief I felt. I wasn't evil after all, thank God.

The witch hunt continued. There were daily reports of new discoveries being made, either in an outer org or at Flag. Hubbard had thought that we would find a small percent of the population, a mere 2.5 percent, but the percentages within our own organizations were very much higher. What did that mean? I remember there was another one-week period in which several people I was very close to got tagged and sent to the RPF.

I was aware that Hubbard had stated that List One RSers hang out in a group and that was why some places would seem to have such a high incidence of them. I couldn't take it any longer. These were people who were my friends whom I loved and admired, people whom I worked side by side with for months. All of them were suppressive people? Why couldn't I see that evil, and what did that say about me? Was I so blind?

I was a friend of the main person who was in charge of isolating or clearing the names of the staff at Flag who could be List One RSers. I took a deep breath and went to see her and told her they must have missed me because so many of my friends were in the RPF as List One RSers.

She laughed out loud. She said that I had already been checked, and besides, if I were one, I would not have come in to her to turn myself in. A suppressive person was incapable of looking at his or her own mistakes, much less trying to atone for them.

Weeks passed. The RPF continued to grow, and those of us who were still on our jobs found ourselves getting less and less sleep while we covered additional duties. The purge of all these personnel had left us very shorthanded.

I don't remember exactly when, but sometime in 1978, the List One era was over, having run out of steam and exhausted the people involved. We were told it was a specific person close to LRH who had instigated everything. Someone named Paulette Ausley. I knew she was being used as a scapegoat because we had been running the List One checks and RPF assignments from the international management in Clearwater, Florida, and she was not even in Clearwater. Mutual friends of ours told me that that was just a bunch of BS, that this person was the nicest, sweetest person and could never have done what it was being said she did. Besides, those of us at Flag in Clearwater knew we were running it from our international point of view. I never found out the real story behind this person's new status of Scientology's scapegoat, but Paulette took the blame for all of it.

It also seemed convenient to several of us in Clearwater that this discovery and disbanding of the RPF occurred at the same time the renovations of the new Scientology Complex in Los Angeles were completed. The RPF had provided the needed workers to complete those renovations. Suddenly, those falsely accused of being List One RSers no longer needed rehabilitation. The RPF emptied and went back to previous much-lower population. We welcomed our colleagues back with open arms, and the cry "I always knew you weren't suppressive!" was heard often throughout the base. All was forgiven, and everyone quickly got back to work.

Chapter 6

The Quiet Witch Hunt

NOT SURPRISINGLY, a new "clean house" was soon begun. This one was much more confidential and targeted the most senior executives of the group. By 1978, I was promoted to a senior position in international management. I was in daily touch with Hubbard, working on many matters from promotional planning of the establishment of the secular organization WISE (World Institute of Scientology Enterprises) to the investigation of why the Scientology Guardian's Office was spending all of Scientology's reserves of money on legal fees and why the Scientology network was not producing enough income.

The FBI raids of Scientology organizations in both Los Angeles and Washington DC had occurred on July 9, 1977. The legal cost of defending the staff members involved was getting very high, and L. Ron Hubbard did not favor the expense, especially since it was coming out of reserves at an enormous weekly rate.

During these few years, I helped research and get Scientology opened up in Japan. I investigated an earlier attempt to do so as well as successful expansion activities in Mexico and Israel. New religions could not be legally set up in any of those countries, so the organizations had to be listed and registered as a nonreligious entity. I studied what had been done successfully in other countries where Scientology operated in exactly the same way as in the United States but was simply not referred to as a religion.

That didn't appear odd to me at all because even though I had belonged to the organization for over six years and was operating as an international executive, I still didn't see Scientology as having any traditional religious aspect in my daily life. There was no prayer; there were no hymns. In the entire time I had been a Scientologist, from the day I first read that poster to the moment I researched Scientology's expansion, I attended only one church service. Even that was put on solely as a public relations action for the local people of Clearwater, Florida. I actually enjoyed it and personally thought it would be nice to have some aspects of regular churches as part of our daily lives.

My personal experience with Scientology up until that time was that it was a spiritual self-help group, a practical philosophy; and if it was to be considered a religion, it was a nondenominational, and you could maintain your own religion and use Scientology as one of your practical philosophies.

There were several countries in the late '70s and early '80s in which we were not presented as churches. The fact that Scientology was not legally recognized in some countries as a church did not translate into the dogma of traditional religion. There were no prayer and church services; when performed, they were performed as public relations for the community. In the Sea Org, our day-to-day religious garb was a naval-like uniform, replete with gold lanyards and mission ribbons.

When L. Ron Hubbard discovered what he felt to be corporations and companies owned by individual Scientologists ripping off both staff and customers from our Orgs, he was incensed. There were public Scientologists (not staff members) who either hired Scientology org staff to work for their companies on their personal off hours or hired them away from the Scientology orgs when their two-and-a-half- or five-year contracts were complete. Hubbard made it plain that he felt that this was just like stealing money from our coffers. He felt that he and the organization of the Sea Org and Scientology had spent much time and money training these people, making them effective, and now others were reaping the financial benefits of their talents.

Hubbard and I had many conversations by telex and dispatch regarding the situation of these commercial entities. He asked me to establish a corporation that would corral them all up and put them under our control. By charging these members a percentage of their gross income, we would at least be collecting some financial return. The question of whether this would be a profit or nonprofit corporation came up. Hubbard expressed to me the thought that going with the whole church angle for Scientology might have been a mistake in the first place. He felt that the trouble we were currently having with the IRS would not exist if he had not listened to those around him at the time and just stayed as a for-profit corporation and just made more money to pay the taxes. This conversation with him was not upsetting to me or out of the ordinary. I myself had often wondered why we were pursuing the church status. Self-help was big business in the late '70s, and I felt that if anyone had the best self-help around, it was Scientology. This questioning by Hubbard about the efficacy of being a church was also known by others and was even published from some of these other sources in a 1982 *Forbes* article written by Richard Behar. These thoughts were definitely on LRH's mind.

Of course, the other side of being a for-profit organization would be that the staff would have to receive at least minimum wages. That would cut into the profits flooding the bank accounts of Scientology's international reserves, those very same reserves that the Guardian's Office was now draining with their legal troubles.

In the end, we did incorporate the World Institute of Scientology Enterprises (WISE) as a Delaware corporation and as nonprofit. In his final decision, LRH told me that WISE should be nonprofit because it went better with the church mock-up we already had.

Chapter 7

Dating and Marriage in the Sea Organization

IN THE LATE '70s, I was divorced and single and would sometimes moan on the shoulder of my good friend Pat Gualtieri. With my 24-7 job schedule and limited access to eligible bachelors who *also* were members of the Sea Org and living in Clearwater, it seemed that finding a partner did not give me much hope.

"Chris Many," Pat said without a moment's hesitation.

"Who is Chris Many?" I asked.

"He's the perfect guy for you. He is currently running the Celebrity Centre in Los Angeles, but I know you both and he is perfect."

Pat's complete certainty did bring a smile to my sad face, and soon after that, my job duties expanded to supervising all the celebrity centers around the world including the Los Angeles one Chris ran.

The first thing I noticed about Chris was that I would have a direction or suggest an idea for something Celebrity Centre should do and send it to him, but before he had time to receive mine, I would receive a dispatch from him saying almost exactly the same thing. This happened between us several times. I had never worked with someone that I was so in sync with.

I started to wonder, "Who is this Chris Many?"

Within a few months, Pat Gualtieri and I were sent on a mission to Los Angeles Celebrity Centre. I finally got to meet this man, and Pat was right; there was an instant connection. It was so obvious that Chris and I even spoke of it.

I returned to Florida, and Chris remained in Los Angeles. We corresponded for some time till it became obvious that I never wanted to live in Los Angeles and he never wanted to leave Los Angeles. Chris had a son in LA; and even though he had been divorced for some years, he did not want to break up the stability his son, Corey, had. We were at a standstill, and our letters dwindled away. Chris got engaged to a woman in Los Angeles, and I began dating in Florida.

One day at the end of summer 1978, my roommate, who was in charge of international personnel, laid out all the personnel file information on Chris Many on the floor between our desks. She commented on how well he was doing as an executive, and she put together a package that would involve several people changing jobs that included Chris's promotion to international management in Florida. I tried not to get too excited.

Chris was asked over to the Flag Liaison Office in Los Angeles and presented with the promotion. He was very polite and said that he was honored but did not want to accept because he loved his job, loved his son, and loved LA.

When my roommate received this information, she became angry. Once again, she pulled out all the information available on Chris. She once again laid out the graphs that had been kept of his tenure as the leader of Celebrity Centre Los Angeles and reviewed her earlier analysis, which she found to be lacking. Two days passed; the person who had been a great, effective leader expanding Scientology in LA and Hollywood now was an incompetent executive who needed to be removed from post before he did any further damage. He was immediately suspended as the commanding officer of the LA Celebrity Centre (CC) and ordered to report to Clearwater on the next flight out.

Chris arrived and we saw each other and talked a bit, but neither one of us came right out and said how we were feeling. I was sitting at breakfast one day when a friend asked, "Why don't you go after him?"

Now I had never made the first move with a guy before; my friend Franny had been married several times and obviously knew her way around these waters. I looked over to the other side of the dining room where Chris was sitting, and I couldn't deny it; my attraction was very strong.

"But he's engaged," I said.

She quickly responded with "Engaged is not married. You will never know until you try." I looked across the cafeteria where we were all eating breakfast, and even though I had never taken the first move, I knew I would always regret it if I didn't with this one.

There was a rule in Florida that for safety reasons, no woman could walk the streets of Clearwater alone after dark; escorts were assigned or required. I made a plan. I had never been the aggressor in a relationship, but our connection was so strong and he was here in Florida now. I realized Franny was right; he was not married.

I planned a piece of business to do with Chris at the end of the work night and then felt I could ask him to be my escort from the office over to the hotel. I planned that I would make the first move during our private walk.

We finished our business; and I was just about to ask him to walk me home when someone came up to him and said, "Chris, we need you to go on a special mission to Los Angeles, we have you booked on the red-eye out of Tampa. Come with me now, we have to get you up to speed, and there is little time."

I was crushed.

Chris went to Los Angeles where his fiancée and son were, and I missed out on my golden opportunity.

The next morning, I decided that I would give it one last shot. I wrote him a letter, just a chatty letter, nothing deep or personal.

He wrote me back and asked me why I had *really* written him that letter. He then took some risks and communicated how he really felt about me and asked if I felt the same.

I was walking on air, and we continued with these daily love letters while he was in Los Angeles. When he returned to Florida, he asked me to marry him, and I accepted.

I remember feeling on the night he proposed that I never again wanted to go to sleep without him at my side. It has been over thirty years now, and it is the one thing that I can say with a true heart it was worth all the pain and degradation I experienced within my many years in Scientology. Corey, Chris's first son, is married to a beautiful woman; and Corey has four beautiful daughters of his own. We had two incredible children together. Carey, a wonderful man who coaches sports and teaches high school, is married to a beautiful woman; and they are expecting their first child in August. And then there is Taylor, a sweet soul who is also soon to become a father with a wonderful woman while he continues to challenge the world.

And for all that love and family, which I now have, I must say that even the time Scientology sent me to it's dark side was almost worth it. It was a rough journey to get here, but we have a good and loving life.

The year 1979 was a personally difficult year for me. Chris and I had married in the fall of 1978, and I became pregnant with Carey almost immediately. I did get health care for my pregnancy, but my job was so high-pressure that I almost had no time off, nor did I get many good nights of sleep, much less any needed naps. Either I was staying up all night, not physically taking care of my growing child, or I was *not* staying up until all hours and therefore not completing the work I was supposed to do.

Being pregnant was looked upon as an enormous distraction and Dev-T, Scientology slang for "developed traffic" or unnecessary things that get in the way of production. Anything not focused on the complete dedication of the expansion of Scientology was considered Dev-T.

I found myself in a quandary.

Chapter 8

Rehabilitation

I WAS FIVE months pregnant and barely coping with the schedule and stress of my job. I was still holding the CS-6 position (Commodore's Staff Aide for International areas pertaining to Division 6;, opening new countries, celebrities, franchises and groups) Hubbard was very involved in my direct and indirect areas of responsibility.

I looked up from my desk and noticed the two men in blue boiler suits coming toward me, looking straight ahead as they entered my husband's office. At first, I wondered whom they were coming for this time. This was the standard procedure that played out each time a staff member was assigned to the RPF. The guards would come to inform the individual of his or her assignment and escort them back to RPF living and working quarters. I had witnessed this scene many times before—the worn-out people in the navy blue scrubs silently arriving on a mission of a dark future for someone.

My husband, Chris, had been promoted up the Scientology management hierarchy to a position called Commodore's Staff

Captain. LRH (the Commodore of the Sea Organization) was his direct senior, and the Staff Captain supervised the many senior management executives that ran Scientology internationally. He was basically in charge of the worldwide management and expansion of Scientology and reported directly to L. Ron Hubbard.

When I saw the blue uniforms, I assumed they were paying a courtesy call to let him know someone under his command was being removed from post and sent to the RPF. Minutes later, the guards came out of his office on either side of Chris. It had never occurred to me that they would be there for him. It took a few seconds for me to catch my breath. I got up from my desk and walked toward him. One of the guards stepped in between Chris and me, not allowing us to get close. The other one put his arm up to stop my forward motion and said with steel in his voice, "You can see him during the dinner hour." Chris and I locked eyes. He continued to look at me with his head turned as they walked him out of the area.

I returned to my desk and put my head down pretending to work. My long hair offered a shield for my red and watery eyes. I knew I was being watched for a reaction from the other staff in the room, but I attempted to show nothing. There were only a couple of hours until dinner; I could wait.

Six o'clock finally came, and as I made my way down the street from the office building we worked in to the hotel where we ate and slept, I realized I didn't know where to go to find Chris. Fifty people dressed in navy blue boiler suits may sound like a group easily found, but these people were members of the Rehabilitation Project Force. They traveled the stairwells and back hallways of a huge multistoried hotel, hidden from view. They lived in the spaces set aside and built by them in the five-level garage. I could see them working the gardens, cleaning the bathrooms, or sweeping the grounds before daylight. But otherwise, when the sun came up and the hotel guests were about, they seemed to disappear back into the woodwork. These RPFers were almost an invisible group, kept out of sight while they worked through their correctional program.

So at dinnertime, I found myself wandering through the back halls of kitchens and dining rooms in the main hotel until I finally found them. I asked a young man in his dark blue boilersuit standing by the door if I could speak to my husband. He pointed to the dining table at the back and told me to sit there; he would get Chris. In a few moments, he was escorted to where I was. If he had been brought out in handcuffs, I would not have been surprised, but there were none, at least nothing physical. He had already been transformed into a member of the RPF, wearing an obviously well-worn blue jumpsuit. He sat in front of me and held my hand while I cried, assuring me everything would be OK and not to worry. A tear or two escaped his eye, and after what felt like ten seconds, the guard stepped back in and said our time was up. I noticed that Chris's handler was wearing a black armband on his dark boiler suit. Scanning the room, I saw quite a few black armbands and even noticed a few gold ones. I wondered what that meant. I was told I could return to the same place tomorrow during dinnertime.

I slowly made my way across the few blocks to my office building. Climbing the stairs to my office felt like moving through molasses. I sat at my desk and pretended to work, but I could not make sense of the words on my dispatches through my tears. My unborn child kicked in protest, and I became aware of my surroundings. Some primal instinct moved over me, and I knew I had to care for my baby. I had to force some food into my body. I would have to sleep.

Later that evening, we were introduced to the woman who took over my husband's job, my new boss. She called me and L. Ron Hubbard's other aides into her office. At the end of our meeting, she asked me to stay behind. Thinking she would offer some kind words for my predicament, I looked up expectantly.

She informed me that I too was being removed from my job. One of my assistants, Kim, was replacing me. I was a bit taken aback by the choice of replacement. He did good work, but many times it was ever so slow in coming, causing deadlines to be routinely missed. But then again so many things had happened this day that were out of the ordinary, why not this as well? The new Staff Captain told me I was being sent to work in the galley (kitchen) and to gather my things.

This final shock had dried up whatever feelings had been welling inside me, and I was an empty shell by now. I packed up my bag with a couple of personal possessions and made my way out of the office building. I took some small comfort in the warm hug of Florida's darkness and made my way back to the hotel.

How sudden one's fall from grace, I thought. I had seen it happen to others before. One day I would be sitting next to a woman at a board meeting of international directors and aides, and the next I would see her dressed in a dirty boiler suit leaning over the toilet she was scrubbing. Now it was my turn, my fall.

The baby started kicking again, and my thoughts turned to the immediate survival matters at hand. I had not eaten since breakfast and knew this was not good, so I headed for the snack bar to buy myself a protein shake. I had barely five dollars, but I knew I had to eat. Composing myself as best I could, I entered the small Scientology restaurant at the main hotel. The café was filled with out-of-town visitors who were booked at the hotel while they received advancement counseling and training. I knew very few of them, and those I did would not have heard of my recent demise. The people I worked with would still be at their desks; they would not be here this early.

This was a relatively safe and quiet place. I would not have to speak or think about any recent events and concentrate on forcing the necessary, but undesired, protein shake into my body.

The baby was awake and flipping around as I sat in a booth and slowly drank sip by sip, congratulating myself as each gulp went down and stayed down. *Poor child*, I thought. *I bet you didn't plan on being born to such losers.* I looked around at the other people in the snack bar and saw only unknown laughing faces. No one I knew; I was safe for now.

I made it onto the 10:00 PM bus to the QI, which was about ten miles from the main hotel. The QI was an old Quality Inn that Scientology bought and used to house married couples and children. The units in the back of the property had been transformed into a nursery for all the children. Chris and I had only recently moved there in anticipation of our baby's birth. Since Chris was living in the garage, I wondered if I would lose our private room now that I was "single." Private space was at a premium, and I now no longer qualified. The thought of moving back into one of the crowded dormitories while being five months pregnant filled me with dread. I looked out the bus window at the streetlights and store signs, trying to shift my thoughts. Colors danced as they reflected in the raindrops beading on the glass and glistening in the puddles we passed. This was surreal. People sat in small groups, and I was surrounded by their laughter. I wondered if any of them knew and just how fast the rumor line was.

News in a close-knit community travels quickly. Who the latest addition to the boys in blue is something discussed over granola and coffee in the morning.

No one on the bus spoke with me, and I was happy to have the peace. I knew this oasis would not last. I was certain to bump into someone I knew, someone who had heard. Then I would have to speak it, speak the tragedy and injustice that had befallen our lives. Once spoken aloud, the words would shatter what buffer I had left. What had happened would then be true; it would then be real.

I was exhausted but did not know how I would sleep. I had already decided I would take my time in the morning. I would take the later shuttle to the Fort Harrison Hotel to report to the kitchen duty I had been assigned. I did not want to run into people I knew. I didn't want their pity or comfort or even the gloating from those who felt we had deserved our fall from grace.

The next morning, I arrived at the main hotel by 10:00 AM. On my way to the food services area, I passed the office of a special project unit that had been under my supervision until reorganization a few months prior. The staff who worked in the unit were dear friends, and as I passed the small office, I caught Pat Gualtieri's eye. That was all it took; not a word had to be spoken. He took me in his arms, and as my body was overcome with emotion, he walked me to a chair. Richard, another colleague, and his wife brought me water and comfort. I felt safe; there was relief in their kindness. I had not eaten breakfast, and a protein shake soon materialized. Richard said I could use their hotel room in this building for some rest during the lunch break. I thanked them and said I would return for the key.

When I reported to the kitchen, the galley steward looked me up and down. It was obvious that he did not expect a woman five months pregnant. He put me to work setting tables for the hundreds of seats in the largest dining room. As I placed the forks and spoons in their proper places, I held on to the knowledge that I would at least get to see Chris at supper; I could last the eight hours 'til then.

As soon as the staff began arriving for lunch, I retreated to the special project office. I sat in a corner chair and listened to their upcoming plans for a San Francisco seminar. When they finished their meeting, Richard walked me upstairs so I could rest in their room.

As soon as I closed his door, the tears began to fall. I curled up on the bed and sobbed. My belly was huge, and the force of my grief scared me as it rippled through my unborn child. *What must my child think of this?* I tried to calm myself by watching the breeze move the orange and yellow curtains, back and forth, back and forth. I had not allowed myself to feel much of anything since the shock of my husband's removal from his job yesterday afternoon. The floodgates opened, and now it was pouring out. *Stop it, Nancy,* I mentally shouted to myself. *This helps nothing and can't be good for the baby.*

I went into their bathroom to assess my appearance. I stared in the mirror and saw myself; my skin was pasty white and my eyes were so red I looked like I was wearing a mask. I was alone. Chris was not there. The crying began again, a real ugly weeping I couldn't contain. I bent over the sink and constantly scooped cold water over my face. I remembered reading somewhere that the most effective cooling method was a wet cloth on the back of your neck, so I tried that. Every time my thoughts would drift to the situation Chris and I were in, I would squeeze my eyes tight and work hard to come back to the moment, a moment with the cold water on my face and neck. I looked at my watch and realized that it was almost one o'clock and I would soon be late in returning from lunch break. *What did that matter now, what else could they do to me?* I was already working in the hot, humid kitchens. I took some deep breaths and softly rubbed my large belly. I was not alone in this and had to be strong for our child. I took one last deep breath, and when I felt calm enough, I made my way back down to the galley.

Charles, the head steward, put me to work at dishwashing. He gave me a rubber apron and showed me how to work the huge metal monstrosity that ate large green trays of silver and glasses. My job was to rinse them off with a hose that dropped down from the ceiling. My body was unwieldy at best, and I was not used to maneuvering around with such a large stomach in front of me. The floor was slippery even with the rubber floor mats, so I was carefully watching my every move. I worked silently for an hour, thankful my tears had finally dried up.

I looked up and noticed two people in boiler suits, a woman with a gold armband and a young man, who were slowly making their way toward me. I had a stab of fear that something was wrong with Chris, but the tall woman with a South African accent assured me he was fine and handed me a piece of paper. It was my very own assignment to the Rehabilitation Project Force; they had come for me. It was dated April 1, and being April Fool's Day, I thought this must be a cruel joke. I had never known a pregnant woman to be sent to the RPF, never. I looked from one to the other and asked if there was some mistake. They assured me this was not a joke and that I was to follow them.

They walked me through the back corridors of the hotel to the garage. The office of the Rehabilitation Project Force was not really a formal space; it was a walled-off part of the existing garage. Large sheets of plywood and two-by-fours outlined the space and created a cubicle of sorts, making a room used as an office. The room where the members studied and slept was also a sloppily built room of old lumber. These illegal constructions were so hastily thrown together that when local building inspectors would come, several mattresses would be stacked in front of the RPF entrances, and the spaces would be labeled storage. No city official had ever doubted this, for who could imagine fifty or sixty or even a hundred people shut off and living in a garage like this? The five-star hotel itself was twelve stories tall; its attached garage facilities, five levels. After midnight, the local Scientology security guards locked all doors between the main hotel and the garage. I wondered how I would get to a bathroom; pregnancy had made me very aware of remaining close to a toilet for the required middle-of-the-night relief.

Chris was waiting for me in the RPF office; that was the one shining moment in all this. Now that we had both hit bottom, we could be together throughout the day although we would not be allowed to spend much time alone. And of course, we would not be allowed to sleep together while we were undergoing our rehabilitation as men and women had separate sleeping areas.

Soon I began my orientation into the inner workings of the RPF. Hanna Eltringham Whitfield, the blond woman who'd gathered me up in the galley, handed me a packet of orders that were written as policy covering the rules and regulations of being a member in my new group. She told me to begin studying it as I was expected to know the rules.

RPFers are allowed to clean buildings, toilets, stairways, garages, elevators, and elevator shafts, I read. I couldn't imagine cleaning an elevator shaft.

RPFers cannot handle any vehicles, have no time off, are restricted to the hotel at all times unless accompanied by a security guard, may not speak to or approach staff or public or any outside public unless spoken to, has to use the bathroom facilities only as designated.

Now I understood why those women were so startled when they ran into me in the bathroom that day.

I continued to read, *May not enter staff or public areas, or elevator except when on assigned cleaning projects*, and then in capital letters, *MAY NOT USE THE SWIMMING POOL AT ANY TIME*. As I read these rules, it was sinking in that I could no longer freely go anywhere. There would always be guards or an assigned buddy watching my every step. The clothing I was going to be wearing would make me stand out if I was ever in a place I wasn't supposed to be.

"You are going to have to finish reading that later," said Hanna. I discovered she wore a gold armband as a designation that she was close to completing her rehabilitation and returning to the main group of staff in Clearwater.

"We are going to have to dash to the mall and get you some navy blue outfits. There has never been a pregnant woman here, and none of the boiler suits will fit. I've called motor pool, and we have to leave now."

We sat in the back of the blue hotel van that carried guests and staff to the area malls in Clearwater. I glanced over at Hanna Whitfield. She sat with her head held high, making no eye contact. Her silence was very focused. We arrived at the mall and got out of the van.

"We have to hurry. The driver will be back to get us in an hour." I had a difficult time keeping up as Hanna was almost running through the mall. I had recently passed that pregnancy signpost where even walking was not an option; waddling was my form of movement. I struggled to keep up with her. She was silent, eyes straight ahead. She asked a salesgirl for the maternity department at the JC Penny's, and we found two simple tops that looked like they might work. They were navy blue with the smallest of ornamentation on them. As I tried the tops on, Hanna looked me up and down and nodded. "These will do fine," she said. We also bought a pair of maternity blue jeans. Hanna paid for the items and hurried us out of there. There were no social graces between us. We had a mission, and our job was to complete it in the fastest, most efficient way possible.

We made it back to the point where the motor pool would pick us up early. Even though we were alone, Hanna did not interact with me. She felt cold and serious. The reality of the new personae I was taking on began to sink in. I was no longer a social person with a personality or anything other than the focus of a job to be done. There was nothing funny about the situation, so the lack of laughter was unstated. What could we chat about anyway?

Hanna and I returned to the RPF office an hour before dinner. Hanna said she would show me around before we would join the other members of the rehabilitation unit for dinner.

The Fort Harrison Hotel had an entrance to the parking garage on each of the four connecting floors. The entrance to the RPF portion of the garage was on the second floor. Two wide doors opened from the garage into the reception room for a large auditorium. If you entered the garage from these two fire doors, you would notice plywood walls on either side of the entryway, extending almost to the ceiling. They jutted out to form an entryway about twelve feet from the door. To the right was the RPF office; to the left was the rehabilitation berthing space and course room.

I had already been in the main rehabilitation office. Hanna now took me to the other side of this space to show me the course room. The cramped room contained four folding tables with chairs around them. It also contained the usual makings of a Scientology training facility: clay for the clay table demonstrations, demonstration kits to show how well you understood something, and dictionaries. This was by far the shabbiest course room I had ever seen. The floor slanted in a slight grade as all parking garages do. To the left of the entrance was a small doorway that opened to a dark dormitory for the women. I could make out the silhouette of tiers of mattresses and pillows. *Oh no*, I thought, *not those dreadful triple bunks.*

Hanna said that due to my pregnancy and size, she had assigned me the bottom bunk near the doorway. Members had a single drawer in which to stow their meager clothing. I placed my newly purchased navy blues in mine and returned to the course room in the darkness. She pointed to the doorway at the other end and informed me that that was where the men slept. I never saw the inside but could assume that the men's dorm was no different from ours.

She said that in the next day or so, Chris and I would go to our room out at the Quality Inn and pack up all of our personal items for storage. Now that we were in the RPF, we only needed a few changes of clothing and a handful of toiletry items. There would be no time for anything else.

Hanna looked at her watch and said, "Time for dinner, let's go join the rest of the group for supper."

We went through the doors to the main part of the hotel and made our way to the side entrance of the auditorium. The staff at the Flag Land Base had grown to such a size that the auditorium doubled as a cafeteria for staff.

Members of the RPF could only eat after regular crew ate and could only eat what the staff had not consumed—the leftovers. If it had been a particularly good meal, regular staff ate heartily, and our offerings were slim.

I entered the large carpeted room filled with round and rectangular tables. The regular staff had left without clearing their tables, so the room was a hodgepodge of chairs in disarray and tables full of half-eaten food and drink.

Small groups of RPFers were clearing several tables near the door, so the rest of them could have a clear space to eat. Another group was going through the buffet line to see how much food was left over in the serving pans. Some staff went back into the kitchen area itself to see if more leftovers could be found.

I noticed some individual people wandering through the tables, looking carefully at each one. I saw someone pick up a dessert plate, and after a quick perusal at the state of the slice of pie, he smiled and carried it over to his place at one of the tables. The food was not yet in the trash, so it was not as demeaning as digging through garbage. However, it was clearly meant to be eaten and left behind by a faceless staff member, maybe a friend. I thought how I would never do that. How disgusting it was.

But I soon discovered that time and hunger has a way of helping a person do what they need to do to survive. Within two weeks, I joined the scavengers; I was trying to survive for two.

On some days, there would be many leftovers and I would not have to search, but often there was not very much. On those days, I found myself joining the members scrounging around the tables, trying to find food that looked untouched.

If the food left on the tables was scarce and no uneaten portion could be found, then the next best thing would be something that had only a bite or two missing. After several weeks in this degrading environment, I found myself doing just that. I would throw away the portion near the bite and then eat the rest. Being pregnant drove me to do things that I would not have normally done and forced me to work toward a better nutrition than just leftovers.

That first night, sleeping in the narrow bottom bunk was frightening. I not only had the normal imbalance of hormones of a woman in her fifth month of pregnancy, but I was now also in a state of shock. I felt void of feelings; I was frozen in place. Just a few days ago, I had been at the top of Scientology's international management. I was working on important and world-changing projects directly with the founder. I had a secretary and personal staff assistants. I was responsible for a network of hundreds of staff in many countries and managed the marketing and expansion of Scientology across the world. The change was sudden and devastating.

During my first week, I had a dream that I died. I could sense there were a couple of people (or spirits) with me, ready to take me onto whatever the next step after death was. They informed me we had a bit of time before we had to go. For that brief time, I walked among the living. I went to all my familiar places, but I was unseen by those around us. I had what I imagined to be a body but had no face. I was invisible to those still living. I could see and hear them but could no longer communicate with them. The sudden loss of what had been my life was irrevocable. I realized that this time of walking among the living was intended to help me comprehend how final my separation from my former life was to be.

That was how I felt that night. I was five months pregnant and taken away from all that had been mine and sent to live in a parking garage with fifty or sixty other discarded souls. At least I had Chris. They couldn't take him away.

After a few days in my new blue uniform and with my newly acquired prisoner status, Chris and I went with an escort to pack up our things at the Quality Inn. The staff member was with us not only to give us a ride but also to supervise us, ensuring we would not leave, disappear, or get lazy with the job at hand. We owned no furniture. Our belongings consisted of clothing, a few books, and several other personal items. It didn't take us more than a couple of hours to box up all of our possessions in the world.

The guard left us alone in the room for part of the time. This was the first real moment that we had to ourselves, alone and unsupervised, in the past three days. No one was scrutinizing our conversations or closely monitoring our activities.

We held each other. We joked about Chris's five-year-old son, Corey. He'd been staying with us in Florida but had left about a month earlier to go on a vacation with his mother. Corey had called his dad two weeks ago and told him he wanted to stay with his mom for a while in LA. Chris was upset with the change of plans at the time, but now we saw that Corey had some serious survival skills. He must have known at some level that a storm was headed our way. We were so lucky that Corey had decided to go back to LA to stay with his mom. We knew that we wouldn't have been able to have care for him while on the rehabilitation force.

I knew I would be physically restrained if I had attempted to leave the RPF without permission. There were no fences with barbed wire and no security guards with loaded weapons, but the specific training of the group was to physically restrain anyone who attempted to leave on their own.

Looking back on it from the distance of many years, my RPF assignment marked the beginning of my long road out of

Scientology. I began to deeply question just what type of group I was involved in. It was this exact moment that I woke up and recognized I was trapped, caged beyond any recognition, and I knew I had to extricate myself very carefully.

Personnel in the RPF spent five hours daily in study and counseling that mostly involved a procedure called security checking, a questioning into our deepest, most personal thoughts and intentions. I knew on a very deep survival level that we needed to extricate ourselves from the hold this group had on us, but I did not allow myself to unfold those thoughts, afraid something would be found in one of their thought-digging sessions.

I got more sleep in the RPF than I ever did on my job; I was allowed scheduled doctor's visits and birthing classes at the hospital with my husband.

Personally, I could not believe that I had been sent to the RPF to live in a garage while five months pregnant. I could not believe that I could go from one of the highest positions in Scientology, from having daily correspondence and working closely with Hubbard himself to living in a dirty, filthy garage just that quickly with virtually no warning, little correction, or the appropriate gradient steps in between. The sudden shock, the unexpectedness, and sheer injustice of it was something that caused a mental shutdown in my personal world.

During the years since, I have studied the research done on the power that groups can hold over individuals and the mindsets and peer pressures that got me to that place. But the finality of it and the knowledge of just who it was who had sent me there is something I may have learned to live with, but it is not something I will ever get over in my lifetime.

During my first week on the RPF, I was shown the Ethics Order spelling out my new assignment. Originally the order had been that I was to be taken to the RPF at the same time as my husband. This had to be approved by LRH himself because both Chris and I worked directly under him and others did not have the power to remove us. However, there was someone else who questioned the part of the order that had to do with me. Although I never found out who it was, that person thought that since I was five months pregnant, it might not be appropriate to have me living in a garage with carbon monoxide and other noxious fumes. The question was sent directly to L. Ron Hubbard; his terse answer was an affirmation of my assignment to the RPF. Hubbard had a group of personal assistants known as commodore's messengers who acted directly on his behalf and spoke for him. If he was too busy to sign a dispatch himself, the messenger on duty could sign it for him, which is what happened on the query sent about me. Messengers were prohibited from signing something that was not LRH's express command. They couldn't act independently. Speaking to a messenger was meant to be the same as speaking to LRH himself as Hubbard himself had dictated. The knowledge that LRH himself had sent me here was almost more than I could bear.

That Hubbard would send a pregnant woman to a live in a garage was shocking to me. My assignment was not due to being found suppressive, which is *the* worst thing you can be found to be in any Scientology group. According to the Ethics Order, I was deemed in need of rehabilitation because of a project I didn't get done on time. Which in a bit of striking irony was a project that had been assigned to my assistant, Kim, the person who replaced me.

For the first time, I began to question the group to whom I had given so much allegiance and loyalty. I buried these thoughts deep inside and did not allow myself the luxury of spending time with them. I knew that this assignment was too harsh and unjustified. I may not have been perfect on my job, but I certainly had not been doing bad enough to deserve the upheaval to my life I was now faced with.

Chris had a different perspective on all this, and it was at this point he told me he wanted to leave not only the rehabilitation unit, but also his career and life in the Sea Organization as well. He missed his son, Corey, who was back in Los Angeles with his mother. Chris desperately wanted to be reunited and was obviously unhappy with our current situation.

We talked about it at length, but I knew I could not leave. I knew no one in Los Angeles, and we had no job opportunities at all as we'd been working full-time over the past six years within the insular society of the Sea Org. Currently Scientology was paying for my health care and would pay for the delivery of our child. How could we possibly manage the expenses ourselves? And with me being five months pregnant, who would hire me? We had burned our bridges with both of our families and non-Scientology friends. The cold fact was that there had been no salary paid to us due to the Sea Org's policy of only doling out a minimal $20-30 per week to its staff including executives. We literally had no money to get to Los Angeles even if we wanted to, let alone get an apartment and cover the cost of the medical care we'd need for the birth of our child. We were trapped. There was no way out except to do the rehabilitation program that Hubbard had ordered us. There was no other way.

Another big part of my decision was the group dynamic I had been taught and was knotted in my head. I *knew* that my being sent to the Rehabilitation Project Force was incorrect. I *knew* that at some point down the road, I would be vindicated. A committee or individual would do a review, and it would come out that this RPF order was bogus and should not have happened. However, I also knew the way my coworkers and friends in this group thought. I knew that if I voiced a desire to leave because I considered this wrong, then that would cement my guilt for the group. People would then conclude, "See, sending her to the RPF was correct all along, she must have always wanted to leave underneath. It's a good thing we uncovered her true intentions."

The truth was I simply cared too much about what others thought. People I knew, people I didn't, friends, acquaintances, strangers. I cared about what they thought and couldn't bear to be seen as a traitor or criminal within Scientology.

Additionally, the reality was that we had no friends who were *not* Scientologists. By simply walking out the door, we would be forbidden to speak or work for anyone who was a Scientologist. If we broke our billion year contract, we would be looked upon as deserters and summarily excommunicated from Scientology. We would be declared suppressive people and shunned by all Scientologists in good standing. Even though in my secret heart of hearts I wanted to leave— not necessarily Scientology itself, but certainly the Sea Organization—I did not see it as a realistic choice.

So after much soul-searching, Chris decided to stay. He would never abandon his unborn child or me despite the conditions we were faced with. He decided we would have to get through this together. I needed him, and he needed me. We would face it together.

Ironically, there were some things that were better being on the RPF than being a regular Sea Org member. I got much more sleep and finally got on a regular schedule that didn't involve eighteen-to-twenty-hour workdays. I saw my doctor and got medical care without the hassle of feeling guilty for taking time off my important job. I studied and coaudited five hours every day in order to complete my rehabilitation program. The stress of running an international division under the founder of Scientology was gone. But on so many levels and so many other ways, the RPF was a horrific experience for me.

The RPF was organized into units of five to six people with one in the group being the assigned leader. Projects were handed out to each group. Sometimes several units would work together on a larger project or all the units would work in a coordinated effort. Chris and I were in different units. His unit would work on things like rat patrol, going around the back hallways, stairways, and attics of the Fort Harrison Hotel and setting and handling rodent traps. Sometimes his unit would be assigned to unload the trucks of food regularly delivered to the hotel kitchens.

The labor the people on the RPF were allowed to do was always manual in nature. In fact, no RPFer was allowed to work with any machinery of any kind. The reasoning was that they were so ineffective that they could harm themselves or others; machines were just too much for someone rehabilitating his spiritual and mental abilities.

I was given the job of watering the lawn and gardens of the main hotel in the early morning hours before breakfast. I would stand near the pool with my hose in hand and spray the water in what I thought was an even and saturating method. As I stood there at 5:30 AM sprinkling the lawns, I would sometimes look up at the windows of the hotel and imagine all the normal people sleeping in their beds. One morning, I saw a mother and daughter, who appeared to be about ten, come out of their cabana room. They were smiling and engaged in some conversation that I couldn't decipher from my distance. I thought of how wonderful their lives must be, how simple to be coming here to downtown Clearwater for some sun and Scientology services. I knew they had to have money because the cabana rooms were more expensive and the services available at the Flag Land Base all cost tens of thousands of dollars. I looked down on my massive belly and wondered if the baby was a boy or girl, and how I hoped that when he or she was ten, we would be going out to breakfast just like this little girl and her mom. We would be like normal people.

I had drifted so far in my imagination that I had lost track of the watering I was supposed to be doing. *Had I already watered this section enough? Should I move on to another section?* I took the hose with me to the area beside the pool and began to water the flowerbeds there. In those early morning hours, I would often imagine what it would be like to be normal, to live my life as a public Scientologist and have a life outside of the dedication of the Sea Org.

I was always a bit nervous with my early morning gardening duties. I was the only person out there, and with my pregnant belly, I was not hard to miss. I was afraid I would run into one of the staff I knew even if it was so early in the day. I was still grasping at the concept that I was now a member of the RPF. I was having a difficult time accepting it and bouncing back and forth from being so numb. I felt like a robot and was trying to get behind the glimpses of the horror that was my new predicament. I felt that if I saw even one person I knew who gave me even an ounce of kindness, I would lose it.

One morning, I had finished my watering chores; and after returning the hose, I turned the corner into the breezeway to the garage. Sandy was just standing up from the water bubbler when she saw me.

"Nancy, what are you doing here?" she asked.

I stopped in my tracks. I knew I was not allowed to talk unless spoken to and then only to reply with the briefest of replies. I looked around to see if there was anyone watching us. When I was confident the coast was clear, I turned my head toward her to speak. I looked into her eyes and felt the deep compassion there. She knew by my navy blue outfit exactly what had happened. I could not speak. My throat was frozen. Tears began to streak my face. This was so embarrassing. Sandy came close to give me a hug and a soft pat on the back. I snuffled up my tears and said, "Thanks, but I have to get going." I turned back to make my way through the breezeway, mentally trying to get my wall of numbness back up. I felt it was better for my health and that of my baby's if I did not dwell on my situation too much.

Soon after that, I lost my morning garden assignment. My watering was found to be poor. Apparently, patches began to appear in the grass where I had watered unevenly. There was not much that I could be assigned that I would be physically able to do, so after a few weeks, I was sent to the technical unit within the RPF. This was the unit that delivered the courses and helped with the needed personal counseling to all the members of our group. It consisted of course supervisors and coaches, and they needed a case supervisor (C/S). I had never really even been an auditor, and yet here I was, assigned to be the case supervisor on all of these other RPFers.

The RPF kept a very strict schedule and had several roll calls throughout the day to count all the people and make sure no one was missing or unaccounted for. The person who was the master of arms (the naval equivalent of an ethics officer) would conduct a roll call and we would answer "Aye, sir" Or "Here, sir" when we heard our names. While the Sea Org was modeled after the navy and used a lot of naval language, both men and women of higher rank were addressed as *sir* instead of *sir* for men and *ma'am* for women. Being in the Rehabilitation Project Force essentially made everyone higher than you, and that was why the people in the RPF addressed everyone as *sir*.

We woke up at 0600 and put in a couple of hours of work before breakfast at 0800. At 0800 was when the dining room was closed to the crew and we could then eat.

Meal breaks were brief, thirty minutes at most, and that included the time to put the meal together. We would have a roll call first thing in the morning, after breakfast, after lunch, after supper, and then again at 2130 during the final muster before lights-out at 2200.

The final muster was in the classroom. We would all sit around tables in the various wobbly chairs. Announcements would be made of upcoming projects we were working on and of completions of courses and auditing that people had done. After these nightly announcements, our leader (called the Bosun) opened the floor to the members. RPFers shared any wins or successes they may have had during the day. These would be things like "I really *have* gotten it!" or "I was able to stay in PT (present time) all day as we carried those boxes from the truck to the freezer" or "We caught three on rat patrol today." Sometimes people would thank LRH for allowing them to do the RPF. At the end, we would have the obligatory clapping and cheering to a large picture of L. Ron Hubbard. That always got to me; we were thanking LRH for the privilege of being sent to live in a garage and being treated by the rest of our friends and colleagues as a lower status of being. I could never voice those thanks with any feeling because I simply did not have any to give.

It always felt surreal listening to people thanking LRH for the RPF and how happy they were to be there, how they needed this kind of rehabilitative supervision, and how they were being made a better person. I wondered if these people truly meant it or were simply saying it because they knew they would get out of the garage more quickly. I didn't speak those thoughts out; I barely voiced them to myself in my head. I had already decided that I was going to get through this in the fastest way I could. I was *not* going to have a baby while living in a dirty garage under guard. In the one-on-one counseling that people received in the Rehabilitation Project Force, individuals were probed for evil thoughts or actions that they may have kept secret from other members of the group. The only way to get through it was to accept it for what it was and to not rail against it. All such opposition against it did was prolong the process of getting out.

It was a catch-22. To get out, you had to exhibit change whether you had needed change or not. To get out, you had to act as if it were a needed action whether it was or not. My survival depended on me being able to just sit and take it. I would make the best of these circumstances but be on guard for any thinking outside of the box rather than the approved Scientology line. If I actually had unfolded any of those thoughts buried deep inside, they would have increased the attention of the people probing my mind to go deeper, and that would only prolong my existence in this awful garage.

Chris and I were allowed to continue with our birthing classes at the local hospital during our stay in the Rehabilitation Project Force. One week, we learned that it was in the third trimester that development occurred with baby's brains. Protein was needed to grow the brain. Eggs were a good source of that, and Chris made it a point to scrounge up from leftovers or sometimes steal eggs so that I could have protein every day. Chris and I would laugh along with the staff seated at our table about the eggs I would have to eat. I would always attempt to put a bright face on it, but sitting in a room full of messy tables among piles of leftovers was a truly sad state of affairs.

I was allowed to ride in the hotel van to my doctor appointments. At first I was not allowed to go alone, but once it was clear that I was quite pregnant and not moving very fast, I was allowed to travel on my own. The fact that they had my husband as collateral for my return cinched the deal. The van would drop me off at the doctor's office where I did not mind having to wait.

It was one of the few times I was allowed to dress in clothes other than the regulation navy or black. I would sit in the waiting room and pretend that I was as normal as any of the other women there. I would read magazines and rub my belly. No one here knew I was walking back to live in an environment of carbon monoxide and grease. They looked at me as if I were like them. It felt good to be thought of as normal.

The weigh-in was always of concern to me because I was not gaining any significant weight, but somehow I kept the weight within an average range. When I was done, I always made it a point to walk back to the garage on Fort Harrison Avenue. Several nurses in the doctor's office saw me and offered me rides. It was two miles and usually during the midday heat in humid Florida. This was the South in summer, and the temperatures rose to well over one hundred degrees with regularity. I always turned the rides down. The staff of the doctor's office could not understand why in the world I would rather walk on such a hot day or why anyone would let me walk at all. They had no idea it was the only time I was alone and walking as if I were free.

I also felt a sense of normality with the baby classes. Every Tuesday night, Chris and I would be allowed to go to our birthing class at the nearby hospital. We would walk the two miles each way. It was a time when we could be alone, hold hands, and just be around regular people. I could simply be a pregnant woman with her husband like all the other pregnant couples in the class.

Our walk back would take us through a neighborhood of single-family homes. I would ask Chris if we would ever have such a home. From where we were right then, the thought itself was quite a leap. He would always comfort me with the right answers, that someday we would have a house of our own. We discovered we both liked Tudor-style architecture. I remember a large Tudor house behind a black wrought iron fence that always sparked my curiosity and wondered about the family living there. Did they appreciate all that they had? One week, as I saw teenage boys playing ball in the front yard, I rubbed my belly and wondered if my child would ever play basketball in the front yard of our home.

If we had time on the way back to the garage, we would sometimes take a short detour and walk to a gazebo at the end of a dock. It was our private spot where we had become engaged. The water from the bay gently lapped against the pilings in a soothing rhythm. Occasionally we would see the shadow of a person walking down the street, but more often we were just alone in the dark, seated on the wooden bench close to each other. We would speak in whispers, giving comfort and hope for the years to come and the baby we shared. Life would get better than this. It had to.

After I had been in the RPF for about a month, I was asked to go to a private area in the empty dining room and speak with a commodore's messenger. Hubbard appointed young teenagers, many of them girls, to act as his personal messengers. They were trained and thoroughly schooled to deliver his wishes or questions exactly as he wanted them to and to gather the information he requested as truthfully and straightforwardly as they could. It was drilled into all Sea Org staff that all commodore's messengers were extensions of L. Ron Hubbard and that we were to treat them with the honesty and respect that we would give if it were actually the commodore in front of us. I didn't personally know the messenger who sat down with me with her pad of paper, but I did know that I had to be careful of what I did or didn't say. I was well aware that my facial expressions and other subtle communications would be duly noted and relayed. I had no idea if this was a friendly visit or a visit meant to revise my rehabilitation.

"How are you adjusting to life in the RPF?"

I thought for a moment of exactly how to respond to this and then decided that short and succinct was safest. "Fine."

"Is there anything that you would like to let LRH know?"

My mind went to the relationship I had had with him over the past two to three years and how supportive and kind he had been to me. My mind immediately went to our very first communication as his aide in managing Scientology's Division

6 activities across the planet. I had temporarily taken over for his daughter Diana while she went on her maternity leave. He was initially quite stern with me and actually sent an angry telex asking if I wanted to be the villain in the next movie for destroying the progress of the world. Over the next few days, he investigated and sent his messengers to write and report on all my conversations and actions. Once he'd gathered the information he was looking for, he then sent me a telex saying he was going to make me the heroine in his next movie. From that point on, we had what I thought was a pretty good relationship. He mentored me and issued corrections, but overall, he was pleased by my actions and accomplishments. So much so that when his daughter Diana returned from her maternity leave, he personally promoted me to be her full-time deputy. Later, when she was awarded the opportunity to train full-time, he named me as her replacement. I was his personal aide for all things to do with the expansion of Scientology across the globe. As these memories and many more skipped across my thoughts, I began to cry. I didn't understand what I had done that he felt was so horrific. I felt so very saddened that I had let him down, so much so that he felt he had to send me to the RPF in a garage.

"Tell him I'm sorry," I answered, though I knew not for what. The messenger calmly noted my words and grief and said good luck and good-bye.

As my pregnancy progressed, some accommodations were made for my state. I received approval to ride the freight elevator so I wouldn't have to continue climbing the twelve flights of stairs to deliver and retrieve the PC folders for my fellow RPF members. As my need for the bathroom increased, I received special approval to use the staff and guest facilities, but only if I was not near the RPF bathroom. At night, this was difficult. As part of the hotel's security, all the doors from the garage to the main building were locked down every night. Of course, the garage itself had no bathrooms so I had to make my way down the circular garage ramp to the bottom floor of the garage and out to the street in front of the Fort Harrison.

I often made this walk after midnight in my nightgown. I had to take care because the ramp was steep and my balance was constantly shifting with my gaining girth. The more pregnant I became, the more frequent the trips. The security guard at the front door of the hotel would give me a nod as I would make my way into the women's room. Sometimes cars would drive down Fort Harrison Boulevard during a 3:00 AM walk, and as they passed, I would wonder what that person thought of a waddling, very pregnant young woman making her way down the street in her nightgown in the early morning hours. Once, as I was carefully making my way down the circular garage ramp, I heard a car coming up. I was a very slow walker at that point and it was too far for me to make it to the safety of either the level I just left or the level I was headed to. I stepped into the concrete alcove on the side and hoped I could fit with my protruding stomach. The car made its way past me; I kept my head turned so I wouldn't have to have eye contact with the driver. It was simply too embarrassing. I was ashamed at what my life had become.

As May turned into June and my belly got larger and larger, I found sleeping in a non-air-conditioned garage in a stuffy wooden shelter to be unbearable. Along with another female member, I took a broken pool lounge chair, added a pillow and sheet, and went to the roof of the garage to sleep. I still could not be with Chris at night, but I finally found a place where I could breathe. Since we woke before dawn to get on with our duties, the hotel guests or regular staff never saw us under the stars.

Then one morning, I was awakened by the sound of an engine being turned on in a nearby car. I sat up with a lurch. The driver saw me and paused for a brief moment but said nothing. He simply backed his car out of his space. I wondered what he must have thought: *what is this very pregnant woman doing sleeping out here with the cars?* I was embarrassed and made my way back downstairs.

During the four months I spent in the clothes marking me as unworthy, I learned how people treated those who were down. It was as if by being on the outside of a society, I could see into their deepest hearts. Some people shunned me; some took pleasure in their higher spot of the pecking order. On the other hand, there were many who went out of their way to treat me like a human being. A smile snuck my way, a nod of the head: those bits of compassion went a long way in the midst of a cold hard group. Those small morsels of humanity meant so much.

I knew I was getting a little extra special treatment due to my condition. I didn't have to run laps, I had special use of the bathrooms, and I would take weekly trips to the doctor and attend local baby classes. The staff that supervised the operation of the RPF allowed me these tiny exceptions to the rehabilitation rules. I was always circumspect with the bending of the usual inviolate policy. I knew someone higher up could just as easily find fault with this and quickly act to remove these few special privileges. I always took care to use them while calling the least amount of attention to myself.

Each person entering the RPF had an exact series of steps that they had to complete to get out. There was no time limit, no specific sentence so to speak; instead, there were milestones that had to be reached. One's success in the RPF involved both the ability to work within the group and a personal and spiritual progress on Scientology's Bridge to Total Freedom.

As a group member, these milestones involved proving that you can work in a diligent manner and produce a product (like a clean toilet) that does not require being redone. The RPFer would then graduate to more complex assignments, acknowledging an increased level of trust the group could have in him or her. Colored armbands worn over the blue or black boilersuits were used to signify the completion of the actions taken toward one's rehabilitation. A black armband was handed out after finishing the first level, meaning that the member was able to be trusted. The second armband awarded was a gold armband signaling that the individual is close to graduating from the rehabilitation program.

These armbands could be rescinded however. Like a game of chutes and ladders, one could lose both his or her gold and black banners and be sent back to the beginning for any one of several violations of any one of the many rules. Members of the Rehabilitation Project Force worked at manual labor for nine to ten hours and then studied or had personal counseling for five hours a day. Three thirty-minute meal breaks were allowed as well as one thirty-minute break to shower and tend to personal hygiene matters.

Part of the rehabilitation back into the group meant that you not only had to demonstrate an increase in your own abilities but you also had to help your assigned partner complete his or her steps as well. Everyone had a partner called a twin in the RPF. This pairing was meant to increase one's responsibility for another where both were made completely responsible for each other's success or failure. If one person made a mistake, the twin would get the same correction.

The main punishment during the time I was in the RPF in Clearwater was the running of laps up and down the multitiered levels of the garage. It would be "Take a lap" or "Take three laps," much as the army would use push-ups to toughen up recruits in boot camp. In my personal case, laps were out of the question, so we devised a punishment that would also serve a purpose for my pregnancy training. I had a series of physical exercise that came from my doctor and my birthing instructor; these functioned as my "laps," lucky.

Scientology has a series of spiritual levels that one passes through in an effort to reach total freedom. In addition, there are specific counseling techniques meant to uncover and confess to evil actions one has done or may have felt embarrassed or ashamed about, a type of counseling called a confessional. During this confessional, the auditor (counselor) asks the preclear (the person being questioned) a series of specific questions while the preclear holds a pair of metal cans. The auditor carefully notes the reaction of the E-Meter's needle to these questions. The E-Meter runs a very low level of electricity to the two cans and through the body of the preclear. A degree of electrical resistance as caused by the energy of spiritual pain or suffering will show up as a codified needle reaction. This measurement of resistance or the release of any energy is that which the auditor watches for.

In order to graduate the RPF, one has to pass several confessionals each containing hundreds of questions. The questions were formulated by L. Ron Hubbard to allow the individuals answering them to unburden themselves of things they might have done or not done that they or the group itself felt were wrong in some way. In many respects, it was like the confessional within the Catholic Church in that the person would feel better by making a clean breast of these things he or she didn't feel comfortable with and hadn't shared with another.

Unlike the Catholic Church or any other group that might use a spiritual confession as part of their treatment, every word the Scientology preclear says is written down and kept in a folder with the persons full name and number of the folder written in large black marker on both the cover of the folder and the binding of the folder. Scientology tells the press and every Scientologist that the information told within the confines of these confessionals are confidential and would not ever be seen or used by anyone other than the person's auditor and the case supervisor assigned to this person's spiritual advancement. This is far from the truth. I had personally seen intelligence reports created by someone culling an individual's PC folder for possible crimes or embarrassing actions. I remember going through hundreds of folders myself when we were engaged in the List One missions just a year ago, and I hadn't been trained as an auditor or counselor.

These confessional contained questions like "Have you ever had thoughts you were embarrassed about?" "Have you ever had interracial sex?" "Have you ever wanted to leave?" There are literally thousands of questions a person can be asked.

These confessionals were always double- and triple-checked by asking a series of questions at the end of each session to ensure all was divulged. Questions like "In this session, have you told all?" "In this session, have you told any half-truths?"

went on for two or three minutes at the conclusion of each and every day. If any of these questions elicited any motion of the needle, the auditor would know to dig deeper to discover what information had been withheld and bring it to the light of day. These series of confessionals would take as long as needed. The pair of rehabilitation members, each of whom had to get their twin through the process, would each have to learn the techniques of how to be an auditor. To be an official certified auditor in Scientology, a person has to take many courses and be validated in a variety of different techniques to help the preclear discover the source of their spiritual suffering. In the Rehabilitation Project Force however, this training procedure was modified somewhat and the rule became "Read it, drill it, do it." This meant that if your twin needed to have some counseling on "apples," you, as his or her auditor, would study the particular technical bulletins pertaining to apples, not the entire course. You would then practice with a doll or another person acting as a coach until you felt confident in applying these materials at which point you would go and carry out the action on your twin. This sequence would be repeated until both you and your twin were complete on all the confessionals and spiritual steps required for your graduation.

Within the RPF, there was a supervisor who oversaw the accurate Scientology application of these processes during these sessions by the twins. This RPF case supervisor was a member of the RPF, but all his or her work was double-checked and supervised by the senior supervisors for the entire Scientology base. These senior case supervisors had done the full training required and could guide the less experienced twins through the "Read it, drill it, do it" process. There were three senior case supervisors who monitored the personal folders of all members of the Sea Org staff including those in the RPF. While these senior C/Ss had regular contact with us, it was only in written form through notes placed inside the preclear folders. These case supervisors were not members of the rehabilitation force; they themselves were regular and trusted members of the Sea Organization.

One of these senior case supervisors found a technical bulletin written by Hubbard that stated that the husbands of pregnant women should give some daily simple assist auditing to their wives during the final trimester of the pregnancy. I had never heard of the bulletin before, and I have always wondered if the C/S dug this out of some long-forgotten archive as a special kindness to Chris and me. She placed it in the official folder of actions I had to complete to get out of the RPF. It was a welcome respite for both of us as now we could have some time alone together each day. We found a storage section in the garage that we used for these sessions. One corner contained stacks of mattresses and offered some privacy. It was a bit of an awkward climb for me to get to the top of the stack, but once we settled down, we had some space and privacy. Chris would do the assists he was required to do, but they would never take the entire hour we reported. We would spend the spare minutes talking, just holding each other or simply lying there with our hands on my belly, feeling our baby move and kick and swim.

One morning, after a couple of months on the RPF, the bosun of the RPF and his deputy, Hanna Whitfield, called me into the RPF main office. As I sat down, I was informed they had received a new order assigning me to the RPF's RPF. The RPF's RPF was a level even below the RPF. An individual assigned to the RPF's RPF is completely isolated, not only from regular staff and public but also from the other members of the RPF. I was shocked. This was the lowest of the lows, the complete rock bottom. I asked where the RPF's RPF was located, and they explained that it was in the boiler room of the basement.

The Fort Harrison did not really have a basement, but when you enter the main building, there was a split-level. A set of stairs led up to the main lobby, and a corresponding set of stairs led down. Under the lobby off to the right, there was a bathroom, a connection to the galley, and a few small offices. The boiler room basement was off to the left. It was a dark, humid, dank space frequented by RPFers and estates personnel.

As I remember it, it was barely spacious enough to stand up.

This was where I was expected to live. As a member of the RPF's RPF, I would remain in that crawl space for days or weeks. I would eat and sleep there. I would have no contact with any person at all, and the time would be spent cleaning the boiler room. I started to panic, and as I looked up, I could tell that both of them thought that this was an insane order. Hanna was actually quite upset about it, and she said that she refused to let it happen.

Watching Hanna spit out her anger and her refusal to obey was incredibly comforting to me. Hanna was almost finished with the RPF herself, almost free of the life in those blue boilersuits and the hot, filthy garage. She was risking her own graduation from the RPF to shield me from a fate worse than the one I was already in. In that moment, I felt some protection for the first time in months. I will never forget that she put herself on the line that day at great personal and spiritual danger.

While Hanna and the Bosun, Clint, discussed the options they could take to avoid implementing these instructions, I reread the order. I had originally been removed from my position because one of my staff, Kim, had failed in his duties and I had failed to get him to complete the compilation of a new series of courses geared toward people new to Scientology. Even though he was directly responsible for his own failure, I was the one held culpable, removed from my position, and ordered to the RPF. In a bit of group irony, Kim had since been promoted to take over my previous job. It was now three months later, and not surprisingly, these same courses had still not been completed. I had been singled out yet again, and as the answer to Kim's continued failure to execute the LRH orders to compile and release these services, I was to be assigned to the RPF's RPF. I knew I was way down the rabbit hole on this one but could not even allow those thoughts to be fully formed.

A friend of mine, years later, told me, "When you wake up with your head inside a tiger's mouth, you remove it very slowly." At the time, I didn't know that that was what I was doing, but in hindsight, I can see that I had a deep survival instinct that took over. I was in deep trouble and knew that it was dangerous to even attempt to fight. I needed to back out slowly not only for myself but also for my unborn child.

The three of us decided to query the order. There is a strict policy by Hubbard that states that if anyone receives an order that they believe would cause more harm than good, anyone has the right to question it and give an alternative solution. I went into another room and wrote an impassioned query to the commodore's staff captain. This was the person who replaced Chris when he had been removed from his previous post. She was a person of high authority in Clearwater at that time. It would be her office I would be returning to upon my graduation from the RPF. I didn't know if my query had much of a chance because the order had come from someone higher up in the organization, and perhaps even she didn't have the power to change it.

I appealed to her with the fact that I was almost complete with the RPF and would soon be coming to work for her. *Wouldn't it be more helpful for her to have an extra staff member than to send me to the RPF's RPF?* That would only extend the time I would spend away from helping LRH "clear the planet" and therefore delay my ability to directly contribute to the work in her office. I sent the query up and waited for an answer. I put my head down and hugged my baby, silently hoping for a glint of sanity. The hours slowly ticked by, and the longer I waited, the worse it felt. Chris didn't know what was happening, and I was as alone as I had ever been. I couldn't imagine living in a small filthy place like the boiler room; I constantly shoved those images out of my head.

I waited . . . and then waited some more.

Finally I was called into the Bosun's office. Shaking, I walked in and quickly sat before I collapsed. Hanna looked at me and smiled. My RPF's RPF assignment was cancelled. The query had been approved. I looked up at Hanna, took her hand, and nodded my head in silent thanks. I was sent back to work. I went back to my space and sobbed in relief. I never did attend the RPF's RPF.

Chapter 9

My Parents' Visit

IN EARLY JUNE of 1979, I received a letter that my parents were coming to Florida and were coming through Clearwater to see me and meet my new husband. They would have a couple of days to spend with us. I was happy to be able to see them and excited about them meeting Chris, but I was ashamed of the situation I had gotten myself into. Even if I had not been too proud to ask, I knew they didn't have the kind of money we would need to get out of our current fix. Besides, I felt a bit of the "You made your bed, you have to lie in it." I knew I was in a corner, but I did not feel I could ask them for assistance. Where would I begin?

The fact was that it was known that my parents had been antagonistic to Scientology and the powers that be did not want this to become a further problem.

My parents were going to want to see where we lived, and showing them around the garage was clearly not an option. So it was quickly arranged that we would move back to the Quality Inn and stay at the room of some Sea Org members who were off on vacation. I do not even know who they were, and I doubt they were ever asked or even told that another couple had used their living quarters. Chris and I were given the keys to their room and told to make my parents think it was ours. Pretending that was where we lived, my parents dropped us off and picked us up there. They were probably not happy to find their daughter pregnant and living in what essentially was a motel room, but compared to where we really lived, it was heaven.

We got several days off to be with them, go to the beach, and out to dinner. Again, ironically, if Chris and I had been on our regular Sea Org executive jobs, it would have been very difficult to get that time off. Since we were now being rehabilitated, our work was of very little relative value in the big picture of things.

I remember one afternoon during this visit when my parents came to pick us up in the lobby of the Fort Harrison Hotel. Hanna Whitfield was just then getting out of the RPF. She was standing on the lobby landing, getting her "liability formula" signed. This was an essay written that detailed what they had done, what correction they'd undergone, all the realizations they'd had and closing with a personal request to rejoin the group of trustworthy and effective Sea Org members. People would read this, and if they agreed Hanna had made up for the damage she'd done that had caused her assignment to the RPF, they would sign it and welcome her back into the group. My father asked who she was and what she was doing. It was so strange . . . knowing that soon I myself would be standing on that same landing, asking for those same signatures.

My mind raced to find a sentence that would communicate truthfully an answer to his questions but at the same time not raise more questions that I couldn't answer.

"She is asking to get her old job back." I felt that was an honest answer and shifted their attention to where we would be going for the day.

My parents were staying at a hotel on the Clearwater beach, and we spent our few days with them, talking, eating, and enjoying the weather and the companionship. We talked about the lives of my many brothers and sisters. My parents got to meet Chris, whom they had never met, and learned more of his background. We spoke of my impending birth and the marriage of my sister Jean to a "nice young man" named Jim whom she had met at college. Chris and I were able to forget, for the most part, what our lives had become. My parents dropped us off at our motel room at the end of the day.

The final night was difficult for Chris and me. We didn't sleep much and simply held each other, trying to hold off the inevitability that we would have to return to the garage the next day. There were no RPF security guards watching us that night, only the regular QI night watch. It would not have been difficult to make an escape, but where to and how? We had no money. Neither of our parents could give us the kind of help we would need to start our lives over from scratch. We had no means to pay for the needed medical supervision and birth of our child. We had no place to go. We comforted ourselves with the fact that we were both almost done with our programs and we would be out of the RPF within a matter of weeks. We vowed that our baby would not be born in any garage. We agreed to just keep our heads down, move forward, and get ourselves in a better position somewhere down the road.

As I mentioned, part of the final process for getting out of the RPF was the writing of a liability formula. The individual would acknowledge the bad deeds they had done that had landed them in the RPF in the first place and then list the corrective actions they had been taking over the past months to make up the damage. I wrote of how I had failed to get the needed projects of my position done on time and how I now knew how to do things better and with a higher standard. I had completed all the requirements of my rehabilitation program and was turning the final corner.

Finally I found myself standing in the lobby in my blue suit on a hot July afternoon, asking regular staff to sign my petition to be allowed back into the group. It was quite an intense afternoon. I noticed most people were happy to sign my petition and welcome me back. There was an underlying knowledge among Sea Org members that either they had been where I was at one time or it could be them at some point in the future. There were a few people out of the hundreds I asked that gave me a hard time as they read and reread what I had written. They asked me pointed questions about how I had changed and what I had specifically done that showed that I should be able to return to the group. The majority gladly signed my papers and shared in my joy of graduating rehabilitation.

I had done it. I was out of the RPF, and my baby would not be born in the garage.

A few days later, Chris completed his stint as well. Our new baby boy, Carey, arrived a week later.

The birth was a very painful experience, but it all melted away when I held him that very first time in my arms. Chris was there with me during the entire delivery, and the nurses said he was the best coach they had seen in ages. We were just so very happy to have each other and begin our new family. The RPF was behind us.

Chapter 10

Adjustments

AFTER THE BIRTH of our son, Chris and I borrowed some money for airfare and left Florida to visit with Chris's parents in New York and then to my family in Boston to attend my sister Jean's wedding.

We again had several weeks during which we were back to normal except that we were poor, dirt-poor. I was so excited to be a mom, and there were lots of family and friends to introduce to our new son, Carey.

I changed diapers and got up in the middle of the night to feed him. I got mothering advice from my mom and all her women friends. It was a sudden shift to become a mother, and I was welcomed into that group of women with all the advice and old wives' tales that came with it.

"Let him cry a bit before you pick him up or you will spoil him," one said.

"Use a bit of whiskey once he starts teething," said another.

Most of these older women would talk of the changes that the modern mom now has. We had the opportunity to use disposable diapers, which seemed like a miracle to them. "When I had my babies, I had to wash three loads a day just to keep up" was an oft-repeated refrain from several of them. As these older women welcomed me to the world of motherhood, they also brought gifts. These were things I could never have afforded, simple necessities like quilts and blankets, clothes and toys. It was a joyous visit. Our family not only had their first grandchild, making my many siblings an aunt or uncle for the first time, but were also celebrating the marriage of my younger sister. My grandfather was alive then and able to enjoy looking into the eyes of his first great-grandson. The time spent living in a garage began to fade like a bad nightmare.

After a couple of weeks of good food, sleep, and the unconditional love of family, we returned to Florida where Chris was assigned a low-level job. It at least allowed him full mealtimes and a full allowance of $25 per week. I still had a few weeks of maternity leave left and spent it with our son. Sometimes I would take a van over to where Chris worked at the Fort Harrison Hotel for a brief visit. Other times I would simply spend the day with Carey at the Quality Inn where we were living once again.

Once Carey was six weeks old, I was expected to return to work full-time while he was watched over in the Scientology day care facility provided within the Sea Org.

There was a woman who lived a few doors down from me who had given birth a few weeks before me. When her six weeks were up, she simply refused to leave her child. She and her husband had decided that they would rather leave the Sea Org than turn their child over to a group of Sea Org nannies for twelve to fifteen hours per day. As much as I supported her opinion and personal choices, I knew I couldn't do that. I simply did not have the strength. With virtually no money or immediate family financial support, it just did not seem an option available to me. I watched as the group ostracized her. When it became clear that her husband was not going to abandon his wife and newborn baby, he too became a target of isolation. They packed their meager belongings and left for their family in England, apparently one that could afford the airfare and was more than willing to welcome them home with open arms.

Soon enough, my time was up and my authorized maternity leave was over. The final day had actually arrived. I sat on the edge of our bed and held Carey in my arms. I talked and rocked him gently as tears streamed down my face. I did not *want* to put Carey in day care, but I felt I had no choice. I talked with him about how bad I felt and promised that somehow I would make our future different. I did not know how, but I knew someday I would. I felt powerless and without choices at the time, but I did have a deep belief that the future held tremendous hope. In the end, I accepted my new job assignment and began working the sixteen hours a day that was the routine of a Sea Org member. Carey went to day care where I saw him at dinner and during the single hour of family time allotted each day.

A few months passed and I was ordered to leave the country and go on a special mission to England. A small part of me wanted to get back in the good graces of all these people who had thrown me out so callously last April, but an even larger part of me did not want to go.

When I mentioned I was a new mother and couldn't be separated for various reasons, the woman who was Hubbard's Staff Captain replied "You're *still* breastfeeding?" like it was a crime. Part of me was embarrassed, and I felt bad like I was somehow not 100 percent behind all the efforts of the group.

The part of me that still valued what the others in the group thought battled the instincts of being a mother. I struggled for a few hours, but eventually my commitment to the Sea Org won out and I made my decision. I flew to England that night, leaving Chris and my four-month-old baby behind.

A couple of days later, I was in England trying to go to sleep one night when I sat straight up in bed. It was an electric jolt I'd never experienced before, but I knew with absolute certainty that Carey was very ill. Chris was with him, but he was not his mother. My son needed me right now, and I was not there for him! In fact, I was thousands of miles away, separated by the Atlantic Ocean.

I felt trapped. I was trapped! Finally, I mentally stood up and realized I did *not* want to be there. I recognized it was not my code of ethics that had put me here but some set of rules that I had bought into. I fell back into bed and wept. I cried the frustrated tears born of having a sick child and not being able to do anything about it. I was angry with the people who would separate a mother from her newborn infant, and I was furious with myself for having let it happen.

I took a deep breath, closed my eyes, and tried as best as I could to communicate to Carey through my heart, letting him know I loved him more than the world. I vowed never to let anyone or anything get between us ever again no matter what the consequences.

As the sun rose the following morning, I called my husband. My gut instincts had been correct. Carey had been very ill just as I had known. Chris had been up all night with him, but the fever had broken and he was now doing much better.

I finished the mission in the UK just as quickly as I could and hurried home. I promised myself that this would never happen again.

Carey continued to have respiratory problems for months. He spent some weeks at the local hospital in intensive care under an oxygen tent as he slowly healed his tiny lungs. I don't know if the cause was the fact that I slept in a garage inhaling carbon monoxide, gasoline, and oil fumes during the final months of my pregnancy but I certainly thought about it often and wondered if I had crippled my child for life. He was hospitalized at least three times in addition to several visits to the emergency room over a period of one year.

In December, I was removed from my position working with the Staff Captain in the International Management Bureau. I never questioned the removal; I was so relieved they had not attempted to send me back to the RPF that I didn't want to risk anything by challenging it.

To my amazement, I discovered that I was being transferred to the Child Care Organization. It was supposed to be a huge demotion as child care workers were not considered very high up on the pecking order. Secretly I was thrilled. It was not demoralizing or degrading like the RPF, and it allowed me to spend the remainder of Carey's first year with him. I would be caring for him along with the children of other Sea Org parents.

When the functions of my job entailed shopping or other errands, I would bring him with me. Because the child care facilities were at the Quality Inn, I adjusted the phone in our room so it worked like a baby monitor, and I would let him sleep in the mornings while I did paperwork in my office. Incredibly, I felt I had the best of both worlds. My life was finally in balance. I was still a member of the Sea Org, but I was also able to be with my son all day long.

However, I also lived with an underlying fear, the knowledge that at any given moment there could be a series of events that could thrust me once more into the position of unbearable choices.

I wanted to leave the Sea Org, but I wanted to leave with my friendships intact and my dignity secure. I tried to discover a middle ground where this might be possible. During Carey's first year, there were moments I was ready to walk away but Chris was not. Then there were the times when he wanted to leave, but I saw hope in staying and fear of the unknown. We struggled with our choices but felt we had no choice but to see it through. It was tough for both of us and for our family.

One day during that first year, I experienced a wave of utter hopelessness. I was in our room at the QI with Carey and desperate to leave the Sea Org. I wanted out so badly. I had called Chris that afternoon and he told me that we would talk when he got home, but I could tell that he was not prepared to walk out just then. I lay in bed and hugged Carey tightly while I cried. I gently rolled him off my stomach where he had fallen asleep and onto the middle of the bed so I would not wake him.

I stood to go to the bathroom as another flood of overwhelming emotions washed over me. My frustration was enormous, my future uncertain. I slid to the floor and continued sobbing. In my grief, my thoughts ran in an endless loop: I didn't want to be in the Sea Org any longer, however, my husband did. Should I leave and lose the love of my life or stay and lose myself?

I couldn't stop thinking that we should have left months ago when Chris had wanted to, and if I'd only listened to him then, I wouldn't be in the situation I faced today. But I soon realized that even if we had left then, it was still hopeless; we had had absolutely nowhere to go and no means of support. Neither of us had any credit cards; we had no assets or even anything to sell. We were trapped with no discernable way out. I cried every tear I had until I felt totally drained. I was locked in a corner. I finally stuffed all those thoughts back in the closet I'd built in the furthest reaches of my mind. I would attempt to make the best of the situation and put a smile on my face; I could do it.

A day or two later, I was walking across the same room when I had a vision. I was in the future. It was many years down the road and I was in a doctor's office. I was *working* in a doctor's office! Chris and I seemed to have our own home, and we were with Corey and Carey. And incredibly, there was another child! I remember wondering how I would ever end up working in a doctor's office, but I snapped back to the present with a certainty that things would not be as they were. In the end, we would be free and on our own, *together*. And we were going to have another child in that future.

So no matter how dark things got after that day (and there were many dark moments), I never lost faith for I had been shown that it would all end up right.

Prior to that turbulent year (1979), I had had a fairly smooth time of it as a staff member, Sea Org member, and Scientologist. I had begun in Boston and worked my way up through several positions to my final posting as a personal aide to L. Ron Hubbard himself. My personnel files during those years were not really worthy of note. The ethics file that is kept on every staff and public member of Scientology was likewise minimal. In it were filed reports of either good actions I had taken or my failures to measure up. I was not the kind of person who got in trouble or did not perform well on the jobs I was given. There were a few bumps and minor troubles, but overall, my experience was positive. The most consistently bad habit I had was showing up late for all the daily roll calls and musters. There was often little compensation despite the long hours, but that was made up for in my mind by the compassion and care I had with my fellow staff members and the thought that I was doing good things for all mankind. I had taken some Scientology courses and counseling myself and found them helpful. I wanted to share that with others, and I felt that was a good and important thing. I was aware of mistakes the group had made or was making and some instances of misconduct, but since I never had expected a perfect group, that did not sway my loyalty. I knew LRH had a dark side and could at times get angry and vindictive, but since I had never looked upon him as some sort of god upon a pedestal, it did not sway my feelings about him if he made a mistake or failed at something. Prior to 1979, I had considered him someone just like us: a human being with strengths and weaknesses.

After the 1979 and 1980 experiences however, my view began to shift. I realized that there were, in fact, things I would not do for Scientology. I would never again place the Sea Org above the proper support and care of my own child. I was no longer the fully dedicated member I had been before. I was a mother now and that, for me, was far more important than being a member of any group.

Chapter 11

Celebrity Centre International

EARLY SUMMER OF 1980, someone in international management did a review that found that the removal of Chris as director of Celebrity Centre Los Angeles had been a mistake. It was decided that he would be returned to this job as the organization had not done well without his leadership and that his reassignment would benefit Scientology's celebrity position.

Chris could have responded with bitterness over the years he had been separated from his son Corey or the months spent in the degrading conditions of the garage, but that is just not the type of person he is. Chris doesn't stay in the past; he moves forward. He was simply so happy to be going back to where he felt he belonged that he was not going to waste any time revisiting past mistakes. Besides, his detour to Florida and to the ranks of international management had put the two of us together, not to mention our young son.

Of course, I wanted to go with him. Not surprisingly, this was not a given; the group is of more importance than any familial ties. I knew of many couples that had been separated for years with one being sent to a different continent while the other remained behind.

I was very determined that the group would never again take importance over family, at least never again with mine. I arranged it so that Carey and I were sent to Los Angeles at the same time as Chris was. My sole purpose in going to Los Angeles was to locate a person who would replace me at my job in Florida. That way, a personnel trade of sorts could be made. The new person would take over my functions in Florida, and I would be free to remain in Los Angeles and work with Chris at the Celebrity Centre. Chris was very excited about finally being reunited with his son, Corey, who had remained in Los Angeles with his mom for these past couple of years. Corey finally had both his mom and dad in the same place.

Chris was assigned to his old job of the day-to-day running of the Celebrity Centre in LA. Once I arranged for the personnel transfer, I soon assumed the position of president of Celebrity Centre, a job title that at the time meant that I dealt with Scientology celebrities directly. Being called president gave a status to the post primarily so that celebrities would come to me rather than Chris and so that he would be free to run the organization, helping it grow and make money each week.

We remained at Celebrity Centre for almost two years. My work involved a lot of direct contact with both Scientology and non-Scientology celebrities in Hollywood. I worked closely with them, helping to strengthen their careers using various sections of Scientology courses I had studied. I also advised budding actors and other artists in the entertainment field build their careers and reputations.

I had already supervised the Celebrity Centre network from a distance, so I was not unfamiliar with how celebrities were taken care of as members. During these and subsequent years, I learned a lot more of what it means to be a celebrity or to have a degree of fame or notoriety. It is not always the dream most people think it is.

One celebrity in particular struck me deeply as an example of this. He lived in the San Francisco area at the time. We sent a trained counselor to his home to work privately with him through several of the beginning counseling levels. I went up for a weekend and spent some time with him.

He spoke of troubles he had with "never being seen" in that when people "saw" him, they didn't see *him*. They saw the persona that had been created through his years of entertainment work and through the publicity machines around him. When he went out in the world, most people could not see past the facade they had created in their minds. He felt that the few people who did get close to him were often there for the money or the cachet of being close to such a big star. With no reflection of his true self in the world or in the people close around him, he was having a hard time staying grounded.

This is a key vulnerability of many celebrities and the lifestyle they adopt. I will say that in some ways, the rich and famous can be more vulnerable to the siren call of Scientology than even I was in my idealistic teenage years.

Most of these stars did not know it, but very often prior to their first contact with Scientology, they were often targeted as a potential recruit. A person who is a celebrity or a Scientologist who is close to a specific celebrity worked with the organization to plan and slowly introduce Scientology to him or her. Personal problems shared by the unsuspecting non-Scientologist with his Scientologist friend or peers would be relayed to trained Celebrity Centre personnel. Sometimes a plan was worked out to arrange a party in which a Celebrity Centre staff member would attend and an introduction made. The staff that worked directly with celebrities were well trained and groomed. They were extremely experienced in how to smoothly introduce someone to Scientology. Sometimes it was more straightforward with the Scientologist coming right out and asking his celebrity friend or acquaintance to meet in private with a trained Scientology counselor.

I myself attended many parties with the intention to make a connection with a specific person or had celebrities brought to my office. The person introducing the celebrity and me always had a plan, and I was always briefed on this particular celebrity's strength and weaknesses and their likes and dislikes. There was a compiled list of celebrities who were targeted for recruitment into Scientology. Years later, when I was no longer president but still working with Celebrity Centre and some of their celebrities, the Celebrity Centre in Los Angeles was required to send a weekly report to international management, listing progress that had been achieved during the previous week to inch along bringing the targeted celebrity into Scientology's fold. Whether this program exists today, I don't know, but I have little reason to think it's been discontinued. The woman who became a close friend of Katie Holmes is actually a high-ranking Sea Org member who grew up in a wealthy family. The fact that such a high-level executive was assigned to her seems to indicate that programs like this continue to be the norm.

Once a celebrity has expressed an interest in Scientology, their initial service is chosen and delivered to them. It is important (for all people introduced to Scientology, not just celebrities) that these first courses or counseling are extremely effective in giving assistance to the individual in an area of his life he is having some or great difficulty with.

Some people introduced to Scientology go no further than this introductory level, but if they are celebrities, they are kept close track of and checked on periodically through the organization's contact person. The person being introduced may or may not know at the time that the friend or acquaintance that brought him or her into the Organization got a 10 percent commission on all monies paid for counseling and a 15 percent commission on all monies paid for training. This has actually been a very effective sales commission program that has been run by all Scientology orgs and franchises for over fifty years and has been a fundamental means of rewarding adherents bringing in more and more potential recruits.

It was important that someone new to Scientology did not hear any negativity, or if they did, "misunderstandings" were handled quickly.

I personally found that most celebrities had difficulty with the process of hiring and keeping their personal staff, especially regarding the maintaining of privacy. I would (during the years I was directly on the lines), as well as other Celebrity Centre staff, sometimes step up and offer assistance in the hiring and background checking of potential people who might be working closely with the celebrity. I would sometimes suggest placing Scientologists within the celebrity's organization or home.

The celebrities may or may not have been aware that while this may have protected them from the prying eyes of paparazzi, these staff were loyal to Scientology first and would report any negativity the celebrity has received about Scientology so that it can be handled, or they would take care of it themselves right on the spot. While celebrities can bring a lot of attention and good press for Scientology, if they fall away from the fold, the impact can be just as negative.

I enjoyed my work as the president of Celebrity Centre very much. I learned quite a bit about the entertainment business and got to use the skills I had mastered while working at the higher levels of Scientology with individuals' desires of expanding their careers.

I remember one actor in particular who was hitting a slow period in his career and his phone had not rung for several weeks. We sat down to do a series of steps called a career consultation, and after a couple of hours, we felt we had discovered the things that needed to be changed in order to get his career back on track. Within minutes of instituting some of these decisions, his phone rang with a call for an audition of a high-profile role. He eventually got the part, and his career began a fresh upswing. Over the two years I worked in the position of president, this sort of result happened several more times. I felt I was helping some good people get better so they could do more good for others.

It was these satisfying actions I was allowed to make during my stay in the Sea Org that would keep me there. These happy times would almost make up for the time spent in the garage or the nights spent cleaning walls and floors. Looking back now, I realize that I was out of step with the real world and had no concept that I could be doing these helpful things without the Scientology's extras of verbal abuse, lack of decent food, minimal sleep, and minimal time with my children.

My stepson, Corey, was now a regular part of our lives and that made both my husband and I very happy. My young son was healthy and growing up, and for those few years at Celebrity Centre, I felt I'd achieved a career-motherhood balance that was working.

During the summer of 1982, my two-year-old's day care situation became unsafe. The child care facility was next door to the Celebrity Centre, and he discovered he could run away or climb the fence to get to me in the next building where he knew I worked. His caretakers would not be aware he was even missing for several hours at a stretch. The director of the day care center communicated that she simply had too many children under their care to be able to keep an eye on everyone. I still felt strongly about my commitment as a member of the Sea Org, but I also knew that in any choices involving my family, I would always choose my family over the group. I'd learned that lesson the hard way.

In the fall of 1982, the communications and activities from management seemed to become erratic. I did not know it at the time, but there was a huge power struggle for the ultimate control of Scientology. At our level in Los Angeles, we could only see the fallout: long-term Sea Org executives were removed from very high positions, and Scientologists who had been active in orgs and franchises for years were declared suppressive people. They lost any and all Scientology assets, not to mention many personal friendships with other Scientologists.

We began to hear of a new form of counseling nicknamed "Gang Bang" security checking. The person under question was placed in a small room and handed the cans of an E-Meter so areas of charge they thought he had could be delved into deeply. Using an E-Meter, these areas of disagreement or upset were detected by specific needle movements. But instead of the counseling being a safe procedure in which one could discuss and better oneself with the help of one counselor, several people bombarded these suspected individuals with accusative and demeaning questions all at once. In these "counseling sessions," the person on the receiving end was not allowed to leave the room until the procedure was finished. Stories were reaching us of friends we knew who had been treated like this. People were being thrown out of the organizations and being declared suppressive left, right, and center. There was a new group established within the Sea Org called the International Finance Police, and it was on a rampage.

Chapter 12

Rehabilitation Revisited

I FOUND MYSELF sitting in the large reception area of the liaison office for the Western United States. Three of us had been called over to this senior management building from our work at the Celebrity Centre in Hollywood: Chris, Pam, and I. Chris and I ran the Celebrity Centre, and Pam was one of our divisional directors. My heart was racing, and adrenaline had started to rise when we got a call to report in the middle of a Friday afternoon. There was work to be done and the week's production to be organized. Why would management want all three of us to leave immediately and go to a meeting?

My husband told me not to worry and attempted to calm me down. He tried his best, but I had a few years more experience with international management than he did. I knew a meeting like this, timed on a Friday afternoon, was never good news for someone.

They asked to see Chris and Pam first, leaving me in the lobby under the watchful eyes of a uniformed receptionist. I observed people moving in and out of the building. The air in the lobby was electric. I was aware of at least four Los Angeles area executives that had been removed from their positions in the preceding few weeks. This new group, the Finance Police, had members here in Los Angeles turning over anything they perceived as questionable. I was more confused than worried. Celebrity Centre had, so far, been immune to their investigations. Of the many Scientology organizations in Los Angeles, Celebrity Centre was running smoothly and having good success. It was making money and had just received a high commendation from L. Ron Hubbard himself. Still, I had worked in international management for several years and knew how quickly the winds shifted.

A young uniformed girl with an emotionless face came to the doorway. She motioned for me to follow her to a room down the hall. I entered to a semicircle of serious uniformed officers. Pam was in the room, but I noticed Chris's absence. No one said a single word. One of those in uniforms handed me a piece of goldenrod paper. It was an announcement to all Sea Org members that both my husband and I had been removed from our positions at Celebrity Centre and were assigned to the Rehabilitation Project Force in Los Angeles, which was located somewhere in the basement of the large blue complex.

The uniformed man in the center of the semicircle asked if I had any questions. I stared back at him and said no.

The young woman who had escorted me into this room now motioned me to follow her. We walked down the hall to a smaller office. The room contained two wooden desks and a uniformed guard sitting in a chair in the far corner. Chris was seated at the desk next to the window and the guard. I was told to sit down at the desk nearest the door with my back to both the guard and Chris. I began writing any information that the person replacing me on my job would need to know. The guard was there to ensure we neither talked to each other nor attempted to leave. I sat and began to write.

My mind was a swirl, moving from thoughts of my three-year-old son to my ten-year-old stepson and to my adamancy about never going back to the RPF again. My hands began to shake as I realized that this might be the end of my marriage.

If I refused to participate in the rehabilitation they had planned for me and if Chris was willing to go, we would be forbidden to be together ever again. What would happen to our son? I snuck a peek at Chris bent over his paper and tried to gauge his views; the guard noticed and told me to get back to my write-up.

Chris got permission to go to the bathroom. During his absence, I pretended to write while I tried to corral my mind and think of a plan. I had to know where Chris stood. I heard his footsteps coming down the hall and stood to leave for the bathroom myself. I was facing Chris as he walked in. With my back to the guard, I silently mouthed, "I'm not going." He nodded, smiling, and whispered, "Me neither."

I left for the bathroom with a lighter heart. I still did not know how we would get out of this, but at least I would still have my husband and not be alone. I also knew we would not be going through the degradation of the Rehabilitation Project Force again.

I crossed the empty hall to the women's bathroom. I didn't need to use the facilities; I needed to be alone. Tears streamed down my face. I saw in the mirror that I was becoming a visible mess, but I also recognized something else—the strength of knowing that this time I was not alone. Finally Chris and I both felt the same way at the same time. We were not going back to any rehabilitation program. I splashed my face with cold water as I tried to regain my composure. I attempted the "cool the back of the neck" trick by wadding up some paper towels and doused them in cold water, making a cold compress for the nape of my neck. I held the soggy paper there and stared at myself in the mirror. It simply brought more tears.

I knew I had to get back to the cramped office or they would send someone after me. I didn't want to be seen like this. I wanted to at least show I still had some dignity. They may have kicked me, but I wouldn't flinch. I splashed my face one last time and took several deep breaths. I could do this. I had Chris along with both Corey and Carey to think about now. The thought of my three-year-old son almost made me tear up again, but I held it down. I took another deep breath, smoothed my skirt, and tucked my shirt in. I felt somewhat presentable.

I would keep my head down and let my hair fall to cover my face. I wouldn't give them the satisfaction of seeing my red eyes. I returned to the room; the guard was still sitting on his stool reading a book and Chris was still writing but he snuck a small smile my way. I could feel his calm energy spreading through me. I didn't know how we would get out of this, but I felt comfort knowing we would get out of it together.

Someone brought us a tray of food to eat. Since we had been removed from the regular staff, we weren't allowed to eat with them anymore, but we weren't yet within the confines of the rehabilitation unit. We were in a sort of limbo. I looked at the food and knew I couldn't eat a bite. At least this time I was not pregnant.

We continued to write down all the projects and things we had been involved in. This would give the people taking over our jobs something to go on. I knew from times past, however, that whatever we said would be given no credence. The removal made everything we had to say untrustworthy.

Someone came to the door and asked the guard to step outside. I could hear loud whispers through the door but couldn't make out the words. Chris and I used this opportunity to look at each other directly.

"You really won't go?" I whispered.

"I really won't go."

"Thank God! I was so worried. I can't do that again."

"I know," Chris answered.

"What are we going to do?"

"I don't know. We'll work it out."

The door opened, and I turned back to my paper, hoping that I had not been seen speaking with Chris.

Our mystery guard said, "We are going to wait till the Celebrity Centre staff have eaten and left the Wilcox. [The Wilcox building was where the Celebrity Centre staff ate and slept.] Then we'll take you over there to get some clothes for tonight. We'll handle packing and storing the rest of your stuff over the next week or so. So let's see if you can finish up these write-ups now."

We nodded and went back to our papers.

Several hours passed, and someone else came to the door. He introduced himself as Mike and said he and Gary would be driving us over to the Wilcox to get some of our things.

We asked about our three-year-old son, Carey, and were told that Chris's assistant, Joanne, had taken care of him during dinner and he was back in the day care center. He would spend this night with her.

We will deal with that tomorrow, I thought. I gathered my purse, and we left for the Wilcox with Mike.

The drive was silent. Mike was driving; and the guard, whom I now knew to be named Gary, was in the front seat. Chris and I were in the backseat. In the shadows, we held hands but did not speak, not even a whisper.

At the Wilcox, we were taken to our sixth-floor room and told to pack up the simple essential items we would need: toiletries, underwear, sneakers, and pajamas. Mike kept looking at his watch. We pulled as much as we thought we could into bags. Chris also took the opportunity to get a stash of cash he had been saving. It wasn't much, but it was over $100, which was a veritable fortune in those hand-to-mouth days.

Chris needed a few more items, so we stopped at the local Kmart on the way back for him to buy some socks and a toothbrush.

They drove us back to the large Scientology complex and brought us down to the basement where the rehabilitation offices were. I knew this was a lot larger than some other RPFs, definitely larger than the one we had been in at the Fort Harrison in Florida. Mike and Gary turned us over to the bosun and left. No "good luck's" or handshakes; they were happy to have delivered us.

The bosun was a member of the RPF himself but was also the leader of the self-sufficient unit. He sat us down and handed us a packet of papers that contained the rules of being an RPF member as well as some additional legal documents for us to read and sign.

I questioned him about the legal forms right away. As part of our assignment to the RPF in 1979, we had been given documents to sign that stated we agreed with the assessment that we were insane and wanted to do the rehabilitation program of our own free will and without coercion. Despite my strong misgivings, I really didn't have any options the first time around; and even though it was not the truth, I did, in fact, sign them in 1979. I was wary of this now, and feeling stronger physically and spiritually, I knew I would not be giving my signature.

Just as I had thought, the legal papers were worded to attest that we were joining the LA rehabilitation unit because we personally wanted to, that we knew we were messed up and truly wanted this chance at spiritual redemption.

I read it over and looked up at the bosun. "I'm not signing this." I turned to Chris as he said, "Neither am I." I immediately asked about our young son, Carey. Fortunately, my stepson Corey's mother was not in the RPF and was still working full-time at Celebrity Centre, so I knew he was being taken care of. Carey, however, was three years old and had no other family than Chris and myself.

We were told that although it was unusual for married couples to get assigned to the RPF together, it had happened before. As the bosun saw it, if we were good for the initial transition of approximately two weeks and adhered to the rules and regulations of the RPF, we might then be given the privilege to go and visit our son twice a week for twenty minutes each time.

The room was silent. I took a deep breath, stared at the bosun, and made it clear that this was completely unacceptable and simply not going to happen. There was no way that I was going to sign any paper that said I was there on my own determination and agreed to such restrictions. I was *not* there by my own volition and neither was Chris.

My protests that Carey was barely three years old and that his supervision at the day care center was inadequate fell on deaf ears. No one seemed to believe the fact that he would sometimes escape the watchful eyes of his nanny by climbing the fence and wandering around CC looking for me.

As we staked out our views, a succession of people took turns attempting to change our minds. I remember one woman in her forties telling me that children are Thetans (spiritual beings) and that they are responsible for their own conditions.

I had nothing to worry about and that my son would make it. She had a daughter who had apparently gotten into some unsecured cleaning supplies and drank from an open bottle; I could not believe this mother blamed her young child. She felt that her little girl may have had a five-year-old body but she was a timeless and infinite spirit and knew what she was doing.

I looked at this woman and felt like I had arrived in the twilight zone. I began to wonder how we could escape but quickly realized my dilemma. Even if we could get through the people that were between the door and me, I did not know where the hallways led in this huge building and had no idea how to make it outside. I was trapped.

After several more hours and many other attempts by numerous RPF members to "handle" us, the Bosun had had enough.

"That's it. We have to assign you to your units and get you moving forward on the RPF program."

Chris looked up at him and said, "This routing form says that we have to sign these legal documents before we can go on to the next step."

"We'll handle that later, just pretend you signed them for now," was his measured response.

I stared at him in shock. I couldn't believe he'd actually said that. As he left the room, Chris reached out, squeezed my hand, and whispered, "It's going to be all right."

We were assigned to two different units. I was taken to the women's dorm, a small room but which contained at least four triple bunk beds. My guard pointed to the middle bunk in one of the beds near the wall and far away from the door, indicating that was where I was to sleep. I got into my pajamas and crawled under the covers. The room smelled of twelve women, and the night creaked with beds teetering and various sneezes and coughs. I knew right then I was not staying in the rehabilitation unit; I just hoped I would never have another night in that room. I fell into a fitful sleep.

We were awakened at 0500 to do chores before breakfast. Chris and I were sent to clean a large empty hall. We needed to move the chairs and sweep under the tables and then return the chairs to the appropriate position. A young tattooed man was already working there. We spoke with him even though it was against the rules. He was not in the RPF and should not have spoken to us, but he did anyway.

We learned he was new to staff. He had been a drug addict and was fresh out of prison by way of a homeless shelter. He had been hired a few days ago, and we were surprised to hear that he did not even know what Scientology was. He liked the people, the food was good, and the bed was better than the ones at the shelter.

I went back to work wondering what kind of a group this was becoming. Chris and I continued to sweep until we were gathered up for breakfast. The Los Angeles RPF contained about seventy-five people at that time and ate in a long narrow room near the kitchen. Since Chris and I were in different units, we were not allowed to sit together and were placed at opposite ends of the room. While I pushed the food around my plate, I surveyed the motley group I found myself with. There wasn't anyone that I recognized. Although I'd been in LA for over eighteen months, Celebrity Centre's facility was located at a distance from the other Scientology organizations. Not knowing anyone, I heard the morning chatter around me, but none of it registered.

When the meal ended, we were assigned the job of clearing the tables. This simple job gave Chris and me a few moments to pass some whispered communications. He'd worked out an escape plan. After our morning chores, we would once again help set up the dining room for lunch. He told me that we should wait until everyone was seated and focused on eating their food and then separately mention that we forgot something in the galley. The room was long, and we were at opposite ends with different doors that lead to a common hallway. The hope was that no one would notice we both were leaving. We'd then meet in the galley by the large dishwashing equipment.

The rest of the morning, I was filled with a nervous energy. I was put back to sweeping the floor and tried to just keep my attention on that as I chewed on our escape plan. *What if they noticed? What if we couldn't find our way out of the building? What if a guard stopped us?*

After what seemed like hours and hours, it was finally lunchtime. Just as we had thought, Chris and I were part of the table setup. When everyone was seated, chatting with each other, passing condiments and sandwiches, I saw Chris leave the door at the other end of the room. I looked to my assigned buddy on my right and said, "Oh, I forgot something in the kitchen, I'll be right back" and headed out the door at my end of the room.

I frantically looked around and saw Chris standing by the dishwasher waiting for me. There was no one else around. Chris grabbed my hand, and we started quickly walking out of the kitchen. I had absolutely no idea where in the building complex I was much less where the closest exit would be. Chris seemed to know where he was going; I just followed. We were careful to move quickly but not so fast as to draw any extra attention to ourselves.

We snaked our way through several underground halls, and finally Chris pushed open a door and we were outside. We were on the east side of the building and a block from the Children's Hospital Los Angeles. There were lots of Sea Org members in uniform as well as public Scientologists on lunch break from courses or counseling, so we acted as normal as we could and made our way up the street, heading past Sunset and up to Hollywood Boulevard.

As we turned a corner about a block away and we were out of sight, we began to run. We made it to the bus stop on Hollywood Boulevard and hoped that we could navigate to the day care where our son was being kept.

I had never rode a bus in Los Angeles before, but Chris knew what to do. It was not too difficult to find the day care as we knew it was a straight path down Hollywood and then a right on Franklin for a block. We worried that someone would catch up with us while we waited at the bus stop, but there was nothing we could do at that point.

The bus came, and as it pulled away, we both took a deep breath and held hands. We didn't say much. We were both very focused on getting Carey before anyone noticed that we were missing. We got off the bus and quickly walked to a doughnut shop across the street from the day care facility. We went into a doughnut shop and had a cup of coffee to collect our thoughts and plan what we were going to do next. It was usually me who picked Carey up from day care, so we decided that it would appear more normal if I was the one to go in and get him. I needed to act calm and nonchalant like nothing was out of the ordinary. Chris would remain in the doughnut shop and serve as backup in case anyone had called ahead or RPF members had been sent there to stop us. If the plan went as we hoped, I would just collect Carey and hurry back to Chris.

I walked toward the child care entrance slowly. The child care organization had its own entrance, but immediately behind it was a direct connection to the Celebrity Centre. I was not only concerned about people having been sent over from the RPF but also about being seen by anyone from Celebrity Centre since it was well known what had happened to us.

I made it through the front doors without being noticed. The few adults that were around were busily involved with the children in their care. I headed down the hall to the room where Carey was usually supervised. I could feel my breathing deepen as I prayed that I wouldn't be stopped. *Please God, please God, please God* was my simple refrain.

And then there he was. I found him playing with a large group of children. His nanny was covering for another nanny's lunch break so she actually had thirty kids under her care. I had an overwhelming urge to run and pick him up, but as soon as he saw me, he flew into my arms. I glanced at the nanny and said, "I'll bring him back later." She nodded and went back to cleaning up the mess on the floor.

It felt so good to hold my son. His blue eyes lit up as soon as he saw me. He snuggled into my neck as I carried him back out the front door into the bright sun. I felt safer now than ever because I knew that if I were stopped at this point, they would never get Carey away from me.

We made it back to the doughnut shop without being noticed. Chris hugged us both, and we sat down. Carey was happy with a doughnut and some juice while Chris and I looked at each other and wondered what to do next.

We had the clothes on our back and around $100. We just needed some time to relax and try to forget about everything if even just for a few hours. We talked it over and decided we could go to the movies. It would be dark and relatively quiet and would give us a moment to ourselves to step back and think of what to do next. No one would find us or even think to look for us at a movie theater. We walked the back streets to Hollywood Boulevard and spotted a marquee. We bought three tickets and some popcorn and sat down to watch *Tron*.

The lights dimmed, and the movie began. Carey was excited and was the only one watching as he enjoyed the bonus time with his mom and dad. My thoughts were wild and random. We had very little money and nowhere to go. I remembered when Chris had wanted to leave the RPF in Clearwater and I felt then that we had no options. Now here we were in Los Angeles just as Chris had wished, but still with no money or options. Our families didn't have the resources to bail us out even if we could get over our sense of injured pride. We'd made our mess, and it was ours to sort out.

The next two hours passed in the blink of an eye. The movie ended, and we went back out to the now-darkening light of Hollywood. It was only at that moment that I realized it was Halloween. The streets were filled with costumed people on their way to celebrate. It was beyond surreal.

We had no other choice by now. We slowly walked to the Wilcox building,. By the time we got there, it was dark. We sat in the shadows across the street and watched our coworkers leave to return to their jobs at the Celebrity Centre. By 7:00 PM, the majority of staff had cleared out, and we cautiously made our way across the street. We could already see through the plate glass windows that there were people from the RPF camped out and waiting for us. Chris's son Corey was sitting in the lobby, visibly upset.

We found out later that the people from the RPF had been telling Corey, who was nine years old at the time, about how bad his father was and that he was in big trouble. Ronnie, Chris's ex-wife and Corey's mom, stepped in and stopped the verbal attacks.

She told Corey that no matter what happened, his dad was still his dad and was a good person. I'll never forget her for that.

We made our way across the street and entered the Wilcox lobby. Chris refused to speak with the people from the Rehabilitation Project Force and went straight to Corey. While Chris and Corey talked, I sat in a chair in the lobby with Carey in my lap. Chris comforted Corey until he felt calm enough to go off with his mom. He said a few more words to her to ensure that she would be taking care of Corey until everything was sorted out and then gave her a brief hug good-bye. Only then did Chris turn his attention to the people from the RPF. He said point-blank, "We're not going back. We're going upstairs and packing our things." Chris, Carey, and I got in the elevator and the two RPF guards muscled their way in with us. We made our way back to our room on the sixth floor in silence. We walked down the long narrow hallway to our room at the end. Most married Sea Org members lived in a single hotel room with one private bath, but because Chris had been the Captain of Celebrity Centre, we were assigned a small apartment as our living quarters.

We had a small couch in the living room and a couple of chairs. The two people from the RPF and Chris and I talked briefly. Chris reiterated that we would not be returning with them to the RPF headquarters and would not be doing the prescribed rehabilitation program period. I left to put Carey to sleep in the bedroom. I could overhear bits of their conversation. I could hear Chris continually repeating that we were not going back there while the two people from the RPF kept trying to break him down and talk him into it. When I reentered the living room, I could see that Chris had tears streaming down his face. I went to sit beside him on the couch, held his hand, and joined his tears with my own. It was heartbreaking to realize that we'd both given ten years of our lives to this group and that we were now being forced to make a crucial choice. Either stay and report to the RPF and do a new rehabilitation program or leave the Sea Org in disgrace. We knew that we really had no choice at all. We were not in Clearwater anymore, and we now had two children to think about. The cold calculation with which these people attempted to change our minds and manipulate us was astounding. They had an expectation that we would allow our young son to become parentless for an undetermined amount of time that made my blood boil. They might have thought we would eventually see the light, but there was never going to be acceptable compromise when it came to our children.

I realized that I had changed a lot since I had become a mother. My commitment to care for my son and the love I felt for my family had actually made me stronger. I could say *no* to this group no matter the consequences. I had come a long way since living in a Clearwater garage.

Finally at midnight, with both sides at an impasse, the two people from the RPF reluctantly left. They made it very clear to both of us that if they left the room without us, then we would both be declared as suppressive persons.

This meant that we would be excommunicated from Scientology. Suppressives are outcasts and must be shunned by all Scientologists anywhere in the world. Even Scientologists who did not directly work for an organization would be forbidden to speak with us let alone hire us to work for them. We would be forced to start over, leaving behind every friend, every colleague, and every connection we had made in the last ten years. We had no money, no credit cards, no bank accounts, and no marketable skills. All we had was each other.

The three of us slept in our bed together one last time that night. In the morning, Chris went to speak with Corey's mom, Ronnie. He told her of our decision and that once we were settled, we would be back to either get Corey or work out how they would share custody. Then Chris went down to the pay phone outside the lobby to make a few phone calls to people he knew who had been in the Sea Organization but had left some time before us. These old friends were now established out in the real world with apartments, cars, and jobs. We were thrilled when one friend offered us her couch to sleep on. We packed up what we felt was important to bring with us within the limits of what we could carry along with a three-year-old.

We rode a city bus to our friend's house. By car, the trip would have taken thirty minutes, but we had no driver's licenses much less a car and were lucky to be able to use public transportation. There were several changes of buses. With our bulging bags of belongings and a small toddler, we looked right at home with some of the other travelers we saw.

After a couple of hours, we finally made it to our friend's apartment. It was a very nice townhome in the middle of the Valley in LA. I thought it was a palace. It was amazing to see her two young daughters simply sitting in their own kitchen and eating snacks or meals of whatever they chose.

Al was another former friend from the Sea Organization who came to our aid. He placed a call to Ken Lipton on our behalf. Ken had once worked with both Al and Chris at Celebrity Centre and knew them very well. He now held a high position in the Commodore's Messenger Organization (CMO) and was senior to the International Finance Police who had engineered our removal. He was able to get an approval for us to come back to the main Scientology complex to work in the galleys. He also arranged for a separate room to be assigned for us to live and sleep in while we got a Committee of Evidence (Comm Ev). A Committee of Evidence was like a Scientology jury trial where it would be determined if the orders for us to be removed from our posts and sent to RPF were valid and correct.

Our only other option was to be declared suppressive persons. If we did not take this opportunity to go back and work in the Sea Org's galley while we tried to sort out our future, we would immediately be declared suppressive. Even these good Celebrity Centre friends would be forced to disconnect from us and be made to withdraw any aid they might want to give.

It was again not much of a choice. If we could get out of the Sea Org without being declared, we could at least get jobs with those Scientologists we knew who owned or ran companies. We would not be separated from Carey, and we would be able to see Corey and make a real home for him. We would not return to the RPF and no longer be under guard.

The die was cast. Al picked us up from the townhome and drove us over to the blue Scientology complex.

No one spoke. We were greeted outside the Scientology complex and were shown to where we would sleep. We carried our various bags of clothing and small son up the stairs to a deserted area on a third-floor section out of sight of the rest of the building. It had originally been a high-ceiling hospital room with large windows overlooking Hollywood. It now held about five of the triple bunk beds, but for the moment, it was empty of people. Perhaps the people that used to live here had been sent to the RPF.

We were also introduced to our new boss in the kitchen. We were going to be assigned to running the dishwasher. I actually found it to be not unpleasant work in the large galley now that I was not a waddling pregnant woman.

Chris and I took turns playing with and taking care of Carey while the other one of us worked. After a few days, we found ourselves settling into a routine.

Occasionally we were summoned to the office of the International Finance Police. We watched the number of newly declared suppressives grow through a daily list they tacked up on a bulletin board. We were amazed at some of the names of long-term and trusted members of the Sea Organization when they were added. It was surreal. I personally knew and was friends with about half of the people being declared suppressive. I no longer had the cognitive dissonance of my early days when I struggled with Tom Atlee's kindness versus his supposed evil suppressiveness. I *knew* these people were not suppressive any more than Tom Atlee had been. This was something else; this was an internal power struggle, and the good guys were not winning.

During this time, the International Finance Police held a huge meeting in San Francisco. They swooped in and revoked the licenses from a number of privately franchised Scientology franchises, demanding money from them and subsequently declaring some of these franchise holders suppressive right on the spot. For something as basic as questioning the actions of

146 | NANCY MANY

David Miscavige and the International Finance Police's actions, one ran a high risk of being declared.

David Miscavige and Bill Franks, the present heads of the Sea Organization, had had a showdown with L. Ron Hubbard's wife, Mary Sue Hubbard; and after much drama, even she backed down. From the highest to the lowest levels of Scientology, chaos reigned.

Meanwhile, my father was retiring from his career as school superintendent back in the small New England town I was raised in. My mother had paid for my airline ticket to go back for the celebration, and there was no longer a high-powered posting that I couldn't be spared from.

A day or two before I left Los Angeles for Boston, one of the assistants to the International Finance Police asked us into his office for a meeting. He showed us a telex order from the highest levels of Scientology. This person had commanded that Chris and Nancy Many be gotten out of Los Angeles immediately. It seemed our very presence in the city was upsetting to the staff at Celebrity Centre, and despite our isolation, we were a major distraction. We were to be sent back to Clearwater in Florida for our Committee of Evidence. It was a bit of a surprise but no more shocking than the other things that had been going on. He told us privately that to be honest, we were going to have a better chance for justice in Florida anyway because the committee in LA had already been appointed and included two of the International Finance Police personnel sent to remove us. We were guilty and the verdict was already in.

Within the next twenty-four hours, I left for my prescheduled trip to Boston. My father had been an educator for many years and had run the school system of the same town for twenty years. Given the usual four- to seven-year life span of a school superintendent, this was no small feat.

It was wonderful to be around my family once again. Of course, I said nothing to them of the drama circulating in my life. How could I even begin to convey the experiences? They were unreal even to me.

I watched and listened to what the people of the community had to say about my father both as an educator and as a leader of other educators. I listened to them speak of how he had changed the town for the better and helped grow a tiny community into a small town by its reputation for an excellent school system. The town honored him in many ways, one of which was to name a school after him.

I thought of the difference between this man and L. Ron Hubbard. Not just the Hubbard the public saw, knew, and read about but Hubbard the father, Hubbard the husband. I was proud of my father that day. I felt that he represented how individuals could bring change and good things to the world through their honesty and good works. I listened as teacher after teacher spoke of my father and how his confidence in them and constant encouragement had driven them on to higher achievements.

The words of Ralph Waldo Emerson came back to me:

> To laugh often and much, to win the respect of intelligent people and the affection of children . . . To find the best in others, to leave the world a bit better, whether by a healthy child, a garden path . . . to know even one life has breathed easier because you have lived. This is to have succeeded!

It became crystal clear then that my days in the Sea Org were over. I just hoped I could get out without the dreaded suppressive declare.

Prior to leaving Boston, I met with my dear friend Joanna Atlee and her husband, Tom. They had left the Sea Org some months before and were living in Boston. They were putting their lives together, and Joanna was back in college pursuing her degree. She had run the Child Care Org with me at Flag for that first year of Carey's life and had previously been a personal cook for L. Ron Hubbard. Being LRH's chef had a very high turnover ratio, but she had survived longer than most.

Just meeting with them gave me hope for the future. I knew I still had to go back and complete this Committee of Evidence thing, but at least I felt that life on the outside was survivable. Chris, Carey, and I arrived back at the Flag Land Base in Clearwater, Florida. We were given a room at the Quality Inn a few doors down from where we had lived just a few years earlier and where the nursery and day care center for the children was still established.

We were housed in a room that belonged to Dave and Tina Meyers. Tina had been declared suppressive so was not allowed on the premises. Her husband wasn't declared but somehow had gotten permission to speak with her while she got a Comm Ev to either clear her of the suppressive declare or confirm it. I never saw them but was told they had rented a double-wide in the trailer park right next door and that was where they lived.

Our three-year-old, Carey, was not allowed to enter the day care center. Not only did they not have room for him, but also since we were no longer official Flag Staff, he was an "unauthorized" child. As a result, Chris and I took turns watching Carey while the other worked. Chris worked in the kitchen located at the QI. It fed adults and children both breakfast and dinner but served only the children and nannies at lunch. I operated the small switchboard in the front office when I was not caring for Carey.

We would call the international justice chief who was responsible for the assignment of our Committee of Evidence in Florida, but with us not being a priority, the progress was slow.

From our position on the outskirts of the International Scientology world, we watched and heard of the turmoil that was going on. We heard that one Committee of Evidence had actually found a person innocent. Unfortunately, the person who had ordered the Comm Ev—David Miscavige, I believe, did not like that finding, so he proceeded to send all the members of the committee to the RPF themselves and convened a new Comm Ev with handpicked members. They learned from their predecessors' mistakes and knew better than to find the interested party innocent.

There were entire departments being removed from their position and sent for rehabilitation en masse.

Then there was the woman who was an executive in the Estates Organization. After a grueling interrogation by some of the Finance Police, I heard that she along with her three-month-old baby were ordered to be removed from the building at 2:00 AM while a heavy tropical rainstorm raged outside. I heard she had no money and nowhere to go and huddled under a tree until dawn as she shielded her child from the storm. I do not know what happened to her after that night. We watched as this chaos brewed around us. I made some discreet queries as to how the organizations were doing internationally. As one could imagine, Scientology's statistics were plummeting. It is difficult to achieve a productive organization when internal politics and personal fights for power rule the day.

Eventually, we had some visitors—two people from our old Rehabilitation Project Force at Flag. They arrived at our door in their familiar blue uniforms one morning to let us know that it had been decided that we would be permitted to have our Committee of Evidence regarding the validity of our assignments to the Rehabilitation Project Force but we would have to get it *while being members of the RPF*. They expected us to come with them back to the RPF offices at the garage of the Fort Harrison and report for duty.

We refused.

We asked what our other options were, and they said that if we cooperated by following a routing form, we could leave the Sea Org in such a way that we would not be put on the list of declared suppressives. Our choice was made for us. After more than ten years of dedication and commitment, we were leaving the Sea Organization.

We would owe huge amounts of money for the training and counseling we were given but would not be shunned. It looked like we would be able to find some sort of work from people we knew. Our friends and colleagues would not be forbidden to speak with us.

After they left, Chris and I sat down and took stock of our immediate situation. We had spent everything we had and had gotten down to literally our last quarter. We made a short list of a few people we hoped that we could borrow a little money from.

Over the next month, we completed the routing form offered us. It was a lengthy process of seeing different people within the organization in a last-ditch effort to resolve our conflicts and remain within the Sea Org. We received confessionals and security checks, talked with ethics officers about our decisions, and did everything asked of us.

I celebrated my thirtieth birthday on December 10, and two days later, we boarded a bus in Clearwater that would take us to Chris's parents in upstate New York.

Chris, Carey, and I sat in the back of the bus on the wide rear seat. I remember the tightness in my gut as we boarded the Greyhound. While I looked through the small windows at Fort Harrison for the last time, I was afraid that we still weren't going to make it away. I worried that someone was going to arrive at the bus station and tell us that it was all a mistake and to please come with him or her. I held Chris's hand very tightly and took long breaths to try and calm myself.

Finally, the bus driver closed the door and pulled out of the station. Chris and I watched out the back window as Clearwater slipped into the background. With each mile that passed between our bus and Clearwater, the knots in my stomach slowly went away.

The bus ride took forty-eight hours. Spending two days on a bus with a three-year-old can be a bit stressful, but we were so happy to be getting away. The farther we pulled away from the state of Florida, the greater the relief. I was leaving ten years of my life behind and yet I hadn't felt such peace in a long, long time. I was so grateful that Chris and I had made it out together. I had kept the vow I had made in England to Carey. I would never again put any group above him, his care, or our family.

Chapter 13

Our Transition

OUR PLAN WAS to spend Christmas with Chris's parents in New York then see my family in Boston and hopefully join Chris's brother, Steve, in New Hampshire. Steve, his wife Bonnie and young daughter, Vanessa, had left the Sea Org over a year ago. They had an apartment; they both had jobs and were creating a future for themselves.

We hardly had any money left after buying the bus tickets we needed to leave Florida. There was a little over one hundred dollars to our name, and with that, we were ready to start our new life. For Christmas, we went to the Goodwill store and found ourselves some warm winter clothing. Carey got a new winter coat and a couple of Fisher-Price toys.

We did not know what lay before us, but we enjoyed this first Christmas outside of the Sea Org as a family with all the hopes and dreams for our new future. After the holidays, we visited my family in Boston for a week before making our way up to Manchester, New Hampshire, to move in for a while with Bonnie and Chris's brother Steve. They themselves were still struggling to get established in the real world. If we could help them with the rent for a while, that would give them a boost as well as giving us a much-needed beginning.

They had a small apartment with two bedrooms, so they arranged for their daughter to sleep with them while Chris, Carey, and I used the second bedroom. Despite the cramped quarters, it was wonderful. We were living with our family without the intense stress and pressure we had been under for the past four months. Despite having nothing much more than the clothes on our back and the love of each other, we finally had a life of our own. We felt free and happier than we had in years.

Chris had never had a job outside the Sea Org except as a musician. In his youth, he'd made money as an organist for local churches in the small town he grew up in. He had summer gigs playing in house bands for the resort hotels in the Catskills. His only other means of making money before joining the Sea Org was as a street musician in New Orleans. He did sell dry-cleaning coupons from door to door for a short while after arriving in LA and had a short stint in a waterbed factory while waiting for the approval to join, but he'd spent his adult life in the Sea Org and that didn't go very far on a résumé. There wasn't much call for musicians in the winter months of New Hampshire, so he got his first job as a video clerk in the Manchester Mall.

I got a job as a waitress, not only because I had experience but also because I knew there would be some money each day as well as a little extra food that I could sometimes bring home.

We muddled through for the first several weeks. The day we broke our children's piggy bank for food money was when I felt we had hit bottom. I picked up the phone and called some people I knew in Los Angeles to see about borrowing some money to help us get started. Chris had a close friend, Bill, who not only was able to help us with a bit of money but also arranged jobs for us back in Los Angeles.

Chris's job was working for a wealthy Scientology investor and real estate broker who also owned several apartment buildings. Part of Chris's payment package would be a rent-free apartment in one of his complexes. I got a part-time job working as an assistant for a lawyer we both knew who was another close friend of ours. We said our emotional good-byes to our East Coast family and flew back to Los Angeles.

We found a beat-up old white Toyota sedan and bought it with $500 borrowed money. We eventually dubbed it the Death Car because the hood had the habit of flying up and covering the driver's sight of all traffic in front. This happened to me twice on the Los Angeles freeway. I was lucky to be able to squint through the little opening between the hood and the top of the car to maneuver the breakdown lane. Chris took the bus from Glendale to Beverly Hills every day. We were soon able to afford a cheap moped, and while slow in the hills of Los Angeles streets, it was a small step-up and it got Chris back and forth from work.

We settled in. We found day care for Carey and were able to have Corey move back in with us once again. We worked out a plan with Ronnie, that he would change schools and move in with us full-time as soon as his current school year was over. The public school for the neighborhood we were in was one of the better ones in Los Angeles and had highly tested students.

We were so involved in the day-to-day challenges of simply surviving; we really didn't have much time to pay attention to the many changes occurring within Scientology. We would hear rumblings and bits and pieces, but nothing definitive.

Months passed. We continued building our new life. We made new Scientology friends and enjoyed creating our family outside of the Sea Org's restrictions and rules. We got a dog. We began going to a gym and took better care of ourselves physically. Carey began elementary school.

The freedom was an incredible feeling. Sometimes I would pick up Carey from his day care and get into my pajamas just because I was free to do so. Going to the supermarket was almost as great as going to Disneyland! All the choices and bright colors. Imagine being able to read a newspaper of your choice each morning and read it while drinking coffee. We had so much happiness in the little things. I took Chris to a parking lot and taught him to drive a stick shift, which he had never learned. It took a few days and a lot of laughter.

We were finally able to buy a car. We went to the dealership, and all went well. I always wanted a Honda. The salesmen was great with us and got us the price we could afford. He asked for our social security numbers and said he would be right back. I saw him slowly crossing the showroom floor, white as a sheet and holding our reports in his hands. When he returned to the table, he asked, "Is there something you are not telling me?" Chris and I looked at each other and said, "No, why?" And he said he had never seen anything like this before: there we were, thirty-year-old people obviously living in the world, and yet, there was *nothing* on our credit reports. He repeated himself and said nothing. It's impossible. We looked at each other not knowing how to explain it.

"Are you in the witness protection program?" he whispered. We denied that right away but then looked across the table at each other not knowing what to say. He said that under these circumstances, he could not go through with our agreement. We said we understood and left without a car. I was thankful then for the two and a half years I worked as a spy for the Guardian's Office for I knew how to open a checking account and pay first and second months' rent and other mundane things that Chris had little clue of so I at least knew more of my way around the real world.

Chapter 14

Espionage, Once Again

ONE DAY I saw an order that declared David Mayo, the senior-most technical person in all of Scientology, a suppressive person. A Scientology issue was released entitled "The Story of a Squirrel." The term *squirrel* is a derogatory slur in Scientology, meaning one who alters the precise steps of true Scientology technology as laid out by L. Ron Hubbard. It went on for pages and pages and was ruthless in its trashing of him and his actions. He was accused of everything, from having a sexual affair to stealing money and keeping the cash in a shoebox in his closet. I decided to reserve my personal opinion until I heard David's side of things. He was a person I knew and respected.

It wasn't too long thereafter that David published an issue of his own. In it he announced that he was opening up his own center and would be using the Dianetic and Scientology materials of LRH, promising to deliver training and counseling in a safe environment. This obviously was unsanctioned by the owners of the copyrights and was the first salvo in an upcoming legal battle. Mayo was announcing the formation of a splinter group of Scientology.

I felt very strongly about copyrights, and while I felt it was David Mayo's right to leave Scientology and certainly to even publicly state all the reasons for his leaving, I did not agree that he had the right to take and use someone else's copyrights without licensing. My opinion was that David's intentions and fight against purported tyranny (some of which I had personally experienced) were correct, but I also felt that the way he was going about it was wrong and could only cause further damage to the group. I still believed that Scientology had some moments of truth it. I did not at that time support the splintering of Scientology as a whole.

I had worked for Scientology for over ten years, operating at the highest levels of the Sea Organization. I knew all the players in the battle for control but didn't really have a clear side for myself. After years of living the structured and cloistered life of the Sea Org, my husband and I were just now getting situated in our new life. We needed jobs, cars, a home, furniture, and child care for our son. I did not have time to think this breach through. I honestly did not take a side until David Mayo opened his alternative center in Santa Barbara. The fact that his group was violating copyrights owned by Scientology did upset me; in my mind, they were taking advantage of the knowledge and experience they had gotten by working for LRH for so many years for their own personal gain.

Several months later, I received a call from Scientology's Office of Special Affairs. I was asked to make a visit to David Mayo's facility as an undercover agent on their behalf, and to be honest, I wasn't surprised; as a matter of fact, I willingly agreed. Part of me was naive, and I felt that this might be a simple misunderstanding and that if I could help repair the breach, that would be a good thing.

I had already had quite a lot of experience with deep undercover work performed by the Intelligence Bureau of Scientology over eight years ago. I would feel fine about doing this work as long as I was not going to be required to do anything actually illegal.

I questioned the personnel who'd contacted me from the new Office of Special Affairs (OSA) about this type of illegal activity within the group. The new command structure of Scientology as led by David Miscavige was proud to express the view that they were not at all like the old Guardian's Office, and I was reassured that this was going to be very different. Illegal activities were forbidden by this new regime, period. I believed them and agreed to help. I arranged to go up to Santa Barbara and pay a visit to David Mayo's new unsupervised center that was using copyrighted material that was not his.

During my first visit to David Mayo's center in Santa Barbara, some old friends welcomed me with open arms. I spent a wonderful afternoon at the facility he'd built in Santa Barbara. Part of me was happy to see the relaxed atmosphere of the center, which had a much different flavor than the driven, controlling, and military-like pace of the Scientology orgs. I had to remind myself that this might all look well and good but that these people were profiting by selling materials and services that they didn't own and were copyrighted to another. That was just not right in my mind no matter how well justified the reasoning.

I returned to Los Angeles to report to my assigned handler, Gary. Gary was the lead executive for a project created by the Religious Technology Center (RTC) of Scientology. He ran a huge program that coordinated all the attacks on the factions that had drifted and splintered from Scientology. It was made clear to me in our very first debriefing phone call that I myself had also been watched on this first visit to Mayo's center. There were obviously other people that had already been put in place there. They had been observing me and reporting back on all my actions. I never knew the identities of all the people that RTC sent to spy on the other camp, but I knew they always covered their bases with more than one agent. They had watchers watching watchers.

The fact that I had private and personal meetings with David Mayo and the executives and people running the center prompted RTC to ask me to continue.

Over the next several years, I engaged in many covert projects for the internal and secretive intelligence department of Scientology. I would meet with various unsuspecting ex-Scientologists and people, gather information, and report what was found. I befriended those close to the leaders of several independent squirrel groups.

Those that had left the mainstream of Scientology educated me as to why they had chosen the path they had. I learned of many horrific abuses heaped on executives in Scientology who had not wanted to support the drive of David Miscavige to take over leadership of Scientology after Hubbard's withdrawal in 1982. If these abuses truly happened, it began causing me to rethink the "rightness" or "wrongness" of each side. *Was it possible that I was on the wrong side?* I would discuss these concerns with my handler, Gary, very frankly. He never backed off from admitting that these atrocities had indeed happened to certain individuals, but he also admitted that it had been wrong and that the new leadership was trying its best in these trying times. The fact that he did not back off from the admission of the new regime's dirty hands did much to assuage my concerns.

In addition, the fact that David Mayo and his group had no legal right to the materials they were promoting and selling kept me in the fold, spying and reporting back to RTC on a variety of subjects and areas.

I was taken into the confidences of RTC in that they had two agents working at David Mayo's center full-time: Bob Mithoff and his wife, Sammy. Sometimes actions would be coordinated between the three of us or we'd exchange information. I was sometimes present for Bob's weekly meetings with Gary and observed his receiving his RTC-approved payment of support money.

There came a point where my support for RTC's actions began to plummet. RTC was in litigation with David Mayo's attorneys and had just come under a restraining order concerning contacting or coming within a certain number of yards of the building. I knew this was in place, yet I was still asked to continue to go up that weekend. I questioned this citing that my appearance in and of it would be considered illegal. I was not pushed or coerced to violate the court order and so did not go to Mayo's center that weekend. However, I did know that the entire time that court order was in place, Scientology constantly did violate it by continuing to run Bob and Sammy (the undercover spies they had already placed) and possibly others about whom I was not directly aware of.

I was involved with some actions directly, but with these other things, I was only privy after the fact. As was the case with working undercover, I often heard the same story from both sides, each with their own spin on it.

Alex and Maude Castillo were two very good people I had known during my time in the Sea Org. I had worked directly with Alex and always found him to be a straight-up guy and a sweet person. He was a Mexican national; his wife, Maude, was an American citizen.

Due to his involvement with these splinter groups, Scientology arranged for Alex to be arrested by the immigration authorities to be deported to Mexico based on some minor discrepancies in his paperwork. I was told this by members of RTC who were happy with how upset Maude and Alex had been. Maude was seen crying as she watched the bus carrying Alex pulled away, Alex with his hands reaching out the window. The individuals relaying this scene to me were laughing at the pain they had inflicted on these two people, the pain they had been put through. This action by RTC along with the violations of the court order that I was all too aware of made me slowly begin to suspect their real intentions and question my support of them.

On the other hand, being within the inner confines of the splinter organizations did not create a sense of loyalty or cause a desire to join them either. I was once at the home of a witness against Scientology in a court case when she returned from spending an afternoon in deposition. She bragged about how she had lied to the Scientology attorneys and laughed about how there was nothing they could do to her. She said that she could not remember things and asked how they could prove the fact that she recalled it or not. She was very proud of her dishonesty and how she had easily gotten away with it and perjured herself.

I learned how two people from one of the splintering factions had dressed up in Sea Org uniforms and simply walked into an advanced Scientology center in Europe. They then requested copies of Scientology's confidential materials while acting with such an aura of authority and confidence that the documents were simply handed over. Copies of these ill-gotten gains were then shipped anonymously to ex-Scientologists all over the world. People could not stop laughing over how easy it was to accomplish the theft.

I was present when several personnel were fired from a software company because they were on the wrong side of the division within Scientology. The company executives had quietly left Scientology and were now supporting the splintered factions. They then fired every employee and outside provider who was loyal to mainstream Scientology. They did not tell them the truth as to their firing because they knew that was illegal and they didn't want to be sued.

RTC sent a friend of mine to meet with a former member, Alan, to attempt to bring him back into the fold or at the very least to lighten the attacks. Instead, he listened to what the departing factions had to say and found much to agree with. I was told by my handler, Gary, that he and Vickie Azneran did everything in their power to get their "agent" back within the group after what he had heard and knew to be true.

Chapter 15

The Third Road

I WAS FEELING confused and uncertain about both sides when I invited Abigail to my home for a weekend. Abigail was someone I knew from the Sea Org, though not well. She had sometimes acted in a callous manner in her position in L. Ron Hubbard's personal department. Several close friends of mine had been the recipients of her harsh handlings. I did not have any qualms about spending time with her, gathering what information I could and relaying it back to the Scientology Office of Special Affairs. She and I had met at David Mayo's Santa Barbara center and had kept in touch. She lived an hour or so south of Los Angeles, and the idea of a weekend was arranged. We could spend some time together and go shopping.

My handler at this time was Donna. She worked at Scientology's International Office of Special Affairs in the Covert Intelligence Unit. A few days prior to the planned weekend, we met so that I could be briefed on what was known and what information was sought after. It seemed

Abigail had testified against Scientology in some major cases. She had also cooperated with the IRS and the FBI in their efforts to gather information on illegal Scientology activities. Abigail had had a very high position while she was in the Sea Org, working for years both indirectly and directly with L. Ron Hubbard so the information she could and did share was harmful to Scientology. Donna briefed me on certain things they already knew about Abigail. I was amazed at the depth of personal information they had, even down to her personal sexual practices. I was surprised yet also felt it a violation that so much had been gathered on this one person. I knew that if they dug this deeply with her, they would (and did) dig deeply with anyone, myself included. I was uncomfortable but didn't express my reservations. I felt in some way that Scientology was justified in attempting to blackball this woman. She was, after all, betraying L. Ron Hubbard personally and taking actions to assist in the demise of Scientology. I felt that even with all its flaws, it was still a group with something valid to offer and didn't deserve to be destroyed, just revamped.

Scientology was especially interested in an upcoming television show they had heard that *60 Minutes* was doing. They had heard that Abigail was involved and wanted me to find out as much as I could about the questions asked, the direction the story was taking, and the possible timing and airing of the show.

Abigail arrived at my door with her suitcase. She seemed like a normal person, but at the forefront of my mind was the fact that she had worked in the personal offices of L. Ron Hubbard. Some childhood imprints of "Tattletale, tattletale, hanging on a cow's tail" ran through my head. She had been in a position of trust and had betrayed that. I had never been comfortable with people who did that, and I was never proud of the times I caught my own self in the act.

Growing up in a large family, its funny the dynamics that develop, and in mine, a tattletale was certainly not welcome. Even if you were revealing the most heinous of crimes, a tattletale was somehow worse than the culprits themselves.

And yet here I was, faced with one of the biggest betrayers that Scientology had ever had.

She appeared nice enough though: beautiful, sure of herself, and put together. She seemed like a person I could have had as a friend. I pushed my conflicting thoughts aside and welcomed her into my house, hoping she would tell me many juicy things that I could then relay to OSA. Somehow I missed the irony of that tattletale connection and what I myself was doing. It really somehow did not apply to me or this situation.

We had dinner; we talked of mundane and of not-so-mundane things. She opened up to me about her journey out of Scientology and how she had felt so lost and traumatized at first. One night she just lost it; her grief was uncontrollable. A friend comforted her. This touched a chord of empathy because I had also withstood incredibly similar experiences. By now, I had heard enough horror stories of what Sea Org members did to people who were not totally with the program that I believed her. I started to feel for what she had been through and found myself walking in her shoes a bit. I quickly caught myself being reminded that she had been mean to and harmed some of my friends. I came back to the reality that she was an enemy and had crossed a line that should never have been crossed.

But still, Abigail was not what I expected. The division in Scientology had created several camps, none of which I found fully appealing. She did not fall into any of those. Instead, as we discussed things, I found that she had an entirely different point of view, one that echoed back to my Christian upbringing and my spiritual and mystical explorations. She took a larger view of the situation. People were people including L. Ron Hubbard. They had their positives and their negatives just as we all did. She had been reading books by Shirley McClain and others from a Los Angeles metaphysical bookstore called the Buddha Tree.

We went shopping. We went to shops in Pasadena that I had never been to but enjoyed. We discovered that we had things in common. I asked her about her philosophy in life and found that what she said touched me deeply. It reminded me of how I felt many years ago before Scientology and even before my hippy days. She felt that life was a school and that we are all here to teach and to learn, that we all have to take the consequences of our actions. She said that L. Ron Hubbard was just a person who had his positives as well as his negatives and that he would have to stand for what he had done, the good and the bad. The fact that he had done some good did not, in her mind, outweigh the real harm he had caused some people. Some of the activities he had been involved in were illegal. He would have to stand up and be held accountable at some point just like the rest of us.

What struck me was the absence of malice and the lack of hatred or any frothing at the mouth. She did not take a black-and-white view. She was so different from any of the anti-Scientologists I had met and been with up to this point. She didn't have the vicious attitudes that Scientology had perpetuated about people who were not toeing the party line.

She was speaking to me. She was speaking to the *me* who had felt many of these things before my years of Scientology.

We were driving back from shopping in Pasadena, and she told me she knew that RTC had sent people to spy on her. My heart rose in my throat! *Does she know that I'm undercover, that I am one of those spies?* I also remembered the personal things that Donna had briefed me on before I met with her. I suddenly walked a few more steps in her shoes and saw how her life had been since she decided she wanted to do something else other than Scientology.

"I gave her something," Abigail said.

"What?"

"I knew that she really wanted to collect brownie points with Scientology so she could get back in their good graces, so I gave her some information that would make her look good."

"You helped her?" I asked.

"Sure. What I told her wasn't that big of a deal, and I knew that that little bit of information would really help her get what she thought was most important thing in her life."

"That was really nice of you," I said, and this time I really meant it.

I wondered if she also knew that I was a spy and was "helping me" as well.

The kindness she was showing me in the face of my own betrayal was electrifying.

I was finally with someone whose path I wanted to be on. I wasn't comfortable with the hatred that spewed out of both the anti-Scientology and the Scientology camps, but until Abigail, I had never thought that there was a third way.

Abigail held a bigger way of thinking that encompassed this paradox. She could see all the evil Scientology promoted while at the same time recognizing the inherent goodness of intentions of most people involved. She did not show any viciousness or hatred at all. As I got to know this tattletale, this big betrayer of the salvation of humankind, I found myself resonating with her and what she had to say.

My thoughts then leapt to the position I was currently in. I was a deep-cover spy for the highest echelon of Scientology. I had pretended to be on the outside of Scientology for several years, gathering information, and reporting it back directly to Scientology's RTC and OSA. And then here in two short days, Abigail, who I expected to be the most hate filled of them all, had shown me that there was a third way. It was a way of nonviolence, both in word and in deed.

She had knowingly helped an enemy. Holding to the truth that we are all humans in the same boat, she questioned how could your brother or sister be your enemy. He or she may do bad acts but is forever connected to you in the mysterious and large world we inhabit. She also believed that there was something larger than this life that we can see and touch. She didn't name it specifically, but somehow she was comfortable with the mystery that we might never know for sure the nature of God, the divinity, or eternity while we inhabit this life. She also held to the truth that while we are here, our acts have consequences and create ripples. We are responsible for the harm we bring to others as well as the good.

Chapter 16

The Messianic Surveys and Plans

I REMEMBERED THAT she was one of the few people in the world I could ask about the messianic surveys and the larger Messianic Program. In the late '70s, I worked on a series of public questionnaires that had been ordered by L. Ron Hubbard entitled the messianic surveys. There were a series of them, and some involved research and finding specialized information. I did the parts that I was handed by going to the library to research information on how individuals and some small groups made it to the international stage. How did these obscure individuals actually make it to the forefront seemingly overnight? I had discovered that while the public seemed to see them as appearing overnight, there had actually been a lot of work behind the scenes to create just that impression.

Cathy was a member of Abigail's group who worked in Clearwater. She had a private office, no windows but very nicely decorated. It was just large enough for her desk and a file cabinet, not the clunky metal ones like the rest of us had but a credenza that matched her desk and gave her space for decorations and another lamp. Image was important when working directly for L. Ron Hubbard, so extra money was allocated. She had a lamp that gave a soft light to her desk instead of the overhead fluorescent glare the rest of us had. The privacy was impressive. Space at the Clearwater base was at a premium, and few people had private spaces. Even though I was working at a senior level of management, I had to wear headphones and listen to music just to block out the ambient noise that surrounded me all the time. But Cathy, she could just close her door and concentrate within the silence of her small oasis.

When I was called to her office, I took the seat opposite her, wondering what the topic of conversation would be. The last and only other time I had been here was when she had sat me down and informed me that L. Ron Hubbard's son Quentin had died in Nevada. "Yes," she said, "the rumors are true, Quentin is dead." Just like that. I had not even heard any of the rumors, so it took me a while to catch up with her thoughts; she knew I was close with Quentin's sisters and did not want me to make some uneducated question that might upset them. So here I was again, sitting in the same quiet office, wondering what she was going to enlighten me with this time.

She informed me she was going to brief me on the overall picture of these surveys I had worked on several years ago. The surveys had been part of something called the Messianic Project. She handed me the project orders that covered the overall program. It was based on briefings that L. Ron Hubbard had had with Abigail, one of his personal PRs. I read the pages and saw that the intention of this program was to create the image of L. Ron Hubbard as the next messiah, just like Christ, Mohammed, or Buddha. I had not been involved with all the messianic surveys or research, so this was the first time I was able to see the entire picture. I suddenly saw that the direction Hubbard wanted to go with the organization was that of his being the next spiritual messiah, the new savior of mankind. As

I sat in the chair in front of Cathy while reading this material, I tried very hard to maintain the appearance that I was excited with these revelations. Meanwhile, within the confines of my head I was screaming, *He thinks he's on the same level as Jesus or Buddha? This is unreal! He can't really be serious, can he?*

I took a break from reading, looked up at Cathy, and saw from the smile on her face that she believed it. She was not only of the opinion that he was as great as Jesus and Buddha and all the other major religious figures from history, but she was going to work very hard to make sure the rest of the world saw him that way as well.

I continued to pretend to read the paper while madly working to control my galloping emotions. I had no doubt that L. Ron Hubbard had something to offer the world; I knew and experienced courses and counseling that helped me in my life and there was much that had worked for others. But to think of him on the same level as Jesus and Buddha, I was reeling.

I flashed at L. Ron Hubbard's treatment of his own family; his own son had just killed himself! His daughters hardly ever saw him. He had at least two children whom he had disowned. Recently I had been listening to a private briefing tape where he had been yelling so loudly that I had to put the headphones down on the floor, but I could still hear the screaming and I could still make out what he was saying. No, this man was nothing like Jesus or Buddha. I didn't know much about Mohammed, but I knew them and LRH was no Jesus; he was no Buddha.

I knew this was not the time or place to discuss this. I had always heard L. Ron Hubbard speak of himself as a normal man, a person just like the rest of us. That's who I knew, warts and all. But this program showed that he had envisioned a plan to impact the world as a modern messiah like Jesus and Buddha. L. Ron Hubbard always said, "What's true for you is true for you," and this was never going to be true for me.

Cathy let me know she had briefed me on this incredibly important project because she needed help to staff this program with additional personnel so we could get the rest of the surveys and research done ASAP. Once complete, they could move forward into an aggressive campaign that would create L. Ron Hubbard's messianic image across the world. His new image was to be built based upon the nine consistent qualities that had been discovered to exist and as perceived by people everywhere to be the essential spiritual qualities of a messiah. L. Ron Hubbard *was* the spiritual leader and messiah of our time, and he would lead the peoples of our world to a spiritual freedom on Earth and beyond.

I told her I would do what I could do to help her and left her office. Shortly after that meeting, I was sent to the Rehabilitation Project Force. No one I knew had even heard of this incredible project. Whom could I discuss it with anyway?

My knowledge and feelings about these inner-circle plans were buried so deeply I honestly did not give it a passing thought for many years. Any negative thoughts I might have had were especially suppressed during my pregnant months on the RPF. If my disagreements had hovered anywhere near the surface, they would have been brought out for analysis and rehabilitation. Instead, as some part of a primal survival instinct, I denied any knowledge of a grand plan to create a Scientology messiah and buried deep my disagreements with it, hiding everything even from myself.

And now here I was years later with the one person Hubbard had actually spoken to, revealed, and tasked to execute his messianic plans with: Abigail. As I grew more comfortable with her, I felt I could reach out, put my thoughts out on the table, and see what else was there.

Sure enough, she confirmed for me that L. Ron Hubbard truly did believe he was as great as Jesus, Buddha, and Mohammed. Not only that but he also had many plans and programs in place and in motion to create that image of himself in the world. I knew from my research and from my years of working at the Celebrity Centre that celebrities and other opinion leaders were a major factor in this plan. If Scientology could get one credible and important celebrity to speak of L. Ron Hubbard as if he were the messiah, then by a careful crafting and guidance of public opinion, others would begin to follow that thought and it would take on a life of its own. I had learned from my own public relations studies that people often don't think their opinions through. They look to people who resonate with their feelings and thus can articulate what their opinions are or even should be. The public relations and marketing world call them opinion leaders.

Celebrities are the most coveted opinion leaders one can have in one's corner. They earn their positions by pure popularity and so can have the power to sway many. That afternoon, Abigail confirmed for me that L. Ron Hubbard really did envision himself as the next messiah, compared himself to Buddha and Mohammed, and that his massive worldwide organization already had the plans drawn up and geared to bring about that reality.

On Sunday afternoon, Abigail and I listened to some metaphysical tapes she had brought along. My mind, however, was unable to keep fully on track with them; it was racing with what she had released from deep inside of me. The position I now found myself in had been simmering for years, and it was now here and tangible.

Chris and I stood in the doorway as we said good-bye to Abigail. She had spent the weekend with us, and unbeknownst to her, it was all a planned setup. I was supposed to spy on her and gather as much information as I could and then report back to my OSA handler who would relay the information to the top levels of Scientology. *60 Minutes* had a show in the works, and Scientology already knew that Abigail had been interviewed. One of my specific targets was to find out what she had told them, the slant the story was taking, and if she got any compensation from them for doing the interview.

I felt so unsettled by her visit that as the door closed, I turned to hug my husband and said, "The only person I trust and care about is you. I no longer care about sides and fights or who is right and who is wrong."

He held me for a while and softly said that I did not have

to do anything I didn't want to do. I told him then that I didn't want to report on Abigail. He lifted my head and told me to look at him. "You don't have to."

I was so confused.

"I don't care about sides . . . I do not care about the Scientologists, and I don't care about the anti-Scientologists. All I care about is you and the kids, that's it. I don't want to report in on Abigail. She's been through enough. She's a good person."

"Listen to me, you don't have to," he repeated as he held me.

I didn't call in that Sunday or the next day, Monday. I replayed my weekend with her over and over in my head.

Tuesday came and went.

On Wednesday, I got a call from Donna, my case officer at the time, at my place of work. I knew it was she on the phone, and I had butterflies when the receptionist told me I had a call. I thought at first of just saying I was busy, but I knew she would just keep calling. I walked into a private room, closed the door, and took the call.

"Hey, kiddo, how are you?"

"I'm OK," I mumbled.

"How did the weekend go?" she asked.

"It went fine." I held my breath for a second. "But I really have nothing to say to you. I don't want to talk."

Donna was silent for a bit.

"OK, well you want me to call you later?"

"Yes," I said.

"OK, I'll call in a few days."

We hung up, and I went back to work. I didn't know what I was going to do, but I knew I wasn't ready to see her or talk to her. I went back to my work.

Several days passed, and my mind was still not clear. Donna called me again, and I gave her a brief overview of my meeting with Abigail. I told her *60 Minutes* was going to do a double segment on Scientology, not just the normal fifteen- to twenty-minute one. I don't know if Abigail told me that to feed it back to Scientology or if at one time that really was the plan because that's not what eventually happened. The piece that ran was the single segment.

After the weekend and a week after my meeting with Abigail, I got a call from Donna and was told that they wanted to meet with me in the main Scientology building. Her superiors had requested it, and even she did not know the details.

I was scared. I was shaking; I knew I was on unstable ground personally, uncertain of where I stood and what was to come of me. It was a big moment when I parked my car and went in the doors and up to the RTC space.

I was brought in to meet with the Scientology's top lawyers. There were several other people in the room. I realized that they wanted me to be a witness in the case they were having with David Mayo. I wondered why because I really didn't have much information for them.

I was being brought in from the cold.

Once you are turned over to the legal machinery, everything seems to move at a rapid pace. They put together a statement for me to sign and placed me on their witness list. I was brought into another room and briefed as to what I should expect as a witness. All the while, I sat nervously and wondered what I would say on the stand. I wondered if I would actually lie for Scientology. There was a time when I had no doubt I would have said or done anything including lying under oath. I was so dedicated that I would have gone to jail or thrown myself on the proverbial sword to protect them. However, I had grown up, I had learned a lot, and I did not think that was true any longer.

Over the next few days, the conversations I'd had with Abigail rumbled through my head. I knew that Scientology had at least two long-term spies in David Mayo's center, reporting every minute bit of information including any legal strategy they could gather.

If I lied for Scientology, how could I live with myself? Moreover, did they deserve to be lied for? Scientology always tells its members that they have to take responsibility. Doesn't that apply to them as a group as well? But I also realized that if I told the truth, the whole truth, and nothing but the truth, I would find myself as a target for Scientology. I would become the traitor that they placed in the center of the bull's-eye. I knew firsthand what they did to people who crossed them. *Was I ready for those consequences?*

In the end, I never did get called to the stand so I never had to deal with the question of honesty. To this day, I don't know for sure if I would have lied for them, but I'd like to believe that I wouldn't have.

Many years later, I found out from someone who was present at a meeting where Gary, my RTC handler, had doubts about me. He had noticed the signs that I was burned out and could see the possibility that I might turn to the other side. He said that was the real reason I was openly disclosed as an undercover agent for them. They didn't need my testimony as a witness in their trial against David Mayo. They wanted me dead-agented, so no one from the other side would ever believe or trust me again. They wanted my connection to any anti-Scientologist to be closed down.

Chapter 17

Becoming a Public Scientologist

A PUBLIC PERSON'S RELATIONSHIP to the world of Scientology can be complex. My experiences while working undercover with anti-Scientologists and other Scientology critics had changed me. Much of what they said I knew to be true, but I did not find their methods or attitude much better than those of the Scientology executives and leaders I was so familiar with. I was still considering the possibilities that Abigail had opened up in me about seeing a bigger picture. I wanted to engage a larger worldview, but so far, I was unable to find a way to activate that direction in my life.

By bringing me forward as a witness for the Church of Scientology, I had been outed as a spy overnight. No ex-Scientologist would ever trust me again.

It was not that I didn't live with my doubts about Scientology; it was that when the questions bubbled to the surface, there was nowhere and no one I felt I could go to help sort them out.

I had been pregnant with my second son, Taylor, during David Mayo's trial. I was working at a job at a computer company until it was time for my maternity leave, and I knew I would have some time then to think and plan things for our future.

As I spent the days nursing and caring for my son, I reviewed where I had come from and where I wanted to go. I took stock of my life and what I had gained from the years I spent on staff in Scientology and the fact that we now had three boys to raise and take care of. My husband's recent career as a music composer was growing, but it demanded odd hours and the income was irregular. I wanted a job where I would have flexibility with my hours but with a stable weekly income. I wanted to be there for my children and available to attend their school functions, but I realized we'd need both of our incomes to support our family, not to mention making up for the many lost years of building a financial base and savings while Chris and I were in the Sea Org.

I felt very strongly that I had learned a lot about business while on staff. I had quite a bit of experience with a large number of organizations, both nationally and internationally. From my work with artists and celebrities, I gained experience working with people in all areas of the entertainment field including writers, actors, and even set designers. I knew what it took to build a career, and I felt very comfortable with helping small businesses grow.

So as to keep Scientology's religious corporations separated from any secular involvement, it had set up and was expanding business elements under the umbrella of WISE (World Institute of Scientology Enterprises). I was adamant from the beginning that I would not mix Scientology the religion with Scientology's secular theories of organization. By translating the administrative principles as laid out in Hubbard's policies, I could find an application in the secular business world. I began working with businesses, using the experience and knowledge I had gained over the years. These were not spiritual in nature, and I was very strict about never mixing the two. If a businessperson I was working with was interested in the more personal and spiritual aspects, I would refer them to someone else for that information.

I decided I did want to help people whom were already Scientologists to continue in their studies and personal counseling and continue moving up the Bridge of Scientology. Despite everything I had gone through and the confusions I might have been facing, I still believed that there was help to be had from Scientology.

My work with OSA as an undercover agent had brought me back to the good graces of my friends and former colleagues. The fact that I'd left the Sea Org seemed to be forgiven, and I was a Scientologist in good standing. Now that I was no longer undercover, I knew that I could join Scientology's sales program where I could act as a field staff member (FSM) and receive a 10 or 15 percent commission on the money paid to the church by the people I was helping move up the Bridge. I disagreed very strongly with the way some FSMs would push their clients to max out their credit cards or even to borrow from someone else's line of credit in order to pay for Scientology services. In the '80s and early '90s, the practice of borrowing from another Scientologist's credit line had become so pervasive that some U.S. Orgs were actually banned by American Express from using their cards due to the amount of reported problems from the original owner of the card.

I realized that there were now three separate avenues of income that I could develop. I could work as a business consultant for an already existing Scientology-based consulting firm. This company would do the marketing and sales needed to get clients for me. I would deliver whatever advice, training, or reorganization was needed for their clients to improve their businesses. I could also build my own business of consulting individuals who worked in the entertainment industry or needed help sorting out their future job and career strategies. The third avenue of income was to work as a field staff member and collect commissions. I had experience in all three of these areas and knew I could do well. I decided to use the experience and knowledge I had gained from working in the Sea Org for the past ten years and use it to help others. So I became an FSM and did business and career consultations.

I raised my children. I was busy with babies and the PTA, Cub Scouts, and work. My life was full. While the personal questions brought up by Abigail bubbled up now and again, life would come and carry me away before I had time to truly unfold those thoughts.

I was conflicted however. Despite the positive and helpful things that I had found within Scientology, I felt certain that the Sea Org was not a good place. I had no doubt that the rehabilitation program was wrong and possibly illegal in and of itself based on my experiences as a pregnant mother and the physical and mental abuse I suffered as a result. Even though I continued to be called by Scientology's intelligence branch in the years that followed, I was free to say no, free of any obligation to help OSA out with espionage tactics. On the occasions they called, I would listen to their proposal, get the details on the operation, and then politely decline; but after the call, I would research what and/or whom they were investigating.

I had never been simply a public Scientologist. I thought that perhaps that would be where I could just take advantage of what I had felt was beneficial and just leave the rest behind: a buffet Scientologist.

Chris and I had been deeply involved in Scientology for well over ten years. Now we were starting out in the real world: in our thirties with no savings, no home that we owned, and three sons to raise. That was enough of a challenge to keep me focused and busy.

I calmed my doubts and confusions about Scientology with the thought that I had never simply been a public member of the group. While I felt that the Sea Org was a totalitarian organization that caused me and others harm, perhaps these islands of Scientology would be immune to the type of abuse that was used in the name of clearing the planet. I certainly had never seen public members and especially celebrity Scientologists treated the way Sea Org members were.

Raising my family was my number one priority now. I felt confident that I could balance being a mother while helping others and, as a bonus, generate some additional income to help create a better future for us.

And so with a mix of both anticipation and trepidation, I set out on my three avenues.

Chapter 18

Business Consultation

USING SCIENTOLOGY TECHNOLOGY in the corporate world as a "business consultant" came squarely under the umbrella of a division of Scientology called WISE. Much had shifted since the original organization that I had been a part of establishing under L. Ron Hubbard's direction. When it was originally registered and conceived in 1979, it was mainly intended to be geared toward Scientologists who owned their own businesses, hence the name World Institute of Scientology Enterprises. Many years had passed and what was originally a small aspect of this group—the exportation of the business paradigm that L. Ron Hubbard had developed to build his international organizations from Scientology orgs to non-Scientology businesses—had become a new source of income for Scientology. Courses had been created in which Scientology policies were minorly edited to adjust any Scientology specific terminology and concepts for the broader public although in fact, not much had to be translated: most of Hubbard's writings spoke directly to a productive business environment just as they were written.

The WISE center in Los Angeles was expanding. Not only did they license consultants, but they also opened up an educational facility called the WISE College. Given my extensive experience and training, it did not take me long to become a licensed WISE consultant. This licensing authorized and allowed me to use the LRH materials I had learned through my experiences and prior training to help improve other businesses. I, or the company. I was hired by, simply had to send in weekly reports and pay 10 percent of the gross income I generated through my consultation activities.

License in hand, it was not very difficult for me to get a job as a consultant for one of the major WISE companies operating in the Los Angeles area. The one I worked for specialized in the consultation of medical doctors. I found that I enjoyed the work tremendously. I traveled, met lots of wonderful people, and I learned a lot about the inner workings of small businesses and the smooth administration of a doctor's office.

I felt free to apply the good and stable business knowledge I had learned while at the same time helping people that were caring for and physically healing others.

I was fluid in the application of my Scientology knowledge including my background and experience in any given situation. In Scientology, expansion is calculated in terms of money, product delivery, and the numbers of people serviced. In interviewing my clients, I found that many of them considered different things to be desirable, which defined what expansion was for them. Some of them wanted the freedom of time. They wanted to be there for their children or to pursue other interests. Several wanted to build up their practices so they could travel and speak, teaching others the techniques they had mastered. It was both refreshing and exhilarating to assist my clients in accomplishing what was important to them.

There came a point when I decided it was time to open a small consulting firm of my own. This business soon became my primary source of income. The clients I worked with and the projects we implemented together gave me a lot of satisfaction and joy. I was still required to pay WISE 10 percent of my gross income to remain a licensed WISE consultant.

I began to examine this licensing agreement, and I realized that I had questions about the validity of it in my consultation practice. It seemed to me that if I went to college and spent a great deal of time and money to learn the materials of my chosen career, upon graduation I no longer owed that institution anything further. There might be the cache of getting a degree at Yale or Harvard and of course I might have had student loans to pay off to a bank or government program, but other than that, I was free to pursue my dreams. WISE's business model was based on the concept that I owed them 10 percent of my gross income for the rest of my career simply because they taught me what I was using. The idea that they owned the knowledge that Hubbard developed and I was going to license it from them to apply in my business seemed extreme. It would be like an author who required his or her readers to pay 10 percent of their gross income if they used anything in the author's book to make money in their business.

Because I refused to mix the spiritual side of Scientology with the business side, I got a lot of business from seminars given by a firm called Sterling Consultants. Sterling was a large consulting group that made no secret of their connections with Scientology. Sterling actually kept a full-time Scientology staff member on their premises. Business owners and professionals would come to Sterling expecting to receive training to become more proficient at running their businesses.

During the first day of arrival for business consulting, new clients were invariably found to be lacking in personal skills. To help them improve these areas of managerial deficiency, they were smoothly routed to the Scientology registrar to be sold additional personal services delivered at a Scientology org that would then resolve any personal issues.

Sterling would collect the business-consulting fees as well as a percentage of whatever the person paid to the Scientology Org. The Sterling Company was considered a field staff member by the Scientology Org and, as such, was entitled to the 10 or 15 percent commission the church routinely paid out to their external sales forces.

Some individuals would become interested in the business techniques that Sterling promoted in their workshops but did not want to get involved in Scientology's spiritual aspects at all. These potential clients simply wanted the business technology being offered even if they were based on Scientology's administrative principles. I soon earned a reputation as a private consultant who would teach clients business techniques that were helpful without pushing other spiritual beliefs on them or insist that they enroll in basic Scientology courses.

Scientology did appear to me to be taking steps to become more of a real church than when I had first joined. The separation of the business side of things showed me that it would like to function as a church.

I felt that Scientology should make the administration of running a business and the spirituality that was the basis of their religion into two separate entities. I never felt I had to use bait and switch techniques by promoting for business consultation as a ruse to sell Scientology.

Consulting was enjoyable to me. I felt I was using all I had learned in working and studying Scientology, but I was able to use it to help people who were out there doing a good job every day and make their little part of the world better.

To be honest, when I joined Scientology, I personally never saw it as a religion. In fact, I don't know if I would have joined the group if I had been told it was a real church. In later years, it appeared that they were attempting to shift more into becoming a mainstream religion; WISE itself was supposed to be the secular arm of their organization, positioned as the business side of things. Since the administrative area was what I had most enjoyed, becoming a secular consultant seemed like a perfect fit.

It worked remarkably well for both my clients and myself for several years. My purpose for being a consultant was to help better the world. I felt that if good people doing good acts could get more training or knowledge to do them better, then the world would be a better place. People did not have to become a Scientologist to do that.

That all changed in 1990. I had a meeting with one of the senior executives of WISE and was briefed on some changes that had been made to the internal structure of the organization. The purpose of WISE had been changed from a beneficent, secular group that disseminated the nonspiritual aspects of running a business using materials that Hubbard compiled to one whose purpose was to introduce and recruit new people to join Scientology itself. It was, to my mind, a bait and switch process, clear and simple. Unsuspecting business owners would contact WISE business consultants for help with their businesses, but the real intention of those consultants was to recruit and turn them into Scientologists.

This did not sit well with me for many reasons. I felt it was deceptive and a mixing of religion and the workplace. This was just plain wrong as far as I was concerned, and it was motivated by money not to mention all the other statistics Scientology could increase by adding to the number of new adherents. And I had thought I was working with a group that was dedicated to bettering the planet.

Now I was confronted with the fact that one of the three cornerstones of the work I had chosen to do with Scientology, which I still believed had tremendous value, was being compromised through a shifty business strategy that went against everything I stood for. I had no problem introducing people and getting them into Scientology. I had done that many times over the years, but I never felt I had to lie to them about it. I never had to create an elaborate outreach into the business world and then surreptitiously transfer the focus toward joining Scientology. I actually felt it demeaned the spiritual aspect of Scientology as if no one would be interested if they were just straight out told about the spirituality it offered. The thought that it was resorting to smoke and mirrors to get people into Scientology was repulsive to me.

Over the years, the number of consulting groups had grown exponentially. Not only was Scientology receiving 10 percent of the consulting groups' gross income, but they also discovered that the professional clientele receiving the consulting had income and assets. It had become a very large cash flow into the organization, and the potential for more was obvious. It became clear to me that this was what Scientology wanted from the licensed consulting companies—new recruits and members and increased income for Scientology.

With this astonishing realization, I felt like I was the odd one out. I had thought the purpose was to export business techniques LRH had developed while putting Scientology together, therefore broadening his image while helping people and the planet along the way. As I reviewed the materials I had been given by the Los Angeles WISE chapter, I realized this was not going to be changed. The expanded promotional materials created for this transition were printed on beautiful and expensive glossy stock. I saw in an instant that the international management of Scientology had invested a lot of money in this shift and any queries or memos from me were not going to change a darn thing. Nonetheless, I still attempted to get a variance for my own consulting firm. The addition of a large annual fee was now mandatory to maintain a license and membership with WISE and was on top of the required 10 percent of the gross already charged. This made it almost impossible for me to operate in the smaller part-time manner that I had developed for myself. To make any profit at all, I would have to expand my organization to a full-time endeavor. I saw that I would have to give up the work I was doing as a Scientology field staff member and as a personal career consultant. After much discussion with my husband and a thorough personal review, I made the decision to end my business consulting with WISE. It took me until early 1993 to wrap up all my existing clients and sell my business to a trusted friend who saw the potential and wanted to make it work on a full-time basis. As a result, I continued to concentrate my time and efforts on my final two corners of deep connection with Scientology: my work as a field staff member and as a career consultant.

Chapter 19

Selling Scientology, Field Staff Member

IN 1987, I attempted to do the field staff member job full-time; I lasted just one week. I quickly realized that as soon as I needed the commission to live on, to pay for groceries or other immediate bills, I was no longer taking care of the person in front of me and what was best for him or her. I was looking at getting the sale so I could pay for my groceries.

From then on, I practiced as a field staff member on a part-time basis. That way, if a person did not have a lot of money to spend on a course but could make some good progress by buying a book or implementing some changes in his business or personal life, then that was the right solution. He or she could handle that financially, and I did not feel any pressure otherwise. In fact, I felt that I was a little bit of a buffer between the individual and the high-powered sales force and hard sell registrars at the organization.

These registrars were well schooled in the art of sales for Scientology organizations, and I knew from my years on staff (and from having been a successful registrar myself) that they received tremendous amounts of pressure each and every day to ensure that the gross income of the organization increased from week to week. I insisted that when I was working with someone as a field staff member, I only had his or her best interests at heart and not any immediate need for personal income from the commissions Scientology would pay me. It did work out to be a prosperous sideline for me, but it was never an income source I counted upon.

I functioned as a field staff member for over eight years, working with Celebrity Centre International, Advanced Orgs, and the Flag Service Org in Clearwater. My work as an FSM ended when two separate things occurred during a period of a month or so. I was offered, along with other successful field staff members, free personal counseling at the Flag Land Base—the mecca for standard technology in Scientology. I was excited about this because I hoped that it would give me additional tools to help people. I also saw it as an opportunity to help quiet the doubts about Scientology in general, which were always hiding slightly beneath my conscious mind.

I went to Florida and stayed in one of the cabana rooms near the large pool. Ironically, these were the exact same cabanas that I had seen that little girl and her mother come out of all those years ago when I was pregnant with my first child and as I watered the lawn in the Rehabilitation Project Force. I was happy to see that I had traveled so far in my life just as I had wished I could. I still had hope that life as a public Scientologist would allow me to access all that I felt was worthwhile about it while not having to partake in the totalitarian control of the Sea Org. It was with great hope that I started my special auditing to improve my skills as an FSM.

The first counseling session was disappointing to say the least. I soon realized after several questions that the purpose of this counseling was not really to help me improve my skills with helping people but rather to enable me to generate greater sales and income for Scientology. The questions were all geared as if I were just another registrar working for the organization whose main focus was cash. I wondered if my definition of a field staff member's being of help to people improve their lives with basic Scientology was, perhaps, not the full job the orgs required. It was rapidly becoming clearer that the real intention of these free counseling sessions was simply to boost up the FSMs to sell lots of services and thus increase the weekly income of Scientology. The series of questions I was asked made it very clear to me that the "help" the organization wanted to give me was in terms of how to get more money from my clients to give to Scientology.

This all gave me pause. I knew several people who worked as field staff members full-time. I knew that their personal income and rent and food depended on what Scientology services their clients were sold and that they lived off the commissions they received in return. As the fees for courses and counseling could easily run into tens of thousands of dollars, a full-time FSM could make a lot of money. It was the first time I felt that perhaps I had been the one to misinterpret the role of the FSM. Perhaps *I* was the odd one out. It didn't change what I felt I could do to help individual people with Scientology, but it did change the support I felt I would get from Scientology itself if I wasn't pushing for big sales.

Within a week of returning home from Florida, I had a problem involving one of my FSM clients who had paid a tremendous amount of money into Scientology. He had supposedly bought everything offered by Scientology at the time, a whole Bridge bundle that initially cost well over $100,000, but even that expense had doubled over the course of just a few years *to* $250,000. My client had received plenty of services and still had enough unused money left in his account to complete the more advanced OT levels given at the Advanced Org. I had worked with him for years. I received a call from Enid Byrne, one of the head registrars at the Advanced Organization in Los Angeles. She told me that despite all the counseling, training, and attention he had gotten, Jason was in horrific shape and would need to pay at least another $50,000 for the preparatory actions he required before he advanced to any higher OT levels that were already paid for. Jason had recently graduated from a lower level org to the Advanced Org in Los Angeles. Before graduating, he (and I) had been told he'd received what they considered all that was needed to enroll on these exciting higher levels. After his $250,000 investment, of which about $150,000 worth of services had been received, I was now being asked to tell Jason he needed to pay an additional fifty grand just to continue to the next step on the Bridge to Total Freedom.

I called Jason but didn't mention the extra $50,000 he would need to spend. I simply listened as he told me how frustrated he was that he had spent all this money, received all these Scientology services, and honestly couldn't see where he had improved or felt better off than several years ago. He listed some of his current complaints, and they were the very same ones he had spoken to me of long before. I told him I understood and I would get back to him.

I hung up the phone and tried to collect myself. I thought about the upper middle-class neighborhood I now lived in. I knew of no one who lived nearby who would be able to afford a quarter of a million dollars to buy his or her spiritual freedom. I had always been told that the goal of Scientology was to achieve those aims of Scientology I'd read on that poster a lifetime ago. If they intended to bring Scientology to the world, it meant all my neighbors would need to receive the counseling that Jason had gotten and more. How could Scientology clear the planet, any planet, if only the richest could afford it? Was it even right to actually charge money, much less pay a commission on the money spent by someone who was promised their spiritual freedom in return?

Later that same month, I had three other clients—all at different Scientology organizations, but all voicing similar complaints. Bottom line: they did not feel they were getting what they paid for.

I finally sat down and wrote a long report to Scientology's Executive Director International about the different problems my clients and friends were having in these different orgs.

I knew I could not ask my client for any more money; I just could not relay to him what Enid had told me. I knew, at that moment, that my days as a field staff member for Scientology were numbered.

I didn't stop working with him or any of my other clients with whom I was helping as a field staff member, but I did stop taking on new people. I made a list of all the individuals I was working with and things we were in the middle of, and began to transfer their care to other FSMs. It took me more than a year before I was able to fully phase out of my being an FSM for Scientology.

During this time of my being a public Scientologist, I encountered many conditions and situations within Scientology that I disliked or disagreed with. I rationalized them, however, and placed them into a perspective that allowed me to feel I could and should continue as an active member. I felt hope that these conditions would eventually change for the better.

I now know more about this condition that is called cognitive dissonance. It is a very uncomfortable place for any human to be in. We want our thoughts and actions to be in harmony and will grasp at the most outlandish explanations or ignore the most ridiculous situations, simply to be able to continue. It is easier for a battered wife to think about the good times of the past and to hold on to those with hope for the future than to confront and really have to deal with the radical changes she needs to make in her life for the safety of herself and her children.

By the mid-1990s, I found my hopes were wearing thin and my doubts and disagreements weren't easily put to rest. While working as an FSM, I learned that not everyone got the same benefits from Scientology counseling that I did. They just didn't. The cost in terms of the time and money it was taking those people to "get up the Bridge" was getting much higher than what I'd experienced, and I found I could no longer rationalize it away.

I knew I was having severe doubts about my personal membership in Scientology. It was a different group than the one I had joined. L. Ron Hubbard had died in 1986, and while the organizations may have looked better and their magazines were glossier, my personal connection to it was getting weaker by the moment.

I had invested many years and felt that I personally had gained some positive things, so I was not quick to abandon it. I sought out several Scientology staff members to talk over my doubts and questions. I took additional Scientology courses in an attempt to resolve the questions and disagreements that were slowly wearing me down.

Chapter 20

The Internet

TOWARD THE END of 1994, I received a call from someone in Scientology's Intelligence Bureau. She wanted me to surreptitiously join this new group that Wolly had started on the Internet. Wolly was the name that the staff at Scientology's Office of Special Affairs used for Larry Wollersheim. He'd won a civil suit against Scientology many years before and had yet to see any of the money awarded. Scientology continued to investigate him and appeal the judgments against them. They had a saying: "Not One Thin Dime for Wollersheim." Scientology would spend millions to ensure he didn't get a dollar.

The woman from the intelligence bureau wanted me to spy on him so they could know what he was up to. I politely turned her down by saying I did not know my way around the Internet.

But her call made me curious, and I quickly learned how to get online. That was how I discovered the Internet.

I was amazed at what I found. During the year 1995, I discovered and read through many affidavits, court cases, decisions, and press information that others had painstakingly put up on a variety of Internet sites. While this information answered many questions for me, it neither eased my doubts nor made me a stronger Scientology member. I took a few trips into AOLA (the Advanced Organization in Los Angeles) and CCLA (the Celebrity Centre International in Los Angeles) to get some further help in sorting out my conflicting feelings. They weren't much help.

These were some of the questions I could not resolve:

If Scientology was supposed to Clear the planet, why did it cost so much? Most of the people that I knew in the regular middle-class world couldn't afford the lower levels of Scientology, much less the higher levels of clearing. Because of the prices, it seemed to be more of an elitist group rather than one that was working to help all mankind.

Where was all the money going? It looked to me like a huge portion was going to lawyers to handle court cases from the people who were hurt by the exorbitant amounts of money being charged for Scientology's services. Did they need to charge that much money because the legal fees ran so high? It seemed like a vicious, endless circle to me, one in which only the lawyers benefited.

Was Scientology really a religion? When I first joined, I was clearly told that the religion aspect was for taxes and legal reasons and that no one had to change their personal faith to become a member. This was even written in a policy letter by L. Ron Hubbard. I knew that after twenty years as a member, I had been to only one church service. Only once in twenty years, and I was in the Sea Org running a large part of Scientology across the entire world for half of that time. Once I tried to find a Scientology service to take my children. One organization told me that they conducted a small service *while* people were eating lunch, which was during a break in a Scientology course room. Another organization spent their Sunday mornings putting on a very large social brunch that they advertised and promoted every Sunday. It wasn't a religious service but simply a brunch held at their organization. I did hear that one organization had services on Sunday nights. My children and I went one Sunday evening. When we arrived, there was only one other person standing in front of the building where we had been told the services would take place. It was dark and locked up tight. We both went into the main lobby of the Scientology Org. After asking several staff—none of them knew anything about a Sunday service—we finally found one person who casually said, "Oh no, that was cancelled tonight." And that ended my foray into looking for Scientology services for my children.

If Scientology was a religion, what were their beliefs regarding God? I had thought that my Scientology counseling would bring me a better understanding and a closer relationship with God—the Divine, the Universal, whatever you want to call it. But here I was some twenty years later, having experienced some of the highest levels of Scientology counseling, and I didn't feel any closer to God through Scientology. Most of the Scientologists whom I knew personally did not believe in God. Were they in the minority, or was that the group belief? I attempted to find a straightforward answer, thinking that that shouldn't have been too hard to do. Imagine my surprise when I discovered the editing, which was being done on Scientology's basic materials. There was one book, *The Notes on the Lectures*, where I found some clear LRH references to the religious basis of Scientology, and I actually had to buy a used copy in a bookstore because the church had cancelled the publication of the entire book.

Why were there always these enemies? I had done intelligence projects for both the Guardian's Office in its heyday and its later incarnation as the Office of Special Affairs. During those projects, I had the opportunity to spend time with some of these enemies. I did not find them to be the ogres portrayed to the group at large. In fact, most had some valid points regarding outrageous behavior by the group itself that led to the basis of their discontent or anger. In other words, from my point of view, Scientology itself had created many of these enemies. The very group that held itself up as the victim under attack was the one creating these enemies.

These were a few of my feelings and concerns as I wandered about the Internet. I worked to sort through my own doubts and find out where I belonged in the Scientology of the '90s.

Scientology is a land of dichotomies for me because I also felt that some of the personal counseling was helpful to me. The structure is one of greatest good: oppressive to the individual, but good for the overall group.

I need to have the balance I want in my life and go forward in the direction I want to go.

The following is from my diary:.

March 12, 1993

I had lunch with a Scientology celebrity today. One of the points she brought up was a public school; she felt they have all been falling apart for years and years. She would never put her kids in there. She took her children out years ago. It made me feel bad because I did not agree and I started to feel alone for those feelings. I don't know any Scientologists who felt as we (Chris and I) do about public school education. It does not change how I feel. It just makes it difficult for me to communicate openly with some members of my group.

I find the greediness of Scientology beyond my level of acceptance. I have not ever been a true believer; I guess I have always tried to be an open and searching member of Scientology. I took to heart the quote by L. Ron Hubbard: "What is true for you is true for you." Some things they (members of Scientology) do are beyond me.

Celebrity Centre International in Los Angeles recently did building renovations. The building and furnishing are beautiful, but did they really have to spend that kind of money?

A celebrity friend of mine was very sick all last week; it was quite a scare. His prostate had enlarged so much he needed a catheter. Thankfully, it is not cancer and he doesn't even need an operation. That was a big relief.

I did not like the comments I overheard from other Scientologists in his life, which came up as a result:

"Well, he hasn't moved forward on the Scientology Bridge."

"His wife is not a Scientologist."

"He has no Scientology training."

If it is cancer, they will shut him off from auditing.

It is not something I am surprised about; these are the thoughts most Scientologists have. Scientologists feel that a person is responsible for everything *that happens to him or her. I am just disappointed. I guess I expected more.*

If I ever get sick, I do not want to tell any Scientologists. I need to make Chris promise me that.

During the spring of 1993, we began to search for a private high school for my son Carey. Because I was a Scientologist, I decided to put some Scientology schools on the list. I had not examined any Scientology schools for some years; perhaps they had improved. We were very happy with the public education in our small city of Burbank, but we wanted something smaller than the large public high schools Burbank offered and began our search.

I called Delphi, the largest most well-known Scientology school that taught a high school curriculum. I asked the Admissions person there for some statistics on their graduates: what their SAT scores were, what sort of colleges they got into, and what percentage received college scholarships. My first clue that this wasn't what I was looking for came when she told me she didn't know what I meant by SAT scores but that a large majority of their high school graduates joined the Sea Org and they were very proud of that.

I continued investigating our options, and the school we all liked the most was a Catholic high school within a mile from our house. Across the street from the Disney headquarters in Burbank, it had a relatively small student body with a great-looking campus. It was modern and clean, their average SAT scores were pretty high, and 99 percent of graduates went on to higher education, most of them to four-year colleges. The tuition was about half the price of the Scientology schools I had looked into. The Catholic church helped to defray the cost of tuition with the students to better the world whereas Scientology schools were charged a fee of 10 percent of their gross income by their Mother Church as a licensing fee, thereby increasing the tuition for the parents to pay.

In speaking with my fourteen-year-old son, it was obvious that he had not had any religious education. I was sorry to say he didn't even know the basic Bible stories. I decided that my younger son was going to be raised with knowledge of religions.

He would not arrive at the age of fourteen this uneducated about religions and the varying beliefs that many people felt.

Scientology had been talking more about its religious status and its efforts to be seen more as a religion but did not even have a Sunday school for children. I'd discovered long ago that there were no regular church services in the Los Angeles area, so I knew I would have to go elsewhere. Since Scientology claimed to be a nondenominational religion, it wouldn't matter what other church we joined as it wouldn't affect our status within Scientology.

Taylor, my youngest son, and I began our tour of local churches, hoping we would find a fit. We went to several and experienced a variety of approaches in faith. After several months of this, I was surprised to find that he enjoyed most the Catholic Church. I could see his point. The Catholics included children throughout the service. The other churches we'd gone to allowed the children to participate in the beginning but then they would go off to another part of the building for their own education. They were not treated as equals. The Catholic Church has many rituals, but its Mass was the same throughout the world and actually seems to move rather quickly. Instead of at least an hour of speaking from a minister, the homily in the Catholic Church was relatively short. The Catholic Church had a continued involvement from the congregation: kneeling, standing, and then kneeling again. The Catholic Mass was a participatory service. The parishioners had parts and lines of their own. There was private time for personal communion with God, but there was also the sense of community. With Taylor expressing an interest in Catholicism and with my older son enrolled in a Catholic high school, I began to feel my way around the changes that had taken place in the Catholic world since I had left the faith. Some of the changes that had taken place during my twenty-year absence were welcomed.

One day, in the middle of a Mass, I realized how my transition into Scientology from Catholicism made sense. As a Catholic, I was taught to treat priests and nuns as special souls who knew more than I did just as in Scientology those on the upper levels were to be respected and followed.

Each professed to the cleansing nature of the confession although in Catholicism, it was kept private between the priest and the penitent and was never written down and I never had to worry about it being used against me.

I could see the path and the consistencies that allowed me to move from one highly structured group to another.

April 28, 1993

I have a deep dark fog over my head and inside my universe. I have been trying to notice where it has come from and how I can kick it back out of me.

It could be several things. I have been doing a lot of soul-searching about Scientology and if it is fulfilling my needs or not. So far, it seems like the only communication I get from any of the staff at the Scientology organizations is for $, $, and more $.

I just talked with Barry, my FSM, and I think he's helped me find the underlying cause of my feelings. I have seen both sides of the game, and I do not want to play with either one of them.

This is a very heavy *cycle for me. Chris feels that I put too much significance on it—well, I cannot help it. That is what it is.*

Moreover, it is *a very heavy area for me.*

I have participated with both sides, *and I cannot be stuck into one side* or *the other. It is like being above or* off *the playing field.*

I guess you cannot go back into *a game once you are out of it. You can never go home again.*

September 8, 1993

We had a small BBQ at our house the other day; it went off without a hitch. We had the perfect amount of food and great weather. I had fun and I think so did others. Two Scientologists showed up on my small-minded list: Martina and Kathy. Martina asked, "Is Harrison (who was another guest at the BBQ) gay?" I said, "Yes, his partner was coming but changed his mind." She said, "Well, that's 1.1. He's 1.1." (In Scientology, the emotional level labeled 1.1 is the equivalent of being covertly hostile; so if all gay people are operating at the emotional level of 1.1, then they are nasty, backstabbing people.) I was too tired. I did not have a good comeback. I wish I could have said something slicing, but I didn't.

Then Kathy made a few comments, also about Harrison. "Boy, they both completely missed the ex-LA Times *reporter and the lesbian!"*

I guess I feel more comfortable around non-Scientologists. Anyway, I need to get involved in more and bigger things.

I need to get my life focused on something else. I need to be so involved with these broader issues that these particular small-minded Scientology issues fall away. Scientologists consider a gay person as at the emotional tone level of 1.1 (the same level as a suppressive), and reporters are considered merchants of chaos.

August 10, 1994

I was on the Internet boards again today. Maybe I should stop for a while. It truly is a shame that most of the bad things I read and heard about Scientology have happened. It is true. It is not just that I have read other people saying it's true, I saw Annie Rosenblum (and others) under guard.

I saw every supposed-confidential preclear folder at Flag being picked through for crimes or high crimes the individual may have done.

I have seen intelligence summary reports of crimes found in someone's counseling folder.

I remember the briefing at Flag when the senior Guardian's Office executives were sentenced to jail. These were key executives that included Mary Sue Hubbard, L. Ron Hubbard's wife. The staff was told that it was a conspiracy by a few evil suppressive persons. Scientology was innocent. It was all justified; all of our actions had reasons. These were the enemies. This was war.

If I go to Scientology events and hear the PR, I am reminded of the truth behind the curtain, which is not so pretty.

November 21, 1994

I feel like I am distancing myself from Scientology even more. I wonder where the sense of community is. I wonder where the care is.

I just found out an old friend, Share Jessup, died. She died while on staff in the Sea Org. I did not know. I heard she went quietly; she did not want her dying to disrupt the production of the Scientology Org she worked at. I wonder if anyone prayed for her.

If a person gets ill in Scientology, it has been my experience that what the person has done to pull it in becomes the object of discussion.

These, as opposed to group prayer, are done to maybe help the person overcome what is going on. The drive for money is amazing, unbelievable, and never ending.

If someone was deathly ill, registrars would say, "Oh good, this is an easy reg cycle.Money, money money and more money." I cannot fault Time Magazine *for its title "Cult of Greed." That is a pretty succinct description of the subject.*

February 4, 1995, Saturday

I had those nightmares again last night. Chris (once again, it's Chris) rejoined the Sea Organization, and I was trapped. I was put under guard but kept trying to escape. It was awful, pretty traumatic chase scenes, fear scenes.

The trauma of being on staff runs deep. It was exciting and oppressive at the same time. A jumbled mix of things, people, and times I loved contrasted with other things and times that I find still unspeakable.

February 22

Chris and I had a long talk yesterday to help me with my mental confabulations about Scientology. The thing that is weird to me is that I do not want *any auditing! The Advanced Org has an offer of some free counseling. I could go in and get a counseling session today, but I have no interest. None.*

I don't have any urge to attack Scientology, but I now know that if I was ever called to testify, I would simply tell the truth; the truth is what I would say.

A couple of months ago, I reread the Scientology Credo of a Group Member. Hubbard said that a group member should never be required to give more than he gets. So that is what I decided; I would keep that code. Since then, I have noticed that I do not get much from this group.

I get what I pay or exchange for. They do ask a lot of their group members.

Anyway, Chris and I talked. He does not go through any of these ups and downs. He just does not expect more, and then he is never disappointed.

February 27

I just finished reading my second Moonie *book. It is amazing to me—the similarities between Scientologists and the Moonies. Granted, there are many differences too, but the totalitarian group focus things like the five-year plan, poor food quality, little sleep that are almost identical. Both groups have two main products: money and recruits. There is a big difference in them. The Moonies do not seem to also have a large public that works in the real world, yet still are members. The Moonies also do not have courses or auditing to give in exchange. The Moonies don't pay commissions to people who get others to donate money.*

I also could see that I had been very vulnerable to recruitment by Scientology those many years past. I was dissatisfied with the drug use I saw all around me. I was searching for structure and purpose. I was not finding it in my college classes. Funny how my life has unfolded, how the years just built one on top of the other.

I did many things for the group when I envisioned that the group would be there for me if I needed them. Little did I know how quickly people could and would be cast aside.

I am so happy to not *be on staff. The freedom I have. I can go to sleep when I want. I can go to the grocery store when I want. I still cannot feel completely free because the fear was ingrained so deeply.*

March

I have been having those nightmares again—the Sea Org ones. How could I not have been impinged upon by the experience? I definitely felt trapped by it. I can remember wanting out, sometimes wanting out so badly but feeling utterly trapped. Friends I didn't want to abandon, lack of money, and nowhere to go trapped me.

I made a list of likes and dislikes about Scientology. Pretty much covers all the practices I just do not agree with. I do not have to agree and I do not. What I do agree with is most of the counseling I received and the business policies. I tend to agree with the spiritual philosophy, and that is what attracted me there in the first place.

April 5

I am finally coming to some real feelings of peace concerning the subject of Scientology. There are two areas. One is my personal benefit, which is mine and mine alone. It is there; there is no question of it. Has the auditing and training I have received made a difference in my ability to help others and myself? YES! Are there parts of it—things I can and always will use? YES!

Do I feel it was worth the price I paid? Definitely not the ten years I spent working for them 24-7 for little to no money. Certainly not $200,000 worth of need! Not $30,000 for my next counseling level, certainly not even $7,000 for one 12.5 intensive of my next needed counseling.

It does not mean I am belittling its worth to others. I am simply saying that it is not worth that to me! Not at this time. I may have enjoyed reading some Hubbard books, but I have realized a few things on my own—I do not feel Hubbard is a greater person than I am. I do not feel Hubbard was better than me. I do feel all the beings on this planet are unique and special. Always have. Are people using their individual talents for the good of themselves and others around them? I certainly never looked up to Hubbard's abilities as a father or husband. He was just not a man I admired for his role as husband and father.

In business, L. Ron Hubbard could be very vindictive. He was prone to anger, and he was demanding. He was always well cared for, but he did not ensure that for his staff.

He had some very simple good things to offer people. These are wonderful, but other philosophies have and do offer a lot too.

April 14

I am very saddened by the new perspective I feel about Scientology. I guess disappointed *is more the right word. Things I did that I did not think twice about. Stealing library books that were negative toward Scientology, I never even thought twice about it.*

I wonder what other little things I used to do that I have yet to examine. I never would have physically harmed someone; at least I know that. I would and did manipulate people, I would lie, and I would say or do things for my group. I knew of outright illegalities going on around me, but I would not do them myself. I would do things that were thought to be for the greater good.

May 18

In a few weeks, I will go into the Advanced Organization. I will give it an honest effort and see if they have anything to offer me. I will speak my mind in a very forthright manner. There are points and issues

I simply do not think they will be able to fix. There are points of personal certainty based on personal experience that I'm never going to see eye to eye with other Scientologists. I come from a certainty and knowledge that is mine. I feel Scientology does not work on everyone; it is not the right time or place for everyone.

The simple truth is that I feel differently than some people do. I guess that could be equated to a divorced Catholic who practices birth control and does not attend church on all holy days of obligations. Are they still Catholic?

It comes down to the simplicity of things. I have major disagreements. Maybe I was partly a true believer. I thought the group cared more for helping the world than itself. I guess, similar to the disaffected who were surprised to find LRH was human, I have been surprised to find my group is still selling things instead of helping the world. The cult-of-greed attitude is choking the group from true wealth.

June 25

I had a major recovery of myself and how I was before Scientology. I was much more a person of "do unto others." I was not a person of the "ends justify the means" or "greatest good for the greatest number" or "never fear to hurt another in a just cause." There are Scientology precepts that are not mine. I don't think they were ever mine.

July 7

I went in and got an interview at the Advance Organization today. The clouds opened and I felt a window. It was smoother than I expected.

July 10

I actually felt good from that interview. Claire happened to be the perfect person to have done it. She not only understood where I was coming from, but also had some similar realities to mine. That was very nice. It was difficult for me to communicate all those feelings, but I got them off my chest and felt understood. I don't know where it is going from here. I do not know where they are going to send me next. I do not mind actually if nothing happens on it. I feel so much better.

Chris said I simply need to find my own peace—I sort of feel that now.

During the summer of 1995, I took several basic courses in Scientology. I felt that I wanted to go back to the simple things I had originally studied and compare it to my current point of view and work out what I agreed with and what I didn't agree with—what parts were workable and what parts were not.

The first speed bump I hit was the religion issue. Was it or wasn't it? I knew they had won their case with the IRS, but, really, did that suddenly make them a religion? I was told and told people new to it that you could be in any religion you wanted to be and also be a Scientologist. This was written in the book *What Is Scientology?* Yet in a very well-known policy by Hubbard called *The Student's Guide to Acceptable Behavior*, he clearly states that students of Scientology could not mix their classes with anything else including religious rites or meditation. I went to see the person in the corrections department at Celebrity Centre International for help in getting this confusion ironed out. He told me frankly that it was a shifting issue—sometimes beginners to Scientology would be allowed to practice other religions and sometimes they wouldn't. I knew he was speaking the truth to me because it had also been my personal experience over the past twenty years. It just meant I wouldn't get a clear answer because the group itself didn't have a clear answer and the winds would shift to suit its needs.

I also reviewed one of the early courses I had enjoyed in Scientology called the Philadelphia Doctorate Course that was a lengthy series of taped lectures by LRH. On the third tape, he spoke of his great friendship with Aleister Crowley who was the head of a black-magic cabal in England and the writer of many books on black magic. In the very first lecture, Hubbard mentioned that people worry about the Prince of Darkness, and he said, "Who do you think I am? Bwahahahaha." I had listened to this tape before, but it didn't upset me as much as it now did.

During that summer, I also found a copy on the Internet of what was purported to be the materials of OT Level 8. Scientology denies that this is the actual OT Level 8 course, but several ex-members who had gotten to that level within Scientology have stated categorically that these materials were exactly what they read and that it was changed at some later time to be less controversial. This supposed-written version of OT 8 included things like LRH's admission that he was the promised Antichrist. He spoke of his mission here on earth as the individual who was L. Ron Hubbard. He said that he had his next mission lined up that was to come back in a healthy body and join politics—a modern-day Damien from *The Omen*. I found it disturbing on many levels. Whether it was true or not, I have never been able to find out. Scientology has denied ownership to my knowledge and never claimed it as their copyrighted article, but it certainly fed into my personal knowledge of his Aleister Crowley comments fifty years ago and my personal knowledge of L. Ron Hubbard's messianic leanings and desires.

September 4, 1995
   I still have the nightmares, the ones trapped inside, can't get out.

Before I was in Scientology, I believed that people should make their own choices about religions and have their own personal connections to God. I never thought mine was better than anyone else's. I just knew what was mine worked better for me.

Scientology, in the broader picture, is a lot different than I thought it was from my personal perspective. What I never noticed was that my view was colored by *me*. It contained what I brought to the table. I did not realize my own power.

When I started off on my own consulting, I wanted to simply use what worked and rid myself of what didn't. I *did* that. I was able to discover that there are many basic simple tools that are very workable. What I did not realize was that the octopus of the group was getting bigger and bigger and going in a completely different direction than I was. Scientology running the world is a very frightening concept for me.

September 4

You will know them by the fruits of their trees. I've always known many of the fruits to be rotten; I just never made the connection that it may be due to the tree. *However, honestly, what else could it be? If Scientology is the truth, then why has it broken the law? Why doesn't it treat its people with compassion? Why does it care for its children the way it does? Why is it always attacking strangers, people who do not even know what they are stepping into?*

September 25, 1995

Chris had a good point that my problem is making things an all-or-nothing proposition. Scientology is hardly all good, but it is hardly all bad either. I just don't feel comfortable in either place. I can't support the close-minded, zealous behavior of so many Scientologists I see. If that's what it is, then I do not want to be a part of it.

But at the same time, auditing has helped me; I have a lot more certainty than before. I have a lot more faith in myself.

October 31, 1995

The counselor (Claire) who did my interview called again. I should call her back. I don't really know what to say, and I don't know how to say it. I guess I know how I feel—how I feel is that I do not want any further auditing. I have had enough (thank you very much). I have had more than enough.

I am no longer going to live a strict, blindsided life. I am no longer going to close my mind from certain places, people, and things. I do know that I feel comfortable having a sense of a higher being, God, or something. Perhaps I got all the gains from scientology I was meant to have, and it's now time to move on.

October 1995

I woke up a few weeks ago, feeling angry with LRH. Angry that Hubbard had promoted and made me feel that there was no other game but his. I had to play his game, and if I didn't, anything else was purposeless and other, intentioned. I have learned that groups do tend to mirror their leaders. Even though so much of this came from people down the line, it starts from the top. The bottom is a reflection of the top. Not the other way around.

It really started to change for me when I had children. Suddenly, things that had been acceptable for me, I would not put my children through. It started to wake me up.

November 28

I have been reading the legal stipulation in the Guardian's Office case when the FBI raided the intelligence bureau of Scientology. Nine senior executives were indicted and found guilty of breaking the law. There but for the grace of God go I. I do know that when I was involved in the things that I knew in Boston, I did them from a sense of belief and duty. I truly felt that what I was doing was the right thing to do. I thought that I was backing up power for the greatest good. If I had been discovered to be an agent of Scientology, I would have gone down alone. I would have denied any attachment or affiliation. I would have protected the group with my silence.

I read these admissions and see what was going on at a national and international basis. It boggled even my mind. These guys were really doing criminal actions on a day-to-day basis and thought nothing of them.

My father made a comment to me once. He said that he understood Scientology had helped me get off drugs and that it helped when he and no one else could have but that I did not owe it my life.

That made an impact on me because it was subtle. It was from his heart. He was also not ignoring the fact that there were some good things about Scientology. Obviously, they were good, at least from my point of view. Otherwise, why would I have given it my life?

So no, I do not feel that kidnapping and violent deprogramming work. I look at how many people slowly drift away from Scientology or other similar groups. Some individuals run from the oppressiveness of the staff. I would like to point out that I've been off staff for thirteen years now—thirteen pretty wonderful years—and I still have nightmares. I still carry that stuff with me. Stuff I did and stuff done to me, those swarming pictures and the ones best kept locked deeply inside.

Chapter 21

The Handling of Nancy

AROUND NEW YEAR in 1996, I realized that I had to tell my husband how I felt even though it was considered a high crime in Scientology to tell another Scientologist about one's disaffection with Scientology. When I told him I might not consider myself a Scientologist any longer, he was visibly upset and was very clear with me that this would be a problem for him. I realized that if I continued in my current direction, my marriage and children could be at risk. I stopped talking with him about my feelings.

On Monday, February 5, 1996, I received a call from Donna, my last case officer, from the Office of Special Affairs. She wanted to meet with me, and I arranged to see her in a restaurant nearby her office. Once we were together, she soon took me into the building where International Scientology was run. To my surprise, she brought another executive I had never met into the boardroom of OSA International on Hollywood Boulevard. Her name was Kirsten, and even though she looked younger than Donna, I got the feeling she was senior to her in the executive strata. To my amazement, they handed me a copy of a private e-mail message I had sent to someone in South Africa several months earlier. Scientology had declared him a suppressive person, meaning the church had dismissed him from membership and severed his ties with the church and active Scientologists. No Scientologist was allowed to have anything to do with him. The person, in his message to me, marveled that I, a Scientologist in good standing, would trust and communicate with him. In my reply, I told the person that I trust him personally but that I was concerned about the spies that I was certain Scientology had close to him.

The two women at OSA International never admitted how they obtained a copy of my private e-mail. The irony that it had to have come from a covert agent of Scientology who had been placed next to him was not lost on me. I told them I was not hiding anything, had signed my real name, and knew they had observers and spies everywhere. I also told them about my visits to both the Celebrity Centre International and the Advance Organization in attempts to sort out my thoughts and feelings about Scientology, including some unresolved issues.

I mentioned that I disagreed with many operations that the intelligence branch of OSA had instigated against its enemies as I found the actions to be unethical. I voiced my disagreement with the Scientology mindset of "the end justifies the means" that govern these decisions, including those I had either personally been involved in or had firsthand knowledge of.

They really didn't seem interested in my point of view but instead seemed to zero in on specific names I had mentioned. They wanted to know if I had talked with this person or that, mentioning all those who were on their enemies list.

At the end of our discussion, they offered to help me sort through my doubts and confusions. They said that a wonderful auditor whom I had known but had not seen for many years had been studying my folders and that she wanted to help. I was not adverse to such an offer. I had been struggling with these confusions for so many months that I welcomed an offer of assistance. I agreed to have the interview.

It was not like any interview I had ever had. This was more like an adversarial interrogation. I was asked if I knew people who were off the Bridge (meaning not actively pursuing the courses and counseling of Scientology). Did I know anyone who is a suppressive person? How about people I chat with? How about what I think? The auditor Joan was difficult to read as she seemed nice one minute and antagonistic the next. I could tell from the direction the questions were going that this was a serious situation.

When I returned home, I was *numb*. I didn't want to talk about what had happened. I knew if I refused their help, I would be declared suppressive. I also knew that my marriage and many other facets of my life were at severe risk of imploding if I got declared.

In an ironic twist of fate, I happened to get a call that same night from a Scientology friend of mine. She was deeply troubled and had been ordered to disconnect from her best friend who had become disaffected as a Scientologist but was not declared a suppressive or an enemy. Her husband told my friend that if she did not disconnect immediately, she wouldn't be allowed to keep moving on the Scientology Bridge and if she was not moving on the Bridge, he could no longer be married to her.

The similarity was chilling. I told her not to worry and it would all work out, but I could hardly breathe as I spoke to her. I knew I had little choice but to appear at the scheduled session the next day.

February 6, 1996 (before my session)

OK, so I went in to see Donna. (She had called yesterday.) Going over, I realized that I had wanted to talk to her—in a way—but not like this.

Donna talked to me into coming inside (damn) the building.

Then she brought another person into the conference room, someone named Kirsten. At one point, I had to go to the ladies' room, but I was not allowed to use the bathroom on the twelfth floor (security reasons) so we had to go to the tenth.

Donna escorted me. "You know this is not normally a public place," *she said. Anyway, we finally all arrived back in the conference room, and Donna handed me a copy of the e-mail I had sent to Kim in September. They thought it was odd.*

I just looked at it. A private e-mail *I had written months ago to another person was staring me in the face on the twelfth floor of the Scientology International Building.*

It was ironic. I had told Kim it wasn't him *I didn't trust; it was the pretend friends Scientology would put around him, and here—right here— was my private e-mail. All tied up in a neat little bow. Now I had two OSA people confronting me with it and persistently asking me questions.*

What did I mean? Do I talk to these people? Who? Do they call me? Anyone else? What do I think? How have I been living my life?

My friends? Who are my friends?

Does Chris know? What does he think?

What have I been doing? Am I on the Bridge?

Who am I?

Then I was told I would have an interview, but it wasn't really an interview—it was an investigation done on an E-Meter.

Do I know people who are off the Bridge? Do I know anyone who is suppressive? How about other people I chat with?

How about what I think?

Breach, you called it a breach, *what did that mean? What did I mean by that?*

I told Donna that if I did run into Abigail, I would apologize. I'm glad I got to tell Donna that. She wanted to know if I saw Abigail or talked with her. I told her no.

I told her Arnie Lerma and I had not communicated for ages.

I felt so set up. I felt like I was being carefully watched for any misstep, but I really didn't have anything to hide.

I returned home numb*—physically, emotionally, and mentally numb. I didn't really want to talk about it.*

What's to talk about?

I could not sleep. I was tossing and turning, very upset.

Headache, I awakened to a headache; however, if I take aspirin, they will know I had a headache. They might think I did it to avoid auditing. (If a person takes an aspirin, he or she cannot receive any auditing until it has passed through his or her system—at least seven days.)

The next day, I was escorted into the auditing room by Donna and Kirsten. The auditor was already set up behind a small desk, and they both followed me into the tiny counseling room. As I looked at these three women and their blank faces, I wondered if this was about to be one of those Gang Sec Checks that I had heard about years ago. It was not. After a stern warning that this was my golden opportunity, Kirsten and Donna left me alone with my auditor, Joan.

The room was cramped with just enough room for a small desk and two chairs. I noticed a security camera in the upper left corner of the room. I had no way of knowing if it was on or off or if they would begin recording us when she started the session. Joan sat in the chair by the door, and I knew from past courses and experience that she had been trained to stop any unauthorized attempts by myself to leave the room. My chair was right up against the single window that overlooked a parking lot many stories below.

What transpired over the next several days was like no auditing I had ever experienced. *Grueling* is a word that seems to fit. Mental torture is more accurate. The sessions were seven or eight hours long with very few breaks and went on for days.

After our initial introduction, the auditor had me read different writings by L. Ron Hubbard to show me that this truly was for my benefit and that these sessions were not meant to be an inquisition or an attack against me. Joan said that she really cared about me and that was why I was being given this help. However, within an hour, she was yelling at me, angry over something I'd said that she disagreed with.

I remember confessing to her something that I had done to a suppressive person that I considered to be an overt, "a Scientology term that describes a bad action or inaction that is committed against another person or group." I was astonished when Joan screamed at me that what I had done couldn't possibly be an overt.

I told her I felt my actions were not good.

Joan shouted, "You cannot commit overts on suppressive people!"

We had several disagreements about the definition of an overt. I said that I did not agree with the concept of an overt being an act that does the most harm to the greatest number of dynamics. Hubbard says that a right action is right to the degree it benefits the greatest number of dynamics: the "greatest good for the greatest number" theory. I felt that this concept had been consciously used to justify many wrong actions that had been done, not to mention my former colleagues and friends within OSA and the Sea Org. If the "greatest good for the greatest number" was Scientology's prime goal with the result being a cleared planet, then almost anything could be justified that forwarded that agenda, even the cruelest of actions. I personally felt that "do unto others" had a much greater validity for me, and I used that as my definition of an overt act to decide if I transgressed or not. Joan vehemently disagreed with my point of view. I did not comply with Hubbard and Scientology's beliefs; this led to several more of the yelling episodes right in the small auditing room.

Another topic we delved into was my feelings about God and his place in Scientology. I told Joan that I had gone to the Catholic church down the street from my house and lit a candle before coming for the first session. Joan seemed surprised and wanted to know more.

I told her of my confusions with Scientology and God over these last few years and how I knew many Scientologists that were atheists. I wanted to know if that was their personal opinion or if that was the systemic view of Scientology. I had found several writings by Hubbard that had been rewritten by others who deleted references to God in his writing after his death.

Joan really became upset when I told her that I knew that Hubbard's children had gone to parochial schools in England

and that supported my feeling that Hubbard himself did not have all atheistic views. She was very angry that I said that and angrily argued that Hubbard had only done that because we had no Scientology schools back then. I pointed out that Hubbard could have sent his children to nonparochial schools.

Joan moved on to other questions: Whom had I spoken these doubting thoughts of Scientology to? What had they said in response?

These sessions lasted almost two weeks. When I wasn't in session, I talked very little. I felt numb all the time. Although I tried, I slept fitfully at best. I had to force myself to eat as I was not hungry at all.

At night, I would feel these sessions repeating over and over, a constant drone in the background. It was like the session never really ended. I had brought the auditor home with me. She was in my mind, disagreeing with me, screaming at me, digging into my head.

February 9 or 10, 1996, was the longest session I'd had, lasting about six hours. I remember desperately wanting to leave; however, I was on one of the upper floors of OSA. When I pictured the difficulties of getting past my auditor as well as the myriad hallways and stairs that had cameras everywhere and were always full of staff and security guards trained to prevent someone leaving such a session, I just gave up. I spent most of those six hours sitting in the stifling auditing room, sobbing and doubled over a trashcan with dry heaves.

I was holding the auditing cans in my hands and was across the desk from Joan, but when she handed me the trashcan, I turned my body sideways. I could see my car parked in the lot below. I would look from the car in the lot to the camera up in the corner above Joan and just know it was hopeless. A new wave of nausea would roll through my body again.

"I'm not going to make it," I cried. "I know I'm just not going to make it."

"Enough of that," Joan snapped. "Let's get back to the question."

Somehow, we got to an answer that Joan was happy enough; with that, we could end for the day. I was able to leave the building and get into the safety of my car. I cried the entire drive home.

That Sunday night, February 11, 1996, I finally got to sleep. It was 2:00 AM that I was violently awakened with an audible cracking of my mind, my soul, my self. I don't know how else to describe it. My mind physically broke, and there was an actual horrible audible sound to me that accompanied it. I was driven to do something I did not know what.

As I leapt out of bed, I heard a voice shout at my husband. "You better get up or you're going to lose your wife!" I knew the words had come out of my mouth, but it did not feel as if I was yelling the words. It felt as if someone else was in my body, attempting to communicate with Chris.

I burst out of our front door, running as fast as I could. My husband ran after me and caught me before I left the driveway. I paced around the car and tried to touch one of the trees in front of our house. I felt I needed to do three things: touch the ash tree in front of our home, find my Helen O'Brien book *Dianetics in Limbo*, and a third thing, which to this day eludes my memory. Chris talked to me softly, calming me enough to go back into the house. I failed to notice that he was trying to corral me back inside while dressed in his underwear.

Deep inside, I was scared to death. Something had happened to my mind, and I knew I was now in a different place. I had no idea where that was and could not hold on to reality; it kept shifting each time I looked at it.

Chris called OSA and spoke with Joan who just happened to be up at 2:00 AM. She spoke with him and then he passed the phone to me. All I remember of our conversation was her saying "There is no technology to fix this." I remember those hopeless words seeping over to where I was in the distance, and I remember thinking "She could have at least lied to me."

It was either on February 12 or 13 that someone arranged another session with my auditor. As soon as she started the session, Joan pulled out a Security Check Correction List, an auditing action that was supposed to detect and resolve the difficulties often encountered in Scientology security checks. Most of these difficulties were thought to come from the auditor missing some sort of secret that the person being interviewed had not divulged. I immediately felt devastated. My case supervisor and auditor thought that this problem with my mind was nothing more than some secret evil deed I had failed to disclose.

I knew that this was not what was wrong with me. I also felt that these people *were* capable of correcting what had happened to me, and I could not understand why they had not. L. Ron Hubbard had spoken on one of the upper levels that sometimes a Scientologist who had reached some of these higher levels could go into a mental spin, called a freewheel. If this freewheel was not stopped, the person would die. I knew my mind was in a freewheel, just spinning on and on until I eventually would die. I knew Hubbard had written a special correction list for this. It did not have anything to do with any undisclosed evil deeds on my part. Joan talked with me for a while and then ended the session. I remember asking her, "But what about fixing what's wrong with me?" She never answered me. I was sent home and told they would call me.

Over the next few days, I stayed home. I was extremely anxious, fearful, and unwell. I would try to fall asleep, but would soon be awakened by frightening things going in my mind. It was difficult to communicate just what those shadows and demons were. I just wanted them to stop; I wanted my clarity of thought back. I increased the dosages of megavitamins my auditor had me taking: melatonin, calcium, magnesium, and vitamin B-1. But my condition continued to worsen, and I found it harder and harder to maintain my grip on the world.

I spent the night of February 13 pacing in our garage so as not to wake any family members. I was trying to keep my racing thoughts calmed down, trying to keep the world from melting around me. My husband could not understand what was happening to me, and I felt very, very alone. I discovered that pacing back and forth, back and forth seemed to calm my inner turmoil. Years before, I had worked in mental hospitals and facilities and knew that pacing was a common activity of people who were crazy. Now I, the ME who was somewhat still there far in the background, understood why. The pacing did help. It gave a focus and slowed down the swirling turmoil of demons and thoughts.

At 5:00 AM, I called a public Scientologist, Bill, who was both my friend and a trained, experienced auditor. He also worked with the intelligence bureau for OSA. I thought he might be able to give me the help I needed. He actually was a great comfort; he likened what I was experiencing to a very bad acid trip he'd had many years ago. It was a comfort to know that someone had been where I was, but at the same time, I was perplexed as I had not taken LSD. I paced while talking with him on my portable phone. I didn't want to stop moving because the mental whirlpool would get worse if I did. I didn't want to stop talking to Bill because the world would then start melting around me.

Bill knew the people at the Scientology Intelligence Bureau and promised to find out why they weren't fixing me. He gave me enough assurance that I finally felt that some help would be forthcoming and I could hang up the phone.

For the four days since my mind broke until this phone call, I was aware that I had had a breakdown. My mind had cracked wide open, and it had broken in the middle of a Scientology auditing session. I remembered some fundamental LRH concepts—"The way out is the way through" and also "What turns it on will turn it off"—so I was waiting for the intelligence unit to just fix what they had broken. I knew they had the tools to fix my broken mind. However, the longer I was like this, things just got even worse. It had been days, hours upon hours, and I was beginning to feel that they were withholding help on purpose. I began to get paranoid.

On February 15, someone from OSA called Chris and told him that I was being ordered to see a Scientology doctor.

I knew enough about the Scientology techniques to know that they wanted a medical opinion about my condition.

By this time, I was starting to wonder if Captain Bill was really right after all. Captain Bill had been a high-ranking Sea Organization officer and executive. He had gone off the mental deep end back in '82 when he left the Sea Org. He had spun stories of how the higher echelons of the Sea Organization had been taken over by the aliens from the planet Marcab called Marcabians. I was intertwined with his European operation, so was in regular contact with him and his followers. I had never given his fantasies a second thought until now. These international intelligence staff from OSA were acting so coldhearted they appeared to be alien.

What if Captain Bill had been right all along?

The doctor I was sent to had completed OT level 8, which was the highest level of Scientology advancement available at the time. I thought perhaps the OT 8's were involved in the alien mind control program, and that is how my mind had gotten broken.

Despite my fears, Chris took me to the recommended Scientology doctor. She told me to continue with the melatonin, vitamin B-1, and the calcium/magnesium that my auditor had me taking. She additionally recommended that I get some other herbs, and she gave me a prescription for chloral hydrate. She said that Dr. Denk, her partner and the doctor who had been caring for L. Ron Hubbard when he died, had done some research and had determined that chloral hydrate was the best "psych" drug that I could use.

Over the next several days, I continued to deteriorate. I was hallucinating more often now. I was still pacing. I was not eating. I felt the universe slowly disappearing on me. Constant movement kept the world present and the demons at bay.

The only helpful advice that Joan gave during this time was to tell my husband not to let me drive a car.

I felt as if I was on a ferris wheel. I had periods of partial clarity where I would know that I was insane, but these were brief and did not last. Each time I came out of my delirium, I knew the moment wouldn't last and that the frightening power of my crumpled mind would soon suck me back under. I was drowning and felt that the Scientology Intelligence Bureau was happily watching me disappear.

I tried many things over the next few days in an attempt to fix myself or get these Scientologists to help me. I spoke with people at the intelligence bureau repeatedly and even gave them my personal diaries and other papers, thinking that they might help the case supervisor understand what I was experiencing.

I was in hell and I told them so. It was like Dante's inferno in my mind. I told them I really needed for them to give me a correction of what had gone wrong and to put my mind back together. The only response I received was that my preclear folders were at their highest levels for a technical review. I would have to wait until the folders were returned to Los Angeles before any correction could be done.

During this time, I religiously took all the vitamins and medications that were recommended. Thinking it might help, I increased the dosages and started taking handfuls of vitamin B-1, but I still could not sleep more than brief bursts of thirty to forty minutes. I would awaken from a dream and think that what I had just experienced had really happened. The division between my dream state and my waking state was practically gone.

My husband did not understand what was happening with me. I felt truly alone. One day, I went into my tiny closet and slid down the wall to the floor beneath the clothes, curled up in the corner sobbing, and began hitting my head against the wall. I just wanted my mind back. I hurt so badly. My mind was destroyed. I would think of eggs for breakfast, but what would come out of my mouth would be chickens. Even though I knew what I was saying was not what I intended, I could not get the thought train back on the tracks. As soon as I would start, spirits, voices, and thoughts that seemed to be sudden realizations would bombard me. My mind was wide open to forces way beyond my control.

I would wake up to find myself at my computer, e-mailing who-knows-what to who-knows-whom. No sooner would my awareness come back to my body on the chair in front of my desk than I would find myself standing in front of the stove in the middle of the night making tea.

So I returned to my little closet, not caring for the clothes that fell around me, not caring about the darkness. I was trying to find a safe place—a place where my mind would work. Perhaps the four walls of this small room could hold my mind and would stop the wild and galloping thoughts that went out of me in all directions. But as I sat there, I realized that there would be no relief. A wide-open broken mind does not heal in a dark closet; it came into the closet with me. There was no relief and nowhere to go. I cried and once again banged my head upon the wall, hoping the pressure or pain would close the hole.

I gave up.

I surrendered.

I believed that dying would not make any difference. In fact, things could be worse because I would still have this broken mind, but no body to contain it.

During the night of February 20, I didn't sleep at all. I was now certain that Captain Bill had been right in his theories. The Marcabians had taken over Scientology's top management. That was the night I untied myself from Chris and made my plan. The next day was when Taylor and I had "opposite day" and the firemen took me to the hospital in restraints.

Chapter 22

Shattered

AFTER I WAS released from the hospital, I was carefully watched. In Scientology slang, it is called a baby watch. Mine was informal because I was allowed to remain in my own home and the people who watched me were people I knew. These others were not forbidden to talk with me although they were not supposed to speak much. Once my husband was home from work, they would leave.

On February 22, Kirsten came to my house to give me a note from the case supervisor. The note read something like this: "Perhaps it would be a good idea if you left town for a while."

I remember it sent me off into a long babbling tirade about how I had discovered that David Miscavige had deleted all references to God when he did his rewrites of Hubbard's policies. Adding to my mental strain was the fact that there were others—another invisible group of beings. Occasionally, one of those spirits would take over my body and begin using it to yell at a particularly annoying spirit standing behind Kirsten. Kirsten left rather quickly and never took a phone call from me again.

My memories of this week are a jumble. I remember waking up in the middle of the night to make a cup of tea. I would turn on the computer and pace. Over the next week, I rarely slept. The hallucinations and paranoia continued; however, I was no longer alone. The only way I can describe it is that Chris somehow got inside the insanity with me. He saw what I saw and heard, or at least he made me feel he did. He helped me calm down. At night, when the waves of terror were the worst, he stayed with me. It was as if he created a lighthouse in my shattered and drowning mind and I followed his beacon back out of the terror.

My husband likens it to the movie *Poltergeist* where the father goes into the other universe to rescue his daughter who had been sucked in through the television. That's what my husband basically did; he came into my psychosis, found me, and pulled me out.

My son, Taylor, had an uncanny ability to know when I was losing it. When my mind would open wider and begin to once again seep beyond my control, he would arrive from whatever part of the house he had been and begin to play with me. He had some balloons, and we would begin hitting them back and forth to each other. The game was to keep them from hitting the floor. How did he know just when to come?

I would tap the balloon and focus on it as it floated back up in the air. I concentrated as he sent it back my way, attempting to judge just the right time and place for me to tap it back. Concentrating on a brightly colored balloon brought focus away from my scattered thoughts and helped me back to a sense of balance.

I needed to keep moving. Pacing helped. When my spiritual self was floating out at a ninety-degree angle, the pacing kept the demons at bay.

Silence and stillness would bring the demons. But it was difficult to hit a moving target.

I remember the running, all the fear, the pressure, the demons, and all things that did not belong there. I remember the cacophony of spirits constantly attempting to take over my body and use my identity to further their own ends.

I wrote a letter to the case supervisor; and as soon as I finished with it, my auditor, Joan, called on the phone and shouted with intention, "What are you doing NOW!" I knew it was a trap to get the mind control back in, and I was very proud of myself that I was able to resist her powers and lie to her. I told her I had just finished breakfast.

One long night, I felt as if Chris and I were in a play and there were hidden cameras in the living room. We had to get all of our lines correct before we could go back to bed. At least a half an hour's worth of dialogue was involved in a scene we had to do. If one of us flubbed a line, we would have to go back to the beginning and repeat it until everything was exact—the exact inflections of voices, the exact words, and everything in a certain order that I was being fed. Somehow, Chris was connected to me and knew the lines he was to say; it took us over three hours to make it back to our bedroom.

The night that has the clearest memory for me was the one when Chris and I were not in our own bed. For some reason, we were asleep in one of our sons' twin beds in their bedroom. They were not sleeping there, and I have no idea where they were. I was so tired of this. I was tired of my body being taken over; I was tired of watching from a distance as this turmoil took place in my mind. Chris was holding me close in his arms. He was trying to get some sleep without my wandering around again and needing to get up with me.

I noticed a light begin to glow in the darkness of my mind. I saw angels coming down—many angels—and there was a leader who spoke to me. With a wave of his sword of light, his energy washed through my mind. I watched as the huge masses of darkness I had been grappling with were being swept away by the light. I could see a battle involving hundreds, if not thousands, of warriors. A battle between the demons and the angels filled with light. It was then the battle shifted, and as it moved, it was swept from my space. It was as if the cavalry had arrived. The dark forces that had inhabited my world were being attacked by light from above. I watched in amazement as the cavalry chased the darkness miles and miles away. I knew the fight would continue, but at least it was now at a distance from me.

The leader remained with me along with three other angelic beings. I was told that my part in the fight was over. The battle would continue but my part in it was done. I was told not to worry any longer and that all would soon be well.

I was wrapped in a blanket of peace as I watched the clouds of darkness moving off, farther and farther away. The leader left to join those that had gone off chasing the demons but left behind three spirits of light.

I nudged Chris and asked him what had just happened. He said nothing. I asked him what he had been thinking of. He told me he had been praying that I would get better.

I felt he had called on the angels.

Chris went back to sleep, and I lay in the peace I could finally feel. Soon after, I climbed out of bed to go to the bathroom.

As I left the room, I noticed the streetlight reflected in the multiple panes of glass of the front window. I had looked out this window many times on previous nights, but on this night, I noticed that the steam had created angelic shapes in each of the individual panes of glass. They were just like snow angels we made in the snow. I knew that the window probably made that scene every time the temperature dropped, but on that night, I took it as a sign that we were no longer alone, that our house had protection.

Everything shifted after that night. Slowly I began to sleep more. Slowly the terrors dissipated. The hallucinations were still there, but they became gentler. The voices I heard were nicer. I now felt the angels surrounding me, wrapping me in peace, and buffering me from the demons. They told me things and they gave me comfort that my mind would heal. They told me that I would return from the awful world I'd been living in.

During this time of my initial slow healing, no one from Scientology called. At one point, I felt an urgent need to get back my books and journals. My husband called Kirsten and did in fact get bunches of my personal things returned. The journals had been opened flat as if they had been copied and certain pages where I had mentioned Scientology had been dog-eared. But at least, I had my originals back.

I kept trying to put normalcy there. In the past, I used to get up in the morning, have juice and coffee, and read the paper. Therefore, I started going through the same routine: getting up, getting my juice and coffee, and opening the morning newspaper. My mind was still broken; I was unable to concentrate and could not read more than a word here and there. I focused on two small concepts of my own: "Act as if" and "Fake it till you make it." I stayed on a newspaper page about as long as I thought it would take if I were really reading it and then turned to the next one.

I was struggling to get my mind back in order, to arrive back in the real world and live day to day. Every night I slept a little bit more, and every day I was a little bit better.

On March 6, I got a call from Bill, my auditor friend who had helped me with his bad-acid-trip story and other actions before my husband understood what was happening. He wanted to interview me and record my experience.

I had already decided that I would never go into a Scientology counseling session again; I would never again pick up the cans attached to an E-Meter. However, Bill was an old friend and I trusted him. Bill pointed out that if I did not document what happened with me, then the people involved would never be held responsible and it could happen to someone else. I finally agreed. I wanted *my* point of view documented. I did not want what had been recorded in my preclear folders to be the only record of this experience. We met in a private safe location.

Afterward, Bill stated that as a trained auditor, he could see there were misapplications and errors in the techniques I had received. His statement did not fix anything for me nor did it tell me anything new, but it confirmed for me that I did not lose my mind through my own fault.

On Friday, March 8, I got another call from Bill. This time, he told me that a woman from Scientology's international legal department wanted me to sign some affidavits. He told me that he had originally been asked to help have me sign these documents. Scientology had not cared for my information and had no interest in interviewing me for my feelings about what had happened. Bill told me that it was he who had demanded that the interview be done for the record.

I was upset. I took the phone number of the person from Scientology's legal department. I was angry that this person didn't even have the decency to call me directly. In fact, my husband and I had received *no* phone calls from Scientology after the day when he realized that the Office of Special Affairs and Scientology would not assist us.

When I called the phone number, a woman answered. She told me that she had a short affidavit and a longer waiver for me to sign. I told her I wanted copies and the time to read them first. As I talked with her, it hit me that after all I had gone through, this was all I would get as a response from Scientology. When my non-Scientologist friends found out I had not been doing well, they sent flowers and good wishes. Scientology wanted me to sign legal documents to protect themselves. Tears filled my eyes and I hung up on her. I called her back a while later, and she agreed to mail the papers to me.

I was saddened and deeply disappointed by this turn of events. I knew this was all I would get from the group I had given so much for the past twenty years.

My husband, on the contrary, was not sad but incensed that all they cared about was covering their own asses.

The documents never did come in the mail. Even so, I wondered about signing them or not. I knew that if I didn't sign them, the intelligence bureau would consider me a threat and would more than likely take further actions against me.

I was doing better, but I was still very unstable. There was a part of me that worried about the alien takeover and those tepaphones the alien Marcabians had placed atop the blue Scientology complex. I knew Scientology could send me right back to the hell I had just begun to climb out of.

On March 13, I got another call. Scientology's legal wouldn't mail them to me but would like me to read them in her presence and then sign them.

My husband was unavailable that day. The only friend I could contact recommended I sign them so that Scientology would leave me alone.

I refused to meet this legal representative in the Scientology building. We agreed to meet in a restaurant. I was too upset, however, to get out of my car, and we made it no farther than the restaurant parking lot. It was only a bit over a month from the beginning of my ordeal and only a week since I began to pretend I was somewhat normal. Not yet having anchors to the real world, I was still pretty shaky. I was seeing things that I knew weren't there, but I was well enough to know not to share that fact with others.

I sat with her alone in the car, in the parking lot, while she read her two documents to me. She said that normally a lawyer would explain them so I knew what I was signing, but as I was in no shape to go into her building and meet with their attorney, I couldn't.

We changed some wording. They called what happened to me my "stressful period." They wanted me to sign that I knew that this was not their fault and that Scientology had actually helped me.

The other thing I was asked to sign was a waiver. She said it was signed by many people every day now. It was a very common act. Everyone leaving staff signed one. Apparently, Scientology's legal department keeps them stacked in boxes in a closet. She said they hoped that those leaving staff would never turn into enemies and that these waivers would never have to be used, but just in case they now got them signed before letting anyone leave the Sea Organization.

She agreed to change some of the wording. She was going to make clean copies and arranged for a time for us to meet again for my final signature. I was about to turn to my car to leave when she turned to me and said, "Oh, one more thing. I would like you to sign these on video. That way, if Arnie

Lerma ever finds out about this, we could prove that they weren't signed under duress."

The irony of sitting in a car in a parking lot, with tears streaming down my face, unable to even make it into even a restaurant due to the stress I was feeling, was unbelievable. I told her I would not be in her video.

I tried to call my husband, Chris, again, but he was still in a recording session and I couldn't reach him. I wasn't sure what to do. I did not want to become involved in a war with Scientology over signing these ridiculous documents; I just wanted my mind back. I reasoned that if signing these papers would keep them from harassing me and aiming those tepaphones at me, I should do so and get on with my life.

I went back to Hollywood to meet with this legal-department woman and a notary public. I picked them up in front of Scientology's main building on Hollywood Boulevard in Hollywood. The building houses Scientology's international legal and intelligence department as well as one of the international organizations that manage Scientology around the world. We went around the corner and parked. I signed the documents in my car. I got my copies, which she cautioned me to keep safe and not to show anyone. The way she said it made it seem as if it were unusual for people to even get copies.

When Chris found out, he was very angry, especially when he found out that OSA had arranged this on a day he was unavailable. He took a deep breath and gave me a long embrace. What's done was done.

Life goes on. Life went on. I continued to slowly mend. I remember it was end of June or early July 1996 when I felt the "walls" return to my mind.

In those months, I never spoke of what happened, not even to my closest friends and family. I did not discuss it even with those who knew what had occurred. At that point, it felt better to just live each day and act as if it hadn't happened. The more I pretended to be normal, the more normal I became.

Early in the summer, a friend told me she had seen my counseling folder at the Advanced Org. I was pleased to hear that at least my folder had moved out of the Office of Special Affairs and the intelligence and legal loop. I called Claire, the same person who had given me the interview months before, and asked her if she could look inside the folder and see if there was a note for me from the case supervisor. There were no notes, and the interview done by my auditor friend that documented all the errors was also missing. In fact, many things were missing. There was nothing in my folder from the time I had been ordered to see the Scientology doctor; there was no information about my collapse or the ambulance or the hospital visit or the hell I had been through—zero. It was as if none of it had ever happened. Persons unknown had vetted my folders. Any and all incriminating evidence had been removed. The echelons of people that manage International Scientology obviously did not like any lower Scientology organizations knowing their business.

On August 14, 1996, I got a call from a very young guy who said he was calling from the Office of Special Affairs. He said he wanted to schedule me to come in and complete the auditing action that they had started in February. I was shocked beyond surprise. I thought I was not hearing him clearly. Then he said that my auditor, Joan, told him to call. He said that I hadn't gotten very far in the security-checking program written out for me. I asked him if he knew anything about what had happened to me. He just replied that I had not gotten far and it needed to get finished. I told him that I ended up in the hospital after the last thing we did. He batted back my comment as if it were entirely my fault, saying, "I've never heard of Scientology giving a bad result."

Overhearing the conversation, Chris grabbed the phone from my hands and took it into the other room to have a few words with the caller. I don't know what my husband said, but no one ever called back again.

Chapter 23

The Healing Begins

FOR THE FIRST year after my psychotic break, I did not speak of it at all. I would act as if all was well even when I knew it wasn't. I was unable to work at any sort of job. Thankfully, Chris was working and we could get by without my income. The boys were in school most of the time and also of an age where they didn't require constant care from me, which was good because I was incapable of giving it. I think my nine-year-old cared for me more than I did for him that first year.

I would start the morning with a challenge to do some laundry. There were days in which even that could not get completed. I spent a lot of time walking on the treadmill in the dark. I would just cry and cry as I walked, wishing I could have my mind back the way it was.

During that first year, I knew I could *appear* normal, but the reality was much further than appearances. I was thankful each morning I woke up to find the walls were still solid and the floor did not move beneath my feet. But I also could feel any slight drift in my mind and knew things could begin to melt away at any time. I struggled to keep my thoughts away from anything that would bring me closer to the edge. Thinking about the things that occurred, the wild carnival my mind had turned into was something I wouldn't go near. I couldn't think the thoughts let alone speak them.

I lived my life mostly among the non-Scientology friends and activities I had built up over the years. I was very practiced at changing subjects or locations if I felt things in my mind began to be triggered.

It was always worse at night. I was often afraid to go to sleep, and Chris would comfort me. We did not talk about it. I had a talisman of sorts, some special wooden runes that were made by an American Indian and were in a deerskin bag. They had been with me when the tide turned and I felt the angels had come to rescue me and they gave me comfort. I slept with them under my pillow, and when my mind would begin to drift to the precipices that were unsafe and not solid, I would hold them and be reminded of the love and hope that had been brought to me by the visitors. I would feel once again a protective cocoon instead of the licking flames of a hellish abyss.

After a year passed, I felt it might be time to begin to tell a few close friends what had happened. Scientology's intelligence bureau, my two sons who were living at home at the time, and perhaps three Scientologists had known what had occurred. It was my first anniversary of that awful cracking sound, and I wanted to mark the day in some way.

The first person I called was Mick Wenlock in Denver, whom I had been in communication with prior to the interrogation. Mick looks all-biker tough with his colors, tattoos, and all but really is a gentle guy. Even though the church had declared him a suppressive, he still wanted to keep up with old friends and know what was going on. He was not vindictive or what could be considered an anti-Scientologist. But since he was on the list of suppressive people, just the fact that he had been in touch with me made him part of my interrogation. The fact that I had sent him copies of recent Scientology brochures so he could keep up to date on some old friends was considered criminal on my part. I was obviously aiding and abetting the enemy.

When I was psychotic, he had gotten somehow mixed up in my irregular and paranoid thoughts. I knew I had sent him some nonsensical e-mails and we had not spoken since. It was a difficult call to make, just to speak the words out loud, and to let him know what had happened to me. It was the first time I shared my experience with anyone who wasn't present for the actual events.

Mick and his wife, Nancy, were very understanding, and their compassion gave me strength. He was not angry about the e-mail I had sent him nor my sudden disappearance from his life this past year. I actually spoke the words of what had happened and the walls were still there and the floor hadn't caved in. It was a major turning point for me to speak of it and still live and breathe.

I remembered when I saw the demons trying to come in through the back of the house. The dogs could see them too. What had always appeared to me to be a random snapping at the air by them I now saw as my three Siberian protectors guarding the parameters of our home by charging away attacking demons.

These aliens could shape-shift; they could do remote viewing and temporarily take over someone's body and use them as their pawns. I had seen them do it. I had. I began to write down the experience.

I called my friend Victoria to take my dog Sasha to her apartment. At one point, she said "You're scaring me, Nance," and I could feel her fear as if it were my own. I had always known we were all connected here in this universe, but incredibly I could feel as if I were she, as if I were walking in her shoes. I realized I had to calm down because my fear was contagious. I pretended to be normal and relaxed and pulled back.

Victoria took my dog home to her small apartment with her cat Orville. What could I tell her? How could I have explained to her that there was an alien plot to take over the world and that they were using Scientology to assume world domination? Besides, what would that do except put her in danger? I felt better pretending all was well and that she simply needed to help by getting the dog out of the house for a while.

I had another close friend, Mary, who was a part of the Hubbard family. She had actually spent some time during this first recovery year staying in my home. I was unable to speak of it during that first year. She had enough troubles of her own and simply thinking of sharing with her would bring me back to the brink.

During this time, I was aware, from visits to the Internet, that non-Scientology people were looking for her along with other Hubbard family members. These non-Scientologists had come across information from staff members leaving Scientology that L. Ron Hubbard's will might have grounds to be contested. Apparently, he had signed the new will after he had a stroke and, a few days before his death, changed everything and left very little to his family and almost everything to the people representing Scientology organizations that were there in front of him at the time of his death.

I knew these non-Scientologists had some valid points. I knew from my friend that no member of her family had been informed that Hubbard was even ill, let alone on his deathbed. He died with none of his family by his side.

My mother-in-law had suffered a stroke, so I had seen close-up how a stroke can ravage a person physically and impair his or her ability to speak and think clearly. Hubbard's stroke had proven fatal. I can only imagine his state of mind at the time of the purported new will. It seemed odd that this new will gave custodianship of his assets to people present at his death and very little for his immediate family.

The Scientology hierarchy was aware that these ex-Scientologists were looking for Mary and other members of the Hubbard family. They took Mary to a sequestered location. I knew where she was; she had even visited me, accompanied all the while by a security guard during this time.

I was still very unstable mentally. I was uncertain of what to do. Should I tell her what I knew? Should I tell the ex-Scientologists anything? How could I sit here in the middle of everything and do nothing?

I felt very strongly that this new "regime" run by David Miscavige had tremendous ill will for the Hubbard family. A vast majority of my interrogation by the intelligence unit was spent digging into private conversations I had had with Mary or with Hubbard's daughter Diana. The attitude toward the surviving Hubbard family members seemed to be not one of goodwill but more of distaste with a reluctant tolerance thrown in. I knew that Scientology was being nice to Mary at this moment because they feared that she had the power to do, not because they really cared for her. I personally felt that it was not right or fair that the family be so removed from the inheritance of even his personal effects. At the time, an official biography of L. Ron Hubbard had been begun. The family was left out as if they had never been there, right at his side, during all those years. I needed some help and guidance. I not only was fearful of my mental stability, but also cared deeply for Mary. I had been Catholic and still had some contact with a local parish. I arranged for some spiritual counseling on what course of action to take. After much review with Sister Margaret and personal soul-searching, I decided that the Scientology hierarchy did not have Mary's best interests at heart; they had their own ulterior motive in keeping her tucked away. Additionally, however, the ex-Scientologists also had their own ulterior motives. While they held no disrespect for the family directly that I was aware of, the ex-Scientologists were not looking for Mary or other family members because they cared for them as people, but rather for what they represented as colored by their own motives.

I decided first and foremost that I was her friend. So as her friend, I should be looking out for what she wanted in her own life. I did nothing either way; I was simply there as a friend for Mary as she went through this turmoil.

I felt comfortable that this decision was not being made because I had also feared for my mental well-being. It was not because I was afraid to rattle the cage of the Scientology or afraid of letting the ex-Scientologists down in what I knew was a valid point. I felt comfortable that it was in the best interest of Mary at the time for me to simply be her friend.

In the end, she did get some support and money from Scientology, and I knew that the ex-Scientologists would never have been able to accomplish that.

Chapter 24

Lisa McPherson

IT WAS IN early 1997 that I first heard about the death of Lisa McPherson. Lisa had died after having a mental breakdown while receiving Scientology services at the Flag Service Org in Clearwater. She was then cared for and kept on the premises of Scientology's Fort Harrison Hotel, the very same hotel where I had assigned to live in the garage. It was very sad and it struck me very hard. Like me, she had been a long-term Scientologist. I discovered many similarities between us. When I read over the daily notes that her caregivers had written, I understood exactly Lisa's seemingly crazy comments and actions. I knew precisely what was going on in her mind. It was where I had been and was not a place I would wish on anyone.

I did not make a connection between the drugs, vitamins, and herbs that Lisa and I both took until I stumbled across a TV show in the summer of 1997. I had already studied sleep deprivation and its effects on mental stability. But in this television story, the doctor laid out that it wasn't that all the medications and megadoses of vitamins each by themselves would have worsened Lisa's condition, but it was the *combination* of them all that furthered her deterioration. I remember sitting on my bed, watching him list the same vitamins and medications that I had been prescribed, and knew that I too had been getting progressively worse, deteriorating each day until the day of my collapse and restraints.

But that day was also the day that Chris told me he was with me as well as the day I had overheard the nurses laughing at the medicine I was taking. Since I was certain the Marcabians had taken over Scientology and they were after my family and me, I knew we had to do the opposite of what I was being told to do. Over the following weeks of *not* doing what the Scientologists recommended, I improved. I started to get better. I could actually sleep. Angels arrived and I began to heal.

Even at this point, I had not yet decided whether or not to continue as a Scientologist. I had hoped that the supposed help I had been promised by the international Scientologists would have helped to settle that question, but it did not. During my first year, part of the healing was not to think about Scientology one way or the other. Thinking in that direction only made the walls of my mind thinner.

I eventually wrote to David Miscavige, Scientology's leader, about what had happened to me and pointed out the striking similarities with Lisa McPherson. I wrote of how it was only after I *stopped* taking the megadoses of vitamins that I had improved. I was not certain if he would get my letter, and I didn't know how it would be received or if it would bring about any changes; but I felt I had to write it for myself. If there was a future Lisa McPherson, at least I had attempted to get the information out there.

I never got an answer from him, but my neighbors mentioned to me that within the week, there was a woman in a white Mercedes taking pictures of my house. Was I selling my house and leaving the neighborhood?

I knew from my work in the covert intelligence area of Scientology that one of the first things that gets done when a person is being looked at as a possible or suspected threat is to begin a photographic record of the subject. That way, in the future, they can show their agents pictures of the targets and the subject's places of business and home.

Part of me knew this could just be my simple paranoia stemming from my psychosis, but sometimes there really is someone out to get you. Although I never did get a direct answer from David Miscavige or his office, I have always felt that the white Mercedes was the only answer I would get.

During this second year, I felt strong enough to share with a couple more of my close friends what had happened.

One friend I had known for years asked if I could please wait before telling her my story. She was a Scientologist and in the middle of her own security checking to see if she would be accepted to do her next level. She knew without me having to say a word that what I was about to tell her would not shed a good light on Scientology. The eligibility counseling alone cost around $400 an hour, and I knew my friend well enough to know that if and when I sat down with her, she would become very upset with Scientology and this would therefore cost her a lot of money.

"Oh sure, I understand," I said and I did.

Months later, I finally told her what had happened to me. Her response surprised me.

"Of course, that happened. Those people over at OSA are suppressive."

"What?" I was a bit surprised by her knowledge of interrogations performed at the Office of Special Affairs.

"Sure, I know that they're nasty and not applying Scientology correctly, but what can I do?"

She took another bite of her salad, and I nodded my head. These were things that were spoken in private moments to private friends, but there was always the risk that the information would come up in an interview or someone else's counseling session. If such divisive thoughts did get reported, the public Scientologist would be sent to an ethics counselor to help them get their viewpoints back in line with the group. Although public Scientologists did not have to fear being sent for rehabilitation, they did have to worry about being declared suppressive or ordered to spend a lot of money on security checking to help get themselves back to thinking in the right Scientology direction.

———————

In September of 1998, I finally made the leap out of any doubts I had about Scientology. It happened when Chris and I were on a vacation and were watching television in the hotel room. The Dalai Lama was speaking about the relationship between Tibet and China and why he would not promote the Tibetan people to raise arms against China. He explained that Tibet and China were neighbors and lived in this same world. As neighbors, they had to learn to live together. Violence would only breed more violence. He was basically saying to turn the other cheek, a mainstay of my Christian upbringing. In that moment, I was no longer lost among the trees but could finally see the forest. I no longer had to go back and forth with "This part of Scientology is good and was helpful" and "This part of Scientology was bad and harms people" that had been the seesaw of my condition of doubt. Suddenly, I saw the bigger picture. Scientology, as they have often said to the media, is *not* a turn-the-other-cheek religion. In fact, I had studied numerous articles by Hubbard wherein he had written that Scientology procedure was to "attack the attackers." He had established the rule that we sue those attacking Scientology, not to win lawsuits or to get justice, but to get them to shut down or at least get them to stop saying bad things about Scientology.

I thought back to the fight I had had with Joan during my interrogation when I told her that I believed the definition of a bad act was defined as one you would not want to have done to yourself as in the golden rule that runs through most religions and philosophies in the world. I believed in that much more than Hubbard's definition of a good act as being one that was the greatest good for the greatest number. I felt that it was this "greatest good" measuring stick that had allowed myself and other Scientologists to justify breaking the golden rule.

In that moment, as I listened to the Dalai Lama, I realized I could no longer be a Scientologist. I believed the golden rule was a greater truth. It was that simple. It had taken me a lot of years; a lot of blood, sweat, and tears; and a tremendous amount of pain to arrive at that one simple point.

Chapter 25

My Internet Posting as Kathryn

IN THE FALL of 1998, almost three years after my incident and Lisa McPherson's death, I wrote a story under the pseudonym Kathryn. It is still available on the Internet on several Web sites, one of them being "Operation Clambake." My husband had read that sometimes the simple act of writing about negative incidents could help with the healing and suggested I try it. I left out everything about my son and the McDonald's ballroom and some of the ins and outs of the insane days, but it was the basic story of what had happened to me.

I no longer felt an obligation to keep their secrets. That was a good feeling.

I (as Kathryn) e-mailed it to Arnie Lerma and asked him to post it on the Internet for me. I had not spoken to Arnie Lerma since before government officials, as a result of reports given by Scientologists, raided his home. In sending the post and asking for him to post it, I did not use my real name; we were friends, and I just wasn't ready to come out to him. Somehow because he had won a court suit against

Scientology, I felt protected with him being the first one to post it. I also remember when that legal person wanted me to sign those papers; she was afraid Arnie would find out what happened to me and think that I had been coerced.

Arnie uploaded the story, and I waited to see how quickly there would be any effect from it. Within twenty-four hours, Bill, the same friend I turned to for help in my mental crisis—I knew he still worked for OSA Intelligence—wanted to see me and talk; so we arranged a lunch meeting.

It was good to see him after such a long time as he had been a friend to me during my turmoil.

"So did you read my story?" I asked.

"Yes. OSA International had me read through it to see how accurate it was."

"And?"

"Well, I told them it was a pretty accurate and an honest account. Your story laid things out like who, what, when, and where."

"I'm glad you thought that. That was what I tried to do."

I wasn't out to embellish, but I did not try and hide what they did. At one point in the conversation, Bill asked, "Do you talk to Arnie much?"

"Is this you who wants to know, or your intelligence handler?" I shot back.

Bill did not answer and was silent for a moment. "You know, I used to know Arnie, he was a pretty good guy."

"Yeah," I said. "He helped me out of some rough times in New York."

We talked of other things, my kids, how Chris was doing. And then the conversation circled back.

"You know Kirsten and Joan really care about you and how you are doing."

"Really?"

"Really. They ask me if I've seen you and how you are doing."

"Bill, they only care about whether I am going to cause trouble or not. They care about what I might *do*. They don't care about me."

"No, seriously, Nance, they do care."

"Well, my phone number is in the book and neither of them have called to see how I was doing these last few years. The only call I got was from someone who wanted me to come back in to finish what they started. That's it. If they really cared, they would have called and said so."

Bill nodded.

"Tell them they can call me whenever they want, they have my number."

Our lunch ended. I do not know what Bill had expected from our meeting, but I left knowing that the personnel at the Scientology Office of Special Affairs had read it and knew I hadn't lied about the events that had occurred. They were not disputing my side of things. They couldn't.

I felt sad about Bill and the friendship that was rapidly drifting away. I did not understand how someone could know what was done to me as intimately as he did and still have his own support for Scientology, not even miss a step. In addition, the information on Lisa McPherson was out on the Internet, and she had died. *She had died.* It didn't seem to cause a blip on Bill's radar about Scientology. As a friend, that hurt; not that I expected him to give up his life's beliefs in what Scientology promises (Lord knows that hadn't been easy for me), but I would have expected that at least some questions had been raised in his mind.

It was an amazing thing that not one of my Scientology friends (once they found out) questioned Scientology itself due to my experiences. They felt that what happened to me was an anomaly. A big part of the Scientology's philosophy is assigning the cause of anything that happens in life to the individual. Scientology takes the idea of being responsible for your own condition to the fullest imaginable effect, teaching that you are in control of *every* single thing that happens to you. If you get cancer, you must have done something for that resultant effect to occur. If you break a leg, have a car accident, or are in a building that explodes, the Scientology credo is "You are responsible for your own condition."

I read the court reports of what Lisa's case supervisor said when interviewed by the police. He felt strongly that what had gone wrong was that he had failed to find the suppressive person in Lisa's life, and because Lisa was connected to this unfound and unnamed person, *that* was why she died. If she had only discovered and disconnected from this mystery SP, then she would not be dead. It was that simple; in Scientology's view, she was responsible for her own death.

Some press and legal representatives contacted me, indirectly, after my story hit the Internet. I was still withholding my real identity from the world at large although, of course, I knew that Scientology was aware of who Kathryn really was. I wasn't healthy enough to speak out, and I certainly wasn't ready to publicly testify. I was tempted many times to contact the district attorney in the Lisa McPherson's criminal case in Florida, but I was simply not mentally or physically up to do so.

On June 12, 2000, the criminal charges were dropped against Scientology. The medical examiner had changed her original findings to that of an accidental death. The prosecutor attempted to question the medical examiner on why she made the changes. Even though he was not in an adversarial role at all, he felt she could not stand up to questioning in the case. She had been his key witness, and he felt he had no choice but to withdraw the criminal charges.

However, the civil case brought by Lisa's family and being run by Florida attorney Ken Dandar continued. Mr. Dandar had asked me to be a witness for him in the civil case, but I felt I was still not strong enough to come forward with anything. If I had been a witness in a criminal case, I would have been offered at least some form of protection, but civil cases are different. I would have felt more exposed and be putting myself out on a limb, so I withheld any decisions other than "not right now."

March 28, 2001
I guess the thought that my words may be taken out of context really do bother me. I do not write near as deeply much as I used to, and I don't write in my journal as often. I think I have to get over this feeling that it's

not safe—that I am not safe. I mean, granted, I am not safe. I need to acknowledge deep inside myself that things are not as they should be and that that's OK right now. Perhaps this is where my higher power comes in and my faith that everything is happening for a reason. Things seem to be shifting in my universe again.

As time would have it, there was a retreat for women offered at my Catholic church. The theme of the retreat was forgiveness, and it was to be a silent and contemplative experience. I knew that I needed to dig deep within myself to be able to let this area of my life go. To allow myself to go forward without feeling there was this undropped shoe, I spent time reading, meditating, and praying. I was seeking guidance for what I needed to finally close that chapter and begin to open new avenues in my life.

March 31, 2001
   I'm at the retreat house.
   Kindness—that's what the guy at breakfast was talking about. And it's true that's what it comes down to—kindness. I was so starved for kindnesses while I was in the Sea Org. A simple kindness sent my way could send me into tears. I do feel this other direction building within me, and that is good.

I had thoughts of suing Scientology for what they had done to me. I am certainly not the person I used to be. I have been damaged in some unspeakable ways, and I do worry that this may be permanent. When the thoughts of suing them arose in my mind, they would be held in check by my husband's feelings. Chris felt very strongly that we had already given them so many years of our lives that we didn't need to give them anymore. I had lived and we were coping. "Let's take what we have and go on." I knew that was his point of view. I also knew there was some truth to it. Scientology had pockets full of money and would throw all they could at anyone attempting to speak out against them. If I did initiate a lawsuit over what they had done to me, it could drag on for years. It could get ugly.

I never allowed the thoughts to go further than "Chris won't let me sue." One day, I was journaling on this matter and realized that Chris and I had been married for a long time and that there was nothing that either of us truly wanted to do that the other would stand in the way of. I knew that if I fully thought this out and felt I *had* to sue them, he would be right there with me. He might disagree, but he would be right there with me. I realized that I always stopped the thought with a "Chris won't let me." It was easier to blame him for my inability to sue Scientology than to really think the thought through for myself. If I decided to sue or not, I would have to be fully responsible for that decision.

So I spent some time weighing my options and desires. I realized that what I really wanted was an apology. I really wanted the people directly involved and the hierarchy of Scientology to communicate some compassion for me and some recognition that they had done me harm. I realized that if I had to instigate a lawsuit to get that, it would not be heartfelt and therefore would not be what I wanted anyway. I was able to freely make the decision not to sue them. I did not want their money. I already felt that they were in an endless cycle of overcharging people for the services they had just to make the money to pay attorneys and injured for the pain they caused. I did not want to contribute to that any longer.

March 31, 2001

Had a great retreat day. It has been good for me so far—very restorative, nourishing, peaceful.

Great gardens, perfect weather, and good prayers.

By the end of the weekend, I had composed a letter to Mike Rinder. Mike Rinder was the international head of the Office of Special Affairs for Scientology. The Office of Special Affairs contains the intelligence, legal, and public relations branches for International Scientology. I had known him personally many years ago, and I knew he was well aware of the incident that went down with me. I wrote him that I knew

Chapter 26

Jeannine and Greg

WITHIN A WEEK of my silent retreat and with my decision to forgive and move on with my life, the families of two separate individuals reached out and contacted me: Greg Bashaw and Jeanine. Both Greg and Jeanine had been long-term members of Scientology, over twenty years each, just the same as Lisa McPherson and myself. They each were suffering from a complete mental collapse and were experiencing psychosis. Each situation had happened differently and was unrelated, but both had happened within the past few months. The families had read my Kathryn's story on the Internet and contacted me for help. I felt like God or some force in the universe was clearly telling me that my connection to this area was not yet over and that I could not leave this alone.

How could I not try to help these people and their families?

Greg lived in Chicago. The first time we spoke on the phone was moving for both of us. I had never spoken to someone who knew from personal experience the place I had been to, and we both knew in an instant we had been to the same hell. I told him I felt compelled to call him that I wanted to give him some hope that things would get better; it would just take time. I said I was someone who had been where he was and had come back. He almost broke down and cried right then. He said he had been hoping so hard that he even put a prayer out to God to send him something, some sign. Within twenty-four hours, I called him.

We talked about Christopher Reeve's trials and agreed that we understood why he fought so hard to stay alive. That life was worth it when you had your mind but that when that basic essence was gone, there was no quality of life. We both agreed we would rather have completely ruined bodies than the broken minds we were experiencing.

Greg and I had other similarities. He had also done some volunteer espionage work for Scientology. He had been one of the key people in Scientology's grand plan to close down and subsequently take over the Cult Awareness Network.

Greg was also abandoned by Scientology—the group that he had given so much time and money over the years. Greg told me that he had been on one of the upper Scientology levels, OT 7, for some years and that he had gone down to Florida for his mandatory six-month checkup regularly. (This level is audited by oneself at one's home and needs minimal supervision but does require you to make biannual trips to the Flag Service Org.) On his last November trip, he commented to a counselor that he felt mentally unstable. He said, "They packed my stuff and had me off to the airport and back to Chicago so quickly it would make your head spin."

We spoke of the pain we had caused our children. Both of our young boys had found us in such horribly negative situations. He had a son close to my younger son's age so we could relate to the trauma we were causing, but we both felt unable to stop it. We shared a feeling of helplessness that was so strong.

Greg wanted to get better *now*. He wanted to find a way that his healing could take place quickly so that he could go back to being the breadwinner of the family. I didn't tell him that it took me years just to get back to where I was now. I didn't tell him that I had still not fully recovered to where I had been before it happened. I just tried to give him the hope and truth that each day, things were getting a little better and that if he worked at it, he would get through to the other side.

We both spoke of how it wasn't so much that Scientologists had messed us up and broken our minds but that once they had made such an incredible mess, they *abandoned* us. The most shocking concept to both of us was just how quickly they disappeared.

We spoke of how help had come from where we least expected it from friends and family who weren't Scientologists. Greg spoke clearly of the assistance he had gotten from Christians in his life.

We spoke several more times after that, and I tried to give him a sense of hope that things could get better and that he should seek help wherever he could find it. The last time I spoke to him, he was still not in very good shape, but he assured me he was taking it day by day.

Jeannine's family contacted me after reading my story on the Internet. Since Jeannine was still in contact with her Scientologist best friend, I did not want her to know my real name; she could speak to me as Kathryn. Although her non-Scientology sisters had my real name and phone number, we spoke freely.

Jeannine had been the top salesperson for the WISE consulting group Sterling Management. She kept feeling that she'd had a mental breakdown because of something that she had done wrong. She knew that there must have been some bad thing she had done and hadn't fully confronted or some piece of Scientology technology she had not fully applied to herself or to a situation. Somehow she knew it was her own fault. By that time, I'd read the notes Lisa had written during her breakdown as they had become available on the Internet. I also knew well my own thoughts when I was trapped in mental turmoil. It was painful to listen to Jeanine continually blame herself for the broken mind she now had. I would often find myself getting off the phone with her and crying. It was all so familiar.

Jeannine was lucky that she had the support of her family. I knew from my own experience that things were worse inside her head than anyone in her family possibly knew and that she should not be driving a car. Just as I had held back and tried to pretend to be normal, Jeannine was doing the same. Her family wanted to see her as better, but they were not seeing the danger she was becoming to herself and others.

June 2001

I heard that Greg might sue; he may have a civil lawsuit going. He may want to settle for lots and lots of money. I didn't sue. I wonder sometimes if that was a good decision. I know lawsuits aren't fun, but at least it would have given me some closure.

June 20, 2001

What a great day! I am just opening up to the comfort and letting go. Just doing what I should be doing and not overstressing myself. I am feeling calmer and filled with more faith than before. I have to feel that I am part of some larger play and we have a director and it is not I. I need to create to the best of my ability the one or two things in front of me and know that all will be well.

June 24, 2001

Greg killed himself.

He actually committed suicide.

He felt it was a way out that he felt he would get relief; I hope he did. I hope he was welcomed to the other side with open arms and healing comfort. I hope his pain and confusion are gone. He just didn't see another way out. He just could not see one. He felt suicide was his way out. I hope it was. I hope and pray it was.

I feel so bad. I feel so saddened and I feel so helpless.

I am going to still take things a bit at a time. I still feel very certain that now is not a good time for me to come forward with these ongoing legal cases. But I am open to that changing. I know of a few things I need to do, and as I do each of them, the next will become clear. I don't need to jump to step 10; I only need to do step 2.

Of course, I am not ready for step 10; I haven't done steps 2-9, and when I do, things will be clear.
"In every moment, there's a reason to carry on."

When I heard the news that Greg had died, I was devastated. I hadn't talked to Jeannine for a week and was actually frightened to call her. She was still alive, and I was thankful for that. She actually sounded somewhat better. She, like Greg, wanted to be better quickly, but she was frustrated; she was in mental anguish because she was so incapable of doing even the simplest of tasks. At least she was still alive.

June 27
Jeannine seems to be doing better. She went down to her sister's house in San Diego.
I've decided I'm going back to college. I am going to complete the college education that was interrupted when I drifted into the world of Scientology. Vermont College has a great program where you attend their sessions for eight days and work out your coming semester's work. Then you go home and do it for six months under the close watch of your advisor. It involves a lot of work and a lot of writing, but I will earn fifteen credits each semester. This will work out better for me. I only need three more semesters for my BA, and I can get it in writing and literature. Vermont College also has graduate studies, and their MFA program for writers is one of the best in the country. I hope to benefit from some trickle-down effect into the BA program. I am excited; this is the future for me. This was my personal future, not one that anyone else chose or directed me to.

July 2
I would like my own room in the dorm in Vermont. I am not going to like not having any time alone. I do enjoy my time alone. I was not used to like it. I used to work at doing anything so as not to be alone with myself. That was the scariest. It was also very painful; the voices were just so negative. I would keep busy just to shut them out. They were not there when I was a child. I enjoyed myself when I was younger. Once again, it is OK to be alone with myself. Now I can

welcome myself again. I've been through lots, and I'm sure I still have more to learn and give and do. I think and pray that I will be able to maintain my balance during that time.

July 4

I am so anxious. I'm sick to the pit of my stomach nervous. I am going away from Chris and the boys for almost a month. It has me scared. I am shaking, just thinking about being away from home for so long. I am worried for my mental stability. I know I need to quiet the turmoil inside. It is a swirling rise of panic, uncomfortable in its fearfulness, just a swirling mass of unresolved and irresolvable fears.

I grieve about Greg being dead while also knowing that if I had needed to work or make money for my family, it could have been way too long a recovery for me to handle either. I would have had that added pressure to get better faster. Trying to get better faster would not have worked; it would have made things worse. I too would have wished for release—relief I would have, just like Greg.

Her mind was broken, and they slapped it together with crazy glue. The cracks showed like ugly purple scars. I have to dig deep in here and get it out. The uninspected fears and feelings—who would want to look at all the feelings? They contradict each other—happiness, sadness; joy, despair; anxiety, relief. I get very productive physically when I have a pot of unresolved stuff. I have to keep moving. There is motion, and it keeps the ocean from rearing up its tidal head.

It feels like an ocean with an unfathomable depth of unspoken feelings.

July 11

Well, I've made it to Boston. Tomorrow is my long drive to Vermont. I called Bob Minton (the millionaire) and Stacy, his partner who had been a long-term Scientologist. I am going to stop and visit with them tomorrow. Just a brief visit so we do not have any more Gregs. I am afraid to call Jeannine. I know I shouldn't be, but I am.

Speaking with her is draining on me; it takes me a while to recover from each call. I feel so bad about Greg.

Over the past few years, I had kept track of the work of Stacy Young and Bob Minton. Bob Minton was never a Scientologist;

he was simply a lover of free speech. He was a millionaire and had some free time when he came across various Internet sites devoted to Scientology and ex-Scientologists. He especially read the information regarding the death of Lisa McPherson while under the care of Scientology at the Fort Harrison Hotel in Clearwater, Florida. He had joined in the fray. He had donated his own money to individuals who were in litigation with Scientology, helping to level the playing field. Stacy Young and her husband, Vaughn Young, had been high-ranking Scientology members. They had left the church and were speaking out to the press, in the courts, and on the Internet. Bob Minton funded the opening of a Lisa McPherson Trust in downtown Clearwater. He opened it as a clearinghouse of information and possible assistance for people leaving or desiring to leave Scientology.

Up until this visit in 2001, I had kept my direct contact with them to a minimum. It wasn't that I didn't like them or had any strong feelings against what they were doing; it was that I knew how the espionage branch of Scientology worked. They not only put the person they felt attacking them into the center of the target, but also worked to collect the names of friends, families, and other connections to get to the target through them. I was still not well enough to withstand such an onslaught.

But at this particular time, I was more concerned with the possibility of additional people dying than I was for my own mental health. I stopped for a morning at Bob's farm in New Hampshire for some communication and coordination as to how we might possibly help prevent another Lisa or Greg.

Bob and Stacy welcomed me with friendship, comfort, and the best scrambled eggs I'd had in years. We spoke of Greg, Lisa, Jeannine, and what had happened with me.

Since Lisa McPherson died on Scientology property, they had vowed never to have another such incident. With regard to Greg, Jeanine, and I, it was becoming clear that it wouldn't happen because they were going to distance themselves from such damaged individuals, not because they were going to stop creating them.

We knew that there would be more people harmed in the way that we had been. Scientology was not changing its operational basis and therefore the same horrific results would occasionally happen.

For the first time, I spoke openly to Bob and Stacy about what had happened to me. Stacy and I analyzed all that we knew about the differences in my care and Jeannine's (who were alive) and Greg's and Lisa's care (who were dead).

We knew that whoever came out of Scientology in that unstable state of mind would also be coming out with intense phobias against psychiatry. In addition, traditional psychiatry would not know what to do to handle such a situation. They, perhaps, might treat the person as a schizophrenic or, in some way, mishandle someone and possibly lock in the psychosis and mental difficulties.

When I left that afternoon, we made an agreement that we would search the Internet and use all our resources to somehow find an alternative form of mental healing that would be available for people in this situation. We knew there would be more casualties, and we felt we should be prepared for them.

I made the drive to Vermont, smiling at the serendipity I had arranged for myself (who lives in Los Angeles) to meet with Bob and Stacy (who normally live in Florida, in the state of New Hampshire). I had confidence that we would find some help.

Over the next several days, the serendipity continued. In order to graduate from Vermont College, one needs to publish a final paper that is called a *Black Book*, so called because the binding of the book is black. The college maintains archives of these books in its library. During my first day on campus, I went to the library to read a few of these books. I wanted to see for myself what was going to be required of me to get my degree.

I entered a room filled with shelves upon shelves of the black volumes from floor to ceiling. I chose a book at random and read the title: *A Compassionate Handling of*

Psychosis by Ben Bashore. *I was stunned.* I began to read. The first section was a well-researched briefing on what it was like to be psychotic, what happens inside a person's mind when he or she is in that state. Tears were streaming down my face. Here I was, face-to-face with someone who had put words to my pain. Someone truly knew where and what that living hell was that Greg and Lisa and Jeannine and I had gone to.

The second chapter delineated a series of steps on how one might help a person come back from such a state. As I read, I was amazed at how intuitively Chris had done each one of these steps with me. I could finally see what I had been unable to clearly envision in New Hampshire. I could see where my mind broke and how Chris guided me back to reality.

I carried the black book to the librarian and asked for the e-mail of the author. I wanted to have an electronic copy of the paper. She said she was unable to do that due to confidentiality requirements.

I asked if there was any way I could get in touch with this author.

She looked at the book's title page. "Oh Ben, he lives in town. I bet his phone number is listed in the directory."

It was. I called him and arranged a meeting for that night.

Ben is a Buddhist. In line with his "letting go" nature, he had not kept a copy of his dissertation. There was no electronic copy to have. I copied the master copy in the college library and over the years, with Ben's permission, have sent numerous copies out to people and the families of people in similar straights. The paper includes an in-depth annotated bibliography that gave exactly the sort of resources that I had been hoping for. I was surprised at how quickly it had fallen into my hands.

I knew Vermont College was right for me, but not that semester. I took a break from college with a promise to return in January. I brought my treasured copy of Ben's thesis with me to Los Angeles.

August 9, 2001

I spoke with Jeannine; she seems to be doing so much better. She can now talk about her crazies and have more awareness about them. She just got a car so she is definitely better. She is still having her episodes and her "floating." She was concerned about floating while driving. I told her to listen more to herself and that her floating was a sign of herself saying something. She is still not ready to give up on all her Scientology friends, and they seem to think she just needs some more vitamins. Everyone seems to have an opinion, and many of their opinions forward that person's own personal agenda. No one in her life seems to be able to do much to understand her position. She is writing poetry, and I told her that's good to do and to continue doing it. She asked me to call her in the next day or so.

Within the week, I had a troubling conversation with Jeannine. She had driven herself to the railroad tracks to wait for a train. She was going to kill herself, but no train came. I knew that no matter how well intentioned her family was, they did not know how to deal with this. Her psychotic state made her use of Scientology arcane language, confusing even to me let alone to her family who didn't understand Scientology terms at all.

I talked with Chris about the situation especially my concerns that she could end up like Lisa and Greg. I could not let that happen. I wouldn't. I asked him if we could take her into our home, and he agreed that we were probably the best people for her at this time, having gone through what Chris had done to help me. Chris knew what he was in for but agreed we had to help her. We talked to the children who still lived at home and asked for their help in having a quiet, peaceful house. They already knew what it was like with me in that state so it wasn't a mystery of what was to come. Some friends of mine picked her up and drove her to our home. Over the next two weeks, I had numerous conversations with Jeannine's family, hours of talks with Jeanine, and calls to some of the resources mentioned in Ben's book.

It was finally arranged that I would fly with her to Boulder, Colorado, where the Windhorse Institute, which was connected to Naropa University, was located. It was not going to be cheap, but it was the only place I could find that I knew had the exact and professional care that she needed. We flew to Boulder the first week in September.

Jeannine's lead therapist was a woman named Jenna. Jenna not only interviewed Jeannine, but she also spoke with me in depth. At one point, Jenna told me that there are many trails and roads in life that can lead one to psychosis, but the things that Jeannine and I had been subjected to were like being on a highway to insanity. Scientologists had pushed us to psychosis through a series of missteps and introversions during their various handlings.

Windhorse did not like to use psychiatric drugs, preferring a more holistic approach and handling. However, they were not opposed to their use, and when they're needed, they were used.

The basis of Windhorse is that the mentally ill person is so wide open to stimuli already that being around other psychotic and unstable people will only make him or her worse.

I remembered I had felt that way when I was psychotic; it was like my mental state was the consistency of tofu. I would take on the emotions and attitudes of whatever environment I was in. If the energy was angry, I would become agitated; if the energy was calm and soothing, I could more easily find my balance. I was now seeing the same phenomenon in Jeannine.

Windhorse counselors operate on the premise that people who are in a state of psychosis always have some islands of clarity. There's usually some period of time during which they are mentally stable and aware of what is going on; sometimes it is only for minutes, but sometimes the clarity can last for an hour or more. The purpose of these trained individuals working with the mentally unstable person is to notice these islands of clarity and help the damaged person recognize them and help to make them larger and last longer.

That was exactly what had happened to me. I had felt like I was trapped on a Ferris wheel. I would reach the top, feel some clarity, and yet know I was about to go back down. I would call out to the Scientologists in desperation during these times, begging for help and assistance that never came.

At Windhorse, the individual is paired up with a person whose primary purpose is to just be with the person, to communicate either verbally or nonverbally, and to involve the person in the mundane activities of daily life. Making the bed, doing the laundry, cooking a meal, going for a walk are all activities that may be done. It takes a team of people to help the person come back. Not one aide is left on shift for longer than four hours. Being around a psychotic person is very draining, and after a certain point, even the most honorable of counselors will begin to feel frustration and that energy does not help the mentally injured person to heal.

I knew how exhausted I was being alone with Jeannine for just two weeks. I cannot imagine how my husband did it with me for months while maintaining his full-time job. I had already appreciated and had been so grateful for his love and compassion, especially his patience, but after only two weeks with Jeannine, it gave me an entirely new level of admiration for him.

Jeannine and I shared a motel room in Boulder while we were working on setting her up in a temporary apartment. There was a moment when I was dialing the long list of numbers needed to make a phone call using a phone card. I looked at Jeannine and in that instant realized how far I had come. I had been in that place; Jeannine now was unable to punch in a phone number. I could see how much progress in healing I had made, and I knew in that moment that Jeannine would be able to make her own phone calls again. She was going to make it out of her mental jungle. We were not going to have another Greg or Lisa.

Jeannine paced, which I knew to be a calming activity. She repeated her thoughts over and over. I knew I had done that myself when I was in that place. It was like a record or CD that skipped over and over. No wonder Windhorse had a limit of four hours with a client. Once again, I was so grateful that I had been given the gift of Chris. Not many men would have had the patience to listen to me repeat something over and over for days, if not weeks, at a time.

While in Boulder, I was invited to sit in on a graduate level class on the handling of psychotics. The teacher was an experienced professional who was teaching students who were going to help heal mental infirmities. His approach was to understand what that client is going through. He said that while most people have never been psychotic, most have at least experienced what he called an extreme state of mind. This could be due to some sudden shock or loss when one felt the boundaries of life, as one knew it, shift. He said if you can recall those brief experiences of yours, you could begin to understand where your clients are and you can then reach them and assist in bringing them back.

I thought of Chris and how he did understand where I was, how he came to that place and helped guide me back out. I looked around the course room and wondered how many others in this room had been in that state and returned.

The professor gave some examples of clients and their individual states of mind and how their progress had gone back. I understood that what was being taught here was not something that was completely new; shamans, priests, doctors, and others had been doing it for centuries.

It wasn't until after my breakdown that I learned of shamans and mystics and their work with spirits and the underworld. I couldn't help but find resonance in the writings of *Shamanic Journeys* and parts of the places where I had mentally and spiritually gone. The difference being that shamans are guided on these journeys and the way is somewhat mapped out. There are corners and turns that these shamans are taught to avoid. I'm sure it was because others before them had gone and found it not a pleasant place to be in. I realized that many people over the centuries had been to the place where I had fallen into; I had just done it alone and unexpectedly. I had no spiritual teacher to guide me and keep me from the demons.

The professor was very clear that once a person goes over to that other side, there are no guarantees that you will be able get the person back. Some people cannot make the journey back to a stable mind. He told his students to be prepared that in their work with the psychotic, they could lose some.

The professor explained that the triggering episode that dropped the person into their particular black hole also contained the ladder that would help him or her out. When I returned to Jeannine, I paid attention to her rambling thoughts and noticed that she would be scattered and disoriented, except when she spoke of one particular incident. Whenever she spoke of that incident, I could see her mind clear, and I was aware that she was having an island of clarity. She had a boyfriend who had taken her American Express card and, without her permission, had charged over $10,000 worth of equipment. The bill came in to Jeannine, and she had thirty days to pay. She called American Express and informed them that this was an unauthorized expense. Several days later, she was called into the Scientology Ethics Office of the Advanced Org in Los Angeles, but instead of being supported, she was berated for turning against her Scientologist boyfriend. Mistakes were only to be handled within Scientology by the organization itself. The ethics officer raked her over the coals and made her call American Express and withdraw the charges she had made against her boyfriend. It was wrong and an injustice, but she was forced to make the call.

I noticed that whenever she relayed that tale to me or someone else, her entire demeanor shifted. She had clarity on the subject, and she was thinking and speaking in logical terms. I saw that what the professor had said was true as this was one of her final breaking points and therefore could be a ladder out of her personal hell.

This incident was one that I could use as a friend and helper to guide her to her ladder so that she would begin to climb out of her pit of mental chaos.

We organized Jeanine's team of therapists and rented a beautiful apartment in Boulder for her stay. I flew back to Los Angeles, knowing that Jeannine was safe and in good hands.

September 8
I am just so relieved to have found Windhorse and to learn more about how and what they do. I now know we have a place and a treatment

to send these people. That is just such a relief—such a major relief. Now when people like them come across my path, well, it is very difficult. It is so lonely to be trapped and to be so crazed. There seems so much to write, so much to process. I feel like things are just moving forward, and for the most part, that is a very good thing. I had planned on writing and writing; my gosh, I have only been gone from Los Angeles for four nights. I just find that so hard to believe. Seems like forever, and I think that was because I had been with her for so long, so very intensely.

So this is where we are. Making my descent back into Los Angeles, thank God. Thank God I can think clearly. Thank God I am doing well.

In the days that followed, I was so thankful we had moved as quickly as we did to get Jeanine the help she needed. Travel was restricted for some time after the horrific tragedies of 9/11. By the time Jeannine was ready to have her sisters come to Boulder for a visit, air travel was back and running.

I spent that fall in a daze like most other Americans. I had close friends in New York City, and I had even more friends who had family and close friends working in the World Trade Center, or on one of the planes.

The Lisa McPherson case crawled forward. I continued to watch from the sidelines and observed the changes and evolution of the case. The criminal charges had been dropped, and the civil case appeared to be mired in briefs and legal maneuvers.

I continued to stay in touch with Stacy. I was not interested in getting involved with the Trust's ongoing battles with Scientology in Clearwater, but I couldn't help but care about what was happening with them.

I will let Greg Bashaw speak for himself.

To: Debbie Cook, Captain FSO
cc: Mary Shaw President, FSO
cc: Kathy True, OSA/Flag

Dear Debbie:
29 April, '01

I have written many success stories in my years of being a Flag public. This story, however, is one that shares a complete loss at the hands of Flag Service.

First, some background. I had been a Flag public since 1984. I am a Patron. An Executive Planetary Disseminator. I had been On New OT 7 since 1989, and had effectively devoted my life to daily auditing, and coming to Flag for 6-month checks.

You can check my ethics file. It's fairly spotless.

The service disaster I experienced occurred during my last trip to Flag for a Refresher, from Sept. to Nov. 2000.

Specifically, during a review session with Therese Blum in AO-1, I had a psychotic break. This occurred during an arduous session On Oct. 31st that totaled more than 3 hours.

Despite numerous originations after this to my C/S Margaret Ainsworth, and to my D of P, Margarete, this psychotic break was never handled.

I was personally assured by A.J. Specher, the head of the Solo Unit at the time, on several instances, specifically on 5 Nov., that my folder was being studied, not to worry, and something would be worked out for a handling.

Despite many assurances there was urgency behind the cycle, my folder did not come out for a session until November 9th. This was a full 9 days after I had the psychotic break in the session with Theresa Blum.

Needless to say, by this time, I was in considerably more duress, in worse shape, submerged way below my case.

I still complied with what Flag asked of me, buying two new intensives on 11 November in hopes of handling what I was stuck in. After that, I got one session on the 12th of Nov.,none on the 13th, and one on the 14th.

During the session on the 14th, I made an origination about feeling psychotic.

The very next day I was promptly routed out of the org.

What followed was the most bitter charade I've ever been involved with in my life.

Upon being routed out of Flag, I did as I was instructed and regularly reported to my D of P, Margarete.

I let her know the physical handlings I received showed nothing wrong, and that I was In extreme spiritual, not physical turmoil.

Of course, this didn't matter to Flag at that point. There was no way I was going to get treatment, even if the ailment was proven not to have any physical cause whatsoever.

In fact, Margarete's suggestion was to drink some "pep drinks" What an invalidating and viciously heartless statement to someone sitting in a psychotic break, trying desperately to get through the day. Drink some pep drinks!

What followed immediately upon my arriving at home on 15 November, 2000 was this:

- I was intensely suicidal, caught in a psychotic break I had no control over. I had previously never had suicidal thoughts before in my entire career as a Scientologist.

- I lost my job, being unable to work in my mental state. I had been making over $160,000 a year, more than $90,000 of which went to Scientology in the year 2000.

- I decided to file for bankruptcy, as I had always borrowed heavily to finance my donations to the Church, and now could not afford to pay my bills without a job.

- I suffered several "nervous breakdowns," which were nothing more than times I could no longer tolerate the psychotic break, and was hospitalized four times.

When people asked me what was really wrong . . . . what could I tell them? Nothing.

What would they understand about having gone psychotic in a session at Flag, Being turned away, and left to live out the rest of my life in this state?

Debbie, I invite you to check up on me. You will find I had been a loyal enthusiastic, dedicated supporter of Flag for more than 16 years.

You could ask the following people about me: Mary Shaw, Rudy Kempner, Abby Lancaster, the Vice President, Jose, the New OT 7 sups, including Linda Goodwin and Vicki. Ask my long-time D of P, Christina Martinez, if I wasn't always responsible on the Level. Ask Janet Bowes about my dedication and service.

Look at my ethics file. My student file. My thousands of sessions on the Level. I was there for Flag. I completely oriented my life around Flag and Scientology

For example, I quit my high-paying job in 1997 rather than being associated with the company that was going to then start advertising Prozac.

I left my home and work for seven months that year in order to stay at Flag for review and courses. During that trip, I spent my entire retirement savings, and went more than $100,000 in debt beyond that to sustain my stay there.

Then.... on the one trip to Flag when I suffer a psychotic break.... after making more than 20 such trips to Flag while being on New OT 7, I am not handled and sent away.

I'm left to suffer alone in the world.

Yes, Kathy True came up here to visit me and run some objectives on me in December. She got someone to volunteer to let me stay at their place so that I could "destimulate" But the destimulation needed was needed at Flag immediately after 31 Oct., not six weeks later at someone's house.

I consider my life ruined. I am barely able to work. Hardly able to function on a daily basis. Stuck in a psychotic beak that is unrelenting.

In closing, let me say that during my years at Flag, I had much excellent service. In fact, the service was routinely excellent. The people there are my friends.

But from Sept. to Nov. 2000, Flag failed me in the most complete and total way.

When I crashed last Oct.31st, I was told I would be picked up and handled. I was not....

I was personally assured by the head of the Solo Unit, AJ Sprecher, not to worry about anything. That my folder was being worked on, and I would get cleaned up. I did not

I am now in a worse state than I ever have been in my life. That is a very bitter thing for someone who gave his whole adult life to Scientology, in addition to most of the money he made, most of his non-work time and all his heart and soul.

If you want to look in my folder, you will see verification of these statements. Of my originations as things got worse. Of my desperate attempts to get help as the bottom was falling out on me. And of my reports back to Flag that physical conditions had nothing to do with the psychosis.

When Kathy True was sent up here in December to try to help me, she was surprised to find out all this happened at Flag. The assumption was that I was OK there and then came home and somehow crashed.

That is not the case. What happened, happened at Flag.

The psychotic break was engendered by the auditing I received while at Flag.

I can tell you the exact time in the session with Theresa Blum when it happened, and exactly what she did that LRH says not to do.

She asked about a motivator chain ("What are you looking at?") while I was already heavily submerged in trying to handle other case. I immediately was overwhelmed and thrown into a turbulent psychotic break.

Later, upon being routed out of Flag I was told to find a physical cause for this psychosis! This was ridiculous. I was in perfect health. The psychosis was created at Flag, during an auditing session when I had complete faith in my auditor. The psychosis was allowed to continue at Flag while I waited and waited for handlings, and then after I did receive a few very short sessions, I was sent out of the organization.

I did go ahead and get all the physical examinations, as ordered—from a chiropractor, a nutritionist, several medical doctors. I had blood tests, heart tests, brain tests and consultations. Of course nothing was found wrong.

What was wrong was what had been created at Flag during a session there.

I understand the need for the organization to protect itself. If someone falls into a psychosis during his services, Flag is then worried about lawsuits, about its responsibilities, about more situations like the one with L. McPherson.

But I was completely abandoned in my time of most urgent need. I did not come to Flag in a psychosis; I was holding down a high paying job in Chicago, I was auditing every day, I was a responsible faher and loyal contributor to many of Scientology's projects.

I got into the psychosis at Flag and, of course, by my own devices have not been able to get out of it.

The things that are treated in an auditing session at the level of Solo NOTS and NOTs review are treated anywhere else in the world. And so I had no possibility of undoing the psychotic state I was left in.

Do you have any idea what that is like? Can you even imagine it? What it's like to wake up every day and try to get through the day in a psychotic break that won't go away because you know what caused it won't be available to treat it again?

I could try to tell you what it's like, but my description of it would pale to the reality. It has been a living hell.

I understand that the org needs to be protected from people who fall into severe trouble.

That there is worry over legal matters, public relations and other potential damages.

But I want to you know your organization abandoned a comrade in his most urgent time of trouble; did not correct what was created there; did not listen when he said he was in spiritual agony; and did not take action when he said he would be completely consumed if he did not get help.

No help was given. No hope was forthcoming. "Never abandon a comrade" from the Code of Honor was broken.

Flag's "#1 standing order" is to deliver what was promised. I was not delivered what I was promised. When I was told I would be handled after suffering a severe psychotic break, I was not handled and was left to merely fend for myself.

It's a tragedy. Not just for me. But for my family. My friends. And for Flag, who has lost someone who could have remained an ardent, loving supporter for another 20 years. Thank you for taking the time to read this.

Greg Bashaw

Greg Bashaw

Greg Bashaw
September 28, 1954-June 23, 2001

Chapter 27

A Hope of Closure

JEANNINE RETURNED to Los Angeles in December of 2001 in a very much-improved condition. I was so relieved. I had spoken some with Laura Bashaw, Greg's wife, and shared with her the personal pain of her loss as well as the financial troubles that had been left behind. Their credit cards had been maxed out to astronomical levels due to Greg's purchasing of more and more services in Scientology to try to help himself. Now she was drowning in debt. She was also working hard to be a good mom and now a dad as well to their high school-aged son.

One day, my husband and our two younger sons were sitting in the living room watching a show, and a few funny comments were made of "when Mom went crazy" especially "opposite day" and we laughed. I realized how far we all had come as a family when we could laugh at the horrors we had all been through. I also realized that my older stepson was out of the loop. He was not living with us when my breakdown happened.

My stepson, Corey, remained an active public Scientologist. He went to courses and was receiving auditing by our old friend Bill. I thought it was strange that Bill, who was primarily a case supervisor and who supervised and directed the auditing of many other auditors, was the one to be giving personal counseling to my stepson. Bill would make the long hourly drive going there and an hour back to be able to audit at Corey's home in Orange County. That too seemed unusual and extremely preferential. The paranoid side of me felt that because Bill did so much volunteer work for the espionage arm of Scientology, there was an aspect of this being done to keep a connection to Chris and me and to tap into our comings and goings.

But Bill had also been a very long-term good friend and was always close to our son Corey, so the odds that he was doing this because he personally did not want to lose Corey was just as feasible.

I felt that it was a disservice to Corey as a member of our family to have Bill know what had happened and Corey not be made aware of it, especially now that we were finding ourselves able to laugh about what had happened.

I was seriously considering becoming a witness for Ken Dandar in the civil case against the Scientologists. I knew that this would place me on Scientology's enemies list and could cause someone to sit Corey down and demand that he either handle or disconnect from us. I talked it over with Chris, and we agreed that it was time for Corey to know what had happened to me and to Greg, Lisa, and Jeannine.

I had some private time with Corey and told him some of what happened to Lisa, bits about Jeannine and Greg, and most of what happened to me. I reminded him that I have always kept my stepmom distance but loved him as my own. I let him know that while I wasn't antagonistic to Scientology and did not consider myself an anti-Scientologist, I did have my limits. I told him that if he was ever going to join the Sea Org, stepmom or not, I would be all over him about it. I told him that if I ever saw him taking time and money away from his family or children for his support of Scientology, I would have a lot to say about that. However, I told him that I knew he had a great life, a beautiful fiancée, and a career that was growing. He owned a home and had money beyond what he gave to Scientology. For now, he was able to get the benefits from Scientology without paying the high personal price that so many other people had paid.

I also told him that because some people had died, I felt that I might have to do something. I had not yet confirmed with the attorney that I would testify if needed in the Lisa case, but I was leaning in that direction.

This all led up to my major concern that Scientology could simply demand that he disconnect from family. Tears welled up in my eyes at the thought of it. He patted my arm and just said, "Do not worry about it. You just do what you have to do. I trust you." Despite his involvement with Scientology, he had heard and understood everything I said. I know he wasn't happy about the possibility of my testifying, but he was there for me.

After a few months and more research and study, I felt confident to place a message on the ex-Scientology Message Board about having some alternative solutions to help people in the situations that Greg Bashaw, Lisa, Jeannine, and myself had been in. I knew that the staff from the Office of Special Affairs read this board daily and would know it was from me, but at that point, I didn't care about repercussions from them; I only cared that future people who might fall into a similar situation knew that there was some help out there.

The next day, I went to the grocery store near my house, and when I returned to my parked car, I noticed a business card tucked in the driver's side window. It was a private investigator's card stating his specializations, including having worked for the CIA. I thought nothing of it and threw it in the backseat of my car.

The following day, I went to a class and made an unscheduled stop at a mall several miles from home. When I returned to my car, I noticed another one of the same private investigator's card tucked into the driver's side window of my car. I dug the other one out and compared it to the one from the day before. It was identical. Just to make sure my paranoia wasn't running wild, I drove around the lot and tried to find one other car with a business card tucked in the window. I failed. There were no other business cards.

I was frightened and concerned that someone would have been following me in some way that I had not noticed. This trip in the morning had not been part of a regular routine of mine, and there was no mistaking of the purposefulness of the coincidence.

I checked on the Internet and couldn't see anything that would arouse their attention toward me other than my post of the previous day, so I called Bob Minton from a pay phone. He was at his home in New Hampshire, and after I told him what had happened and voiced my concerns, I asked him if there was something going on that I didn't know.

He told me that Scientology was desperate to stop the Lisa McPherson civil case from coming to trial. It was due to begin in a few months. He was involved in some countersuits with them, and as part of the settlements on their part, they wanted him to get the Lisa case to stop. I knew Bob didn't have that kind of power, but I could definitely feel the intention that the Scientologists were working hard to make this civil case go away just as they had the criminal case.

After a week or so, I finally got up the courage to call the private investigator on the cards left on my car. He seemed a nice enough guy. I asked if he worked or had ever worked for Scientology, and he said he didn't and hadn't. I explained what had happened, and he said that he gives many classes and that his cards are handed out a lot. Anyone could have gotten a hold of the cards. I told him what had happened, and he said he had been in the business for too long to believe in coincidences. He said that someone was definitely sending me a message. "Someone's messing with your head." That was his exact wording.

I'd noticed some strange background sounds when I was talking on the phone recently. Our home phones had been clicking a lot lately, but it seemed more often on certain calls. When I would speak with Greg Bashaw's wife, Laura, in Chicago, we would always have to talk over a series of annoying clicks and pops. I hadn't thought much of it, but now I wasn't so sure.

Much earlier, the first time I called Bob Minton in New Hampshire from my home number, I got a call as soon as I hung up. I heard bits of a conversation, but I couldn't get over the thought that I had been an unrecognized number. Scientology most certainly had Bob Minton under surveillance, and they would want to know all of his contacts.

I had done nothing wrong; I was doing nothing wrong; and if there was someone tapping my phone, listening to private conversations, in my home or stalking me, it was on them. I was not going to stoop to their level.

February 15, 2002

I had a meltdown on Wednesday. It hit me so hard and so suddenly. It was like a huge return to that time. Jeannine was talking to me on the phone about her hearing against the Scientology consultation company she had worked with. They had fired her when she decided not to be a Scientologist anymore. She told me how well it went and how great it was that she had the opportunity to sit down in front of people and confront them and what they did to her. She told me that she doesn't want to be defined by what they did to her, and I'm thinking "Gosh, it took me years to get to that point." And then I thought how I would never get an opportunity to confront them face-to-face.

The next thing I knew, I was back to that day, back to being out of the hospital, and it was Ash Wednesday. I was in the midst of my mental waterfall. I soon realized it was Ash Wednesday again. Today was the exact anniversary of my "opposite day." The memory was not a memory but a trigger taking me back to that day, back to feelings of that day, and it just got more real and stronger. I told Jeannine I had to go and we hung up.

The pain exploded out of me in a rush of sobs and spasms. I went to find Chris even though I knew there was nothing that could be done, just nothing to be done.

I know Chris cared, I know he loved me, but I also knew he was not there. He was not in my head where I was. He was just not there. He just held me while I cried and cried.

After I felt spent and drained— that hollow feeling after you have vomited and you know that the ugliness that was buried inside is gone— you just don't know if that means you are better. There was also a part of me in shock over the violence of the pain. Chris took me for a walk, but I knew I could not write anymore that day—just could not—so here I am several days later, back to my desk, back to my homework and other schoolwork. I have to take Taylor to the dentist today.

I had had another lunch with Bill after my talk with Corey. Corey was understandably upset when I told him what had been done to me, and he shared what I had told him to Bill.

When Bill sat down for lunch with me, he said that he knew I had spoken with Corey and that Corey had been upset but I shouldn't worry because he had handled him. I wondered what that meant.

Then he said, "You and Chris have been pretty good at watching what you say to Corey, but he soon will be graduating from the smaller franchise and when he gets to the Advanced Org, they are not going to be so understanding."

I couldn't believe that he was intimating that Corey would have to disconnect from us.

I was dumbfounded. I wished Chris had been here with me to hear him say that. As if I had to watch what I could communicate to my own family because of repercussions from Scientology. Like they had a vote in my life.

Bill said that he really wanted to get my situation handled before Corey hit the Advanced Organization so that that type of confrontation and demand for disconnection from his family could be avoided. He said that Joan and Kirsten still asked about me and wished me well. I reiterated that they cared only about what I did, they did not care about me personally, and if they really did care about me personally, my phone number was still in the phone book. They were welcome to call me anytime. They never had and I don't expect them to.

March 3

    When I discovered the second card from the private investigator, I became concerned; it was a dropping in my gut, a tension behind my ears. Fear *arrived in my body, prone to escalate to paranoia—deep, deep paranoia. I felt an electrical buzz complete with darting eyes and sweating palms.*

    Creation of an effect—that's what these Scientologists want. They could have been right there watching my response to that second card. I know from my past personal experience with their dirty tricks that the reaction and the first person called are important, and I did not want to give them that. Therefore, I waited to call anyone for advice or help in calming down. I drove on to pick up Taylor. I stopped at a payphone.

    I felt violated.

    I felt my other persona come out—the cautious, protective Nancy.

March 23

    I have too many things swimming in my head—too many different parts of myself are scattered all over the place. The individual pieces don't go well together; they are parts that are not in harmony.

    But deep inside, there has to be a balance because deep inside, it's me, it's all me. It has to be all me 'cause I am the only one here and I've been through everything. I've been through it all, the entire journey.

    I find myself so afraid of all the judgments. I have been brave when I should not have been. I have thrown myself at the face of evil. I have entered dark rooms and rattled their cages. I have changed, shifted, and survived. I have survived.

Chapter 28

They Get to the Millionaire

WITHIN A FEW weeks of speaking to Bob Minton, the news became public that Bob had bafflingly changed sides. He, who had donated over two million dollars to the Lisa McPherson case alone and an additional million to individuals attempting to sue Scientology, had now become a witness for Scientology.

This was more difficult to believe than the Florida coroner who, in changing her mind, had shut down the criminal case. I had spoken to Bob Minton just a few weeks prior, and there was not a hint or clue that he felt what they had done was correct in any way, shape, or form.

Bob Minton's defection and his new allegations against the attorneys for the Lisa McPherson case delayed the trial yet again. There would now be hearings as to Dander's actual handling of the case. I watched from my safe distance in Los Angeles.

I had been asked once before by Mr. Dandar to be a witness for him and had never given him a clear yes or no. In July, the hearings were ongoing and I was flying East for the end-of-semester week at my college in Vermont. The thought of coming forward and testifying on a witness stand brought a cold panic to my chest. But the idea that I would close my eyes and turn away brought the same sharp terror. That Scientology could get away with it again, that they actually had a shot at shutting down the civil case made me angry. I had watched the materials posted on the Internet about Lisa McPherson very closely and felt so strongly that Scientology was responsible for her death, that it was hard to stomach the fact that they could get away with it, just as they had gotten away with taking any responsibility for Greg Bashaw's death or the mental breakdowns of Jeannine and myself.

I steeled myself up and finally called the attorney, Ken Dandar. I flat out asked him if he thought he could use my help in these hearings. He answered yes and I told him I would seriously consider it and give him a definitive answer within three days.

I spoke with Chris about this before I left Los Angeles for the East Coast. He said that he was my husband and had his own opinions but that this was my decision and I had to make my choices and live the rest of my life with them.

My trip had already been scheduled to have some time with my family in the Boston area before I had to arrive at Vermont College. I grew up in a large family and am lucky to have two siblings that are both attorneys. I went to them for advice.

It was a Florida court case and neither one of them knew the workings of Florida law; but they knew enough to answer my questions. They confirmed that once I would be an official witness for the Lisa McPherson case, I would be open to depositions by Scientology. Depositions are not an enjoyable experience in any type of legal battle, but I already knew that a Scientology deposition could be especially brutal. I would need a lawyer. Scientology had a written record of twenty years of my most personal thoughts and emotions; I had shared everything with them. In any Scientology counseling session, whatever you say is written down along with needle reactions and other information as reported by the E-Meter. These documents are kept in voluminous files called preclear or PC folders and contain a running written account of every auditing session you've ever had along with everything said, felt, and confided in to the auditor.

It was something I had to put some serious thought into. The interrogations they had with me had driven me over the brink. They had that documented from their perspective, and I had no access to that paperwork. In other words, they had it all, exactly how step by step I was driven insane. Would they repeat those actions, causing me to once again lose the mind I had worked so hard to heal?

The best hope I was given was from my sister-in-law. She had worked as a prosecutor on a lot of sex-crime cases where emotions run high and are similar to what I felt. She told me that while I was in that courtroom, I would be protected and be able to speak. The American justice system is established in a way that the person being questioned has rights. She said, "On that day, you would have the power."

Several transcripts of what went on in the hearings had been posted on the Internet. I read them and could see that this judge was in control of her courtroom and was not allowing either side to abuse witnesses.

I felt I had all the information I needed. I knew the consequences of coming forward for my family and myself. I now had to decide how I could live with myself whichever choice I made. I needed no more advice because as my husband Chris had said, this was a choice *I* had to make and live with for the rest of my life.

In Massachusetts, there is a section that curves out into the ocean; it's actually where the Pilgrims first landed and is a great piece of the earth that contains beautiful beaches on both sides of the outcropping of land. Years earlier, a canal was built to separate Cape Cod from the main part of Massachusetts. There were only two bridges that spanned the canal to reach the cape. More recently, both sides of the canal had been turned into biking/walking/running paths. I had many pleasant cape memories from my childhood; I had even once gone through the canal in a boat. It was a safe place to make such an important decision. It was also in an area where I would not be disturbed, a place where I would be alone for as many hours as it took to walk across the winding canal until the clarity of a decision came to me.

I parked my car and put my headphones on, thinking the music would help keep me focused. The path around the canal is several miles long. I began walking and slowly sifted through my thoughts and options.

I knew Scientology had gotten to the coroner, and that didn't really surprise me. I had worked long enough in their intelligence bureau to know firsthand how smoothly and efficiently they could work. The personnel who worked in these departments clocked in 120- to 130-hour workweeks, seven days a week, and sometimes twenty-four-hour days. Scientology had money, and a large portion of that money was spent on private investigators. to "Shudder Into Silence" people that felt differently than they did. "Shudder Into Silence" is a great article explaining in details Scientology's actions to stop any negative press. It was written by Robert Welkos and printed in "The Quill" in 1991. I remembered reading the Florida district attorney's decision to drop the criminal case. He said he had no choice because one of his main witnesses (the coroner) could not even tell him clearly why she changed the cause of Lisa McPherson's death to accidental. I could feel her confusion and sympathized due to the pressure she had been under. I had heard that she had to go to a sanatorium to recover from a breakdown after that. I don't know if that is true or not, but it wouldn't surprise me. As for the state of Florida, it was very costly because her change on a cause-of-death ruling brought into question the verdicts on many of the people who had been convicted based on her autopsies. If she had made a mistake in this case, a defense attorney could make the case that she could have made a mistake in her other cases. Her career was left in tatters.

Her change of heart did not shock me. The refrain in my head that wouldn't stop was "They got to the millionaire, they got to the millionaire." Who was I compared to a person who had the financial resources Bob Minton had? I had no money and couldn't afford to hire my own lawyer to protect me. My phones were clicking, and I couldn't even afford to get the lines checked for tapping. I was still recovering from a complete mental breakdown three years previously. I felt very vulnerable. If Scientology could get to the millionaire, they could wipe me out with so much as a swat. "They got to the millionaire, they got to the millionaire" became a chant that looped over and over in my head.

As I looked up and gazed around me, I noticed the beauty of the moment—there were people out on their bikes and walking or running in the most perfect weather. I watched seagulls soaring across the sky and tried to take a break from that incessant chant while I soaked up the beauty of life all around me. The boats on the canal were making their way to the other side of the cape, the passengers exchanging the wave of the hand that was unwritten boat etiquette.

I felt my body as it moved along the path, and as my hips shifted leg to leg, I gave thanks that I could walk.

My thoughts drifted to the other side of the coin. *How dare they*, I thought. How dare they make me feel afraid? How dare they have that power over me? I survived. I *am* a survivor, and I still have a voice unlike Greg Bashaw and Lisa McPherson. Did I owe it to Greg and Lisa to speak for them? Do I owe it to myself? I had spoken to both Jeannine, still so fresh from her ordeal, and Laura, Greg's widow, who had lost so much. They were 100 percent in support of me and even offered to fly down to the courtroom if I felt I needed the support. How dare Scientology make me feel that I can't speak when I only want to tell the truth?

And then the fear returned. I felt like a rape victim, but it was my mind that was violated by a powerful group that wouldn't hesitate to use their power. That was my dilemma. It was as if I had been raped by the mafia. That gave me some clarity. If what had happened to me had been done by any other group of individuals besides Scientology, I would not even be walking the Cape Cod canal. There would be no question. I would speak the truth and justice would be done. Being raped by a vindictive group strips a person of the freedom to strike back because the backlash could be worse than the original trauma.

I felt good. I had isolated exactly what my dilemma was: I was afraid of the consequences of speaking out. I was afraid of being moved up to the top tier of Scientology's enemies list. I was frightened that they'd concentrate on silencing me or doing other things to my life that would take up so much time I wouldn't be able to fight anymore.

I remembered what happened to a successful painter. He was suing Scientology and they took him into deposition. One of the deposition questions was where he got his income from which involved giving them the names of his clients. He answered honestly; and within a very short amount of time, each one of those clients had been given a "Dead Agent Pack," a package of negative information compiled and distributed about the person of Scientology's interest—in this case, the artist. Within a month, the artist had no work. He had no money to continue with the lawsuit. He ran out of money and was forced into bankruptcy.

Scientology Intelligence and Operations can be very effective and so brilliantly executed that they can wreak havoc without even having laid a finger directly on you.

"They got to the millionaire" rolled back into my head, followed quickly by the fact that they even got to the IRS. The IRS—who gets to the IRS? That's how well-oiled and experienced they can be in their operations. They had lost their tax-exempt status and lost it all the way to the Higher Courts. With the IRS. Scientology changed tactics and began using private investigators to investigate individual IRS agents and gather dirt on them and sue them as individuals.

One day, David Miscavige, the leader of Scientology, and his deputy walked over to the IRS building without an appointment. David told the receptionist to tell him who he was and assured her that he was sure the head of the IRS would speak with him. Sure enough, the head of the IRS met behind closed doors in an undocumented meeting. At the end of months of negotiations, Scientology not only had its tax-exempt status reinstated in America but also the IRS began mailing letters all over the world, declaring Scientology as a true nonprofit religious group. This action overrode all earlier Court decisions. I wondered if the Scientology's private investigators had found something on the head of the IRS.

Scientology still charges what many consider to be exorbitant rates for spiritual services, but it now calls them "fixed donations". A fixed donation is an oxymoron if I ever heard one. They still have a tremendous sales force, continue to pay commissions to field registrars, and keep a gross-income statistic by which the group's health is measured. This agreement between Scientology and the head of the IRS was supposed to have been kept secret, but it was leaked to and published by the *Wall Street Journal*. Something I found very odd is that on the board of directors of the corporation holding the trademarks and copyrights of Scientology is now a leading ex-IRS executive, never having been a Scientologist himself.

So now I had two mantras in my head: "They got to the millionaire" and "They got to the IRS."

Wow, why would I ever want to think of jumping into that snake pit? I now have a good life and a great family. I would be risking all that.

The other side of the coin would then start talking to me: I survived hell, and during that insanity, I saw many things; but at the end of it all, I felt protection from a power higher than myself. I had to trust in that. Greg and Lisa were dead, and Jeannine and I lived by the skin of our teeth. I owed something back.

I took a number of deep breaths and worked on silencing my mental chatter so I could return to the actual problem that needed answering.

I kept walking, feeling my legs move right,left, right,left.

I noticed the seagulls and the fishermen on the other side of the canal as I walked under one of the bridges. How do they do this? I wondered. I had never seen the bridge from underneath. I looked up and was amazed at how a bridge is built. The detail and mechanical ingenuity was incredible, and it was something I knew I was never going to learn to do. Eventually, I reached a park bench and took a seat to assess my thoughts. I wanted to try on my choices and see how they felt. When I felt like calling Ken Dandar and saying "Let's go for it," the fear welled up to a point where I felt absolutely frozen. Would the stress drive me back to insanity? Would they use the information they knew about me to drive me crazy again? I knew I almost didn't make it back last time; would I never make it back again? Would they destroy the life I had?

When I felt like calling Ken and telling him I couldn't come down to Florida, I felt that Scientology had silenced me. I felt defeated and a coward.

Then I thought of Lisa and Greg and how they would never get the opportunity to speak. I personally knew Jeanine and Laura, I would testify for them in a heartbeat, so why shouldn't I do this for Lisa? Was it because I didn't know her personally?

The thought of me not even trying to help only to watch this case disappear made my stomach turn. Scientology would have gotten away with something again.

So. I came to *maybe*.

But I couldn't get past *maybe*.

Earlier I had felt *maybe* about contacting the Florida DA when there were criminal charges, but I wasn't as strong then as I was now.

I got off the bench and went back to my walk. I was not clear on yes and I was not clear on no, but I was clear on *maybe*. I walked with that for a while.

Maybe is the worst situation imaginable. A yes or no gives you the opportunity to move forward in some way, but a *maybe* will stick you and stays with you. Did I want to live the rest of my life with *maybe*? Especially now that the Scientologists had the millionaire on their side and they were so close to getting away with the death of Lisa. I had lived in Clearwater and knew that a person could literally *walk* to the nearest hospital.

I had done it many times myself, even while eight months pregnant. But instead, the Scientologists' assigned to her care drove past several hospitals while Lisa died in the backseat of their car. This was stated because they wanted a Scientology doctor, and he was at a facility miles and miles away. Who knows? Lisa might be alive today if an ambulance was called or they simply drove her to the nearest hospital. I knew they wanted to be in the hands of a Scientology doctor to help prevent a possible PR fiasco.

In a flash, I realized that I had been living with the uncertainty of *maybe* ever since I learned of Lisa's case and recognized our similarities. It all became clear to me; I suddenly had that lightbulb moment that I did *not* want to live the rest of my life with *maybe*.

It suddenly became very real that this case might indeed be dismissed and with it the justice I was searching for that would never be there for Lisa. I would always regret it if I backed down and decided not to testify. At least if I decided to go ahead, I could speak of what I knew. I had experienced firsthand how Scientology deals with insanity and how they then abandon those in need. I could also speak of how their intelligence system works; who knows, I might even be able to help explain how they got to the millionaire. My testimony may do nothing for the case, but at least I could live the rest of my life knowing I had done everything I could.

I brightened up and my footsteps were lighter. I had to try or I would live the rest of my life beneath a question mark, and *that* would not be a good feeling to have—not at all.

Chapter 29

The Hearing

A S FOR THE things they could or would do to me, well, I'd almost died. I'd faced down insanity, and here I stood. I was still standing. What else could they do? I am a survivor.

It was with a much lighter and determined heart that I returned to my car. I had made my decision. I would call Ken that night, and we would work out the travel arrangements.

I called Chris and told him of my decision. I called my siblings who'd given me advice, a few other family members, then Jeannine, and finally Laura, Greg's wife, but no one else.

I was very nervous moving into a spotlight and stepping up to speak out against Scientology, but then I would think of Lisa, Laura Bashaw, Jeannine, and her family. I would calm down and know this was the right choice. I would remember the night the angels came and the peace and solace they brought with them. I knew, in some way, I had protection and that protection allowed me to survive. As a survivor, I needed to speak for those who no longer could speak. I felt I had to speak the truth and only the truth and not get pulled into saying Scientology was no better or worse than I thought it was.

July 11

    Well, I did decide I am going. I'm in the airport with a ticket to Tampa. I leave in an hour. I have been going back and forth and up and down this past week. Yes, no, maybe, then finally yes. The lawyer said let's see how things go and then he said, "Come, come today—come now." I am very much wired and high-strung and nervous, and I go from "OK, I'm going, no problem" to "What the hell am I doing?" How can I risk this, how can I risk my mental health, my family, and my life?

    I want to.

    I don't want to.

    I'm peaceful and happy about it.

    I'm crazed about it.

    I want to go ahead. I want to go backward.

    I want to take it back, duck for cover.

    Just forget about it, let it go, let it all go.

    So I'm going, no turning back now.

    Talk about emotional—this is a ton of emotion, just a pile, a bucket of conflicting feelings.

    Excited.

    Scared.

    At Peace.

    Parts of myself are flying off in many directions.

    Parts of me want to get out of here. "RUN!" they say. Seek safety. Seek some shelter.

    DUCK—duck and cover, crawl back home.

    We, all the scattered parts of myself, have to do this. We need to do this together. Islands of clarity, clarity, focus, strength in numbers, closure.

    I will have the power.

    On this day, I will not be ignored. I will not be ignored.

    Greg will not be ignored.

    He will not be cast aside. Jeannine, who lives, will speak. I will let it be known that she lives. I am alive, and I will have some power this day. I will speak for kindness and compassion. I will speak for love. I will speak for those that can't.

I arrived at the Tampa airport and was met by Atty. Ken Dandar and his associate. We drove to Jesse Prince's house where I was welcomed by Jesse and his lovely girlfriend Dee. Jesse had been a high-ranking member of the Sea Organization before he left sometime ago. It was already late, and there was no time to talk.

That was where I was able to read the letter that Greg Bashaw told me about. The one he had sent to the head of the Flag Service Organization just weeks prior to his death

I had not read it since his death, the timing of Greg's communication gave me strength and made me feel like wherever Greg Bashaw had moved on to, he was here with me now. It gave me the courage I needed for the witness stand tomorrow. Funny, but neither Greg nor I were nearly as upset about being driven crazy as we were about being abandoned by the very group that we had given our all for years and years.

Reading Greg's letter reinforced my belief that I was on the right path, that come what may, I needed to speak and I would be protected from repercussions. There was a lot of synchronicity in my reading of that letter on that night. It reminded me of our talks on the phone and made me feel that I had still had support from him.

The next morning, Ken picked me up early to go to the courthouse. I was so nervous. I was going numb; my fear was pounding very loud in my head. Ken and I saw the Scientologists and their attorneys arriving at the courthouse. They carried boxes and boxes of material on carts with them. I knew that they had only known since yesterday at 5:00 PM about my arrival and I had no idea what they were able to pull together about me overnight. I kept making myself take deep breaths.

Ken and I spoke briefly in the legal library above the courtroom and then he left me while he did other things. He would, he said, be back to get me. I noticed I was pacing. I hadn't paced like this since I was crazy. I checked around in my head, and no, I didn't feel like I was going nuts again. I was simply filled with so much nervous energy that I had to get it out in some way. I kept checking the clock and pacing up and down the stacks of books. I recognized a Scientology attorney on the other side of the library reading at a table. I made sure not to pace in his area. I didn't want them to know how scared I was. The minutes were moving so slowly on the clock.

At times like this, my husband, Chris, says to find a way to think about what it will be like twenty-four hours from now. "Time will march on, and in twenty-four hours, this will be over. You will get through this. Just take it a moment at a time, and you will get through it."

I attempted to follow his advice as I paced quietly in the section of the library where the Scientology attorney could not see me.

Court began with some court business. Then Ken requested I be put on the stand in the middle of someone else's testimony. After a few protests from the Scientology lawyers, I was allowed to cut in.

Note: What follows are excerpts of my testimony and some of my thoughts as the day unfolded. The entire testimony is freely available on the Internet.

MR. DANDAR: Okay. The Plaintiff calls Nancy Many.
THE COURT: You may proceed.

NANCY MANY

Being first duly sworn or affirmed, was examined and testified as follows:

DIRECT EXAMINATION BY MR. DANDAR:
Q: Please state your full name and spell your last name.
A: Nancy Many, M-A-N-Y
Q: And currently you're a resident of what state?
A: California.
Q: Okay. And at what point in time did you make a decision that you would testify in this case?

A: Pretty much decided Saturday morning, but didn't actually tell you until Sunday.

Q: Okay. What is—what is your date of birth?

A: 12/10/52.

Q: And what is the extent of your education?

A: Scientology or regular?

Q: Regular.

A: Well, I'm back in College now. I had two years before I joined Scientology.

Q: Okay. And when did you join the Church of Scientology?

A: 1972.

Q: And did you join it as a public member or a staff or something else?

A: Pretty much joined the Sea Organization within a month.

Q: What was your highest position in . . . as a Sea Org member?

A: Commodore's Staff Aide for Division 6.

Q: What were your responsibilities?

> THE COURT: I'm sorry, what was that position again?
> THE WITNESS: Commodore Staff Aide for Division 6. I was LRH's assistant for the International Marketing and expansion of Scientology

BY MR. DANDAR:

Q: . . . and when you say "LRH", you're talking about Mr. Hubbard himself?

A: Yes.

Q: And did you ever work for a section called the Guardian's Office?

A: I was a volunteer for the Guardian's Office in the Boston area in '74, I think.

Q: How many years?

A: About two.

Q: Okay. What types of things did you do for the Guardian's Office?

THE COURT: That does seem to be a little far removed from this case; 1974 to 1976?

MR. DANDAR: It's all predicate, Judge. I'll show you . . . I'll show you the connection real soon.

THE COURT: Alright.

A: I did basically undercover work, pretty much what a Private . . . what I feel a Private Investigator would do. In fact, my husband at that time was a Private Investigator and it wasn't that much different.

People would work at companies, myself included. If things came up about Scientology, I would report them. If reports were thrown in the trash, I would take them home. If reports were there that might be of interest, I would Xerox them.

THE COURT: Was this a Scientology run business?

THE WITNESS: Oh no. These were like government offices or companies.

THE COURT: Specifically, like what government offices do you remember?

A: The Attorney General's office a friend of mine was at. I was at the Consumer Council. They handled consumer complaints.

BY MR. DANDAR:

Q: And did you tell your employer you were a Scientologist?

A: No.

Q: So you were undercover?

A: Yes.

MR. WEINBERGER (Scientology Attorney): Your honor, objection. Are we going to now go through the entire Guardian . . . we hear all about this from Mr. Frank. We heard how they were disbanded. We heard how they

were thrown out of the Church, the leaders
of the Guardian's Office, by Mr. Miscavige
and Mr . . . . and others. Why are we going . . .
why is Mr. Dandar going back to 1976, when
he knows that the Guardian's Office hasn't
existed since 1981?

THE COURT: Well, because I suppose there
has been some testimony that the Office
of Special Affairs does the same things the
Guardian's Office does. You may dispute that,
but there's testimony of that.

MR. WEINBERGER: We more than dispute that.

THE COURT: I understand that.

MR. WEINBERGER: And he hasn't put on
evidence of that.

THE COURT: Sometimes your side doesn't seem
to see what I see, and sometimes his side, Mr.
Dandar's side, doesn't seem to see what I see.
It seems like that's the case. I guess that's why
you have a judge.

I think there has been some evidence to
that. Whether or not it's been . . . it certainly
has been refuted.

BY MR. DANDAR:

Q: And did you ever work for the Office of Special Affairs?

*(FINALLY! I know there are very few people in the world (if any) that
actually worked deep undercover for both OSA and the Guardian's Office,
and I was one of them. I've wanted to say this on the record for years. Every
time I would hear a Scientologist say "Oh, we do not do that anymore,"
it would feel like fingernails on a blackboard.)*

A: Well, first it was RTC and then a special mission by RTC
and then that got transferred down, because RTC was
higher than OSA. Then it got bumped down to the Office
of Special Affairs International.

Q: When did you start working for RTC?

A: Probably early '83, 1983.

Q: Okay. So when you became a public member of the Church of Scientology, explain how you were working for RTC.

A: Well, first . . . for the first six months or whatever after I stopped being on staff. After a while they did put me on the list of people that were declared. I was thrown out and . . . which means I would be shunned. But then that got corrected. And at the same time that that got corrected, some friends sent me down to RTC, that the person in charge of the mission there at that time wanted to interview me. And the first thing he had me do was go to David Mayo, who had been one of the technical heads of Scientology, had started a splinter group. And there were concerns about copyrights. And they wanted to see if I could get connected in there, which I did.

Q: As an undercover?

A: Undercover.

Q: How long did you stay working, volunteering working as a volunteer, for RTC/OSA/OSA Int?

Q: Probably two and a half years.

A: And was there any difference between the work in the Guardian's Office when it was called the Guardian's Office and the work for OSA when you were volunteering to work for them?

A: As I knew at that time? The differences were with OSA they used a lot more Private Investigators and they ran things through the attorneys. You would get like . . . there would be an operation or you would get briefed to go do something. And they would say, "Oh, we have to run this through the attorneys first". There was a lot more of that.

But otherwise in terms of the day-to-day, "Go pretend you're a friend and tell us what they're doing" or "Go here and tell us what they're doing", that was all the same. The information and the intelligence gathering was the same.

Q: So—so your activities of spying on people in the Guardian's Office was the same as your spying for OSA.

MR. WEINBERGER: Objection to the form. Could he just ask questions?

THE COURT: Sustained. She used the term "gathering information" She's not yet used the word "spying" so I don't think you ought to use it here.

MR. DANDAR: Okay. All right.

(I was frustrated . . . what did they think gathering information or intelligence gathering was, playing in the sandbox? Of course, I was spying. But at the same time, I was relieved that that hurdle had been broken. I had actually been able to put on the record someplace that there was no *day-to-day difference in the operations of the Guardian's Office and OSA.)*

Q: Did there come a point in time when you gained knowledge that there was a court order prohibiting Scientology from having anybody working for David Mayo?

A: Correct. They . . . during this time a court order that said all people . . . agents of the Church, all members of the Church, have to stay within a certain, you know . . . feet order. You know what I mean?

Q: An injunction?

A: Yes, it was an injunction.

Q: And to your knowledge, your personal knowledge, was that injunction honored?

A: Well, first I was asked to go up there. And I said: "Well, how can I go up this weekend? Isn't there an injunction? And I honestly don't remember. I know there was hesitation and a "I'll get back to you and I've got to check with the lawyers," because everything was checked by the lawyers. So whether I came up or not, I can't honestly say. But I do know that they had at least two agents in there on a permanent basis that were agents of the Church, reporting regularly to the Church, that had staff jobs there. They were there all the time. And they were left just doing their business as usual.

Q: Did they report to the attorneys or someone else?

A: No, they reported to the same person that I reported to.

Q: Was that an attorney?

A: No, it was not.

Q: What post did that person have?

A: Well, initially he was in RTC. There was an RTC Mission there.

Q: was this before OSA was formed?

A: No. This was after OSA. This was during that transition period.

Q: Okay. And then you had people that . . . from RTC who were spying on you?

A: I don't know who they were. But I would report back and people had watched me and observed me and they had reported in on what I had done.

Q: And how would you find that out?

A: I would be told by my Case Officer.

Q: Okay.

> THE COURT: In other words, you were . . . they wanted you to know that folks were watching what you were doing.
>
> THE WITNESS: Exactly.
>
> THE COURT: So they weren't hiding that from you; they were telling you.
>
> THE WITNESS: That I was being watched, but I never knew who that person . . . those people were.
>
> THE COURT: But I guess what I'm saying is you were being made aware that you were being watched . . .
>
> THE WITNESS: Right.
>
> THE COURT: . . . so that you knew this when you were making your report.
>
> THE WITNESS: Exactly.

BY MR. DANDAR:

Q: Who else did you go undercover for in addition to David Mayo?

A: A lot, actually. I would just happen into things sometimes. I went to go get a job at what I thought was a normal computer company and it ended up being someone connected with the European squirrels at that time. Squirrels are people that leave the Church but still practice Scientology.

Q: Were you undercover in that job?

A: Well, I reported it to my Case Officer and he said, "Well, go ahead and just report whatever you have". And he would then report it to the Case Officer running Europe.

BY MR. DANDAR:

Q: OKAY. Did there . . . did there come a . . . well, another operation that you participated in with OSA or RTC?

A: Well, I remember . . . I mean, like there would be like little things, like say, for example, this woman . . . I don't even remember her name . . . but she would be in deposition with Scientology all day. And then I would get a call like, "Hey, she's going to be over at this friend of a friend's house after the deposition," and I would go there just to get their reaction from the deposition.

Q: And you would go . . .

> THE COURT: I don't understand that.
> THE WITNESS: A witness . . .
> THE COURT: A witness for whom?
> THE WITNESS: She would be against Scientology.
> THE COURT: In a case?
> THE WITNESS: Yes. She was a witness in a case that Scientology was deposing.
> THE COURT: OK. She was a witness against Scientology?
> THE WITNESS: Against Scientology. And after the day's deposition, they wanted me there to get her reaction, to get some feedback.
> THE COURT: Did she know that you were doing this?

THE WITNESS: For Scientology? Absolutely not.

MR. WEINBERGER: Could we have a name?

BY MR. DANDAR;

Q: A date? Year?

A: Well it would be between '83-'84.

Q: Okay.

THE COURT: Can you tell me how . . . two questions I would have, maybe. One is; "how did you just end up at somebody's house?" I mean, normally you have to be invited.

THE WITNESS: Because it would be a friend of a friend. They knew that I knew somebody who was friends with her.

THE COURT: Okay. So you'd just try to be at . . . end up at the same place where she was . . .

THE WITNESS: Exactly.

THE COURT: And listen in?

THE WITNESS: Exactly.

THE COURT: See if she said anything, and if so, report back.

THE WITNESS: Exactly.

THE COURT: Okay.

. . .

BY MR. DANDAR:

Q: Were you volunteering for any organization of Scientology in the '90's?

A: No. I would still get phone calls, though, to do things, but I never did them.

Q: Who would you get phone calls . . .

A: Except for once, I did do one thing. After . . . I came forward with the affidavit . . . there were a few other things. I was having a lot of trouble with what was going on, truthfully.

I couldn't resolve for myself who was right, who was wrong, what side, this side . . . I mean, it was really difficult to go back and forth between people that had left the Church and then back to the people in OSA.

And it was ... I ... truthfully, I think I lost myself in there, because it gets very confusing when people are black and white, you know. I'd go to David Mayo or any of the critics, I mean, I didn't ... you know, and they would be like the Church is all bad. And then you would go to the Church, and it would be like the critics are all bad, just this ... you know, and both sides, to be honest, I think from my perspective of going back and forth, they were equally as bad. I mean, they're just ... they do things that are ...

> MR. WEINBERG: Your Honor, objection. Is there a question?
>
> MR. DANDAR: Yes.
>
> THE COURT: I don't remember what it was is this whether she had volunteered to do anything in the '90's ...
>
> THE WITNESS: So what I'm answering is, yes, I was asked to do things.
>
> THE COURT: Counsel, don't be so ... I mean ... this lady is about as fair-minded as I've heard yet. This is a lady that really thus far hasn't said anything other than both sides seemed to be equally rabid, although she didn't quite say it that way, about the other,
>
> MR. WEINBERG: I'm not quibbling.
>
> THE COURT: ... Black and white ...
>
> MR. WEINBERG: I was just asking for questions and answers.
>
> THE COURT: Well, I understand. But I found it rather interesting. It was my observation as well.

BY MR. DANDAR:

Q: Did ... when was the last time that you were asked ...

> THE COURT: When you say black and white, ma'am, that's what you mean, that they're fairly stuck on their position?

WITNESS: Exactly. I call it black and white thinking: all good, all bad. And I saw that because I did have that experience of going back and forth.

THE COURT: And the Church felt like the anti . . . their critics were out to hurt them and they were all bad, and the critics thought that the Church was all bad and out to hurt them.

THE WITNESS: Exactly.

THE COURT: And nobody wanted to waver off of that.

THE WITNESS: Exactly, exactly. And my very last thing before they pulled me into the court case to do an affidavit was a weekend with this woman who had been LRH's personal PR, and she . . .

THE COURT: What is a PR.

WITNESS: Public Relations. But she was his personal. Right?

THE COURT: His personal Public Relations person?

WITNESS: and she . . .

MR WIENBERG: Are we back in the 80's, ma'am?

THE WITNESS: I'm sorry. We are in '85. We're in 1985. And she . . . before I had a weekend with her, I was given a briefing, because that's normally how it works. And they brief you on these various different things. It's just individually, it had taken a toll on me, what side was what. And I remember in the briefing being told things that I felt I shouldn't know.

BY MR. DANDAR:

Q: SUCH AS?

A: Personal, private, intimate things about this woman.

Q: Such as?

A: Sexual practices.

Q: And why did you spend the weekend with her?

A: I had befriended her. She was somebody that I had never been close to her when we were in the Sea Org and she had actually been quite a not-nice executive. I thought she had hurt several of my friends. And I thought it was a little over the top to go testify and be LRH's personal Public Relations Officer and then go testify against him. I did not have any qualms about spying on her.

But through this weekend, this woman actually gave me a way out, which was a third kind of view of it, which was not black-and-white thinking. And it was . . . it actually ended up being quite a gift for me, that woman.

And after that weekend with her, I did not report in to OSA. I would not report on that woman. And within a week, I was pulled in to make an affidavit.

Q: Do an affidavit about her?

A: No. It was about the David Mayo case, which I didn't understand really, why . . . I mean, it was an affidavit and I was a potential witness, but I really didn't have the knowledge of that particular case.

Q: Okay.

A: And during the year when I was pretending—there's somebody called an FSM, which is your bridge between you and Flag Services International Organization, and mine FSM's name was Barry. And even during this year he would call me every couple weeks and say, "Hey, Nance, how are you doing?" And I would say "Okay", because I was in my be normal time. And he would say, "Well, call me if you need me" . . . click.

> THE COURT: I'm sorry, this is a real . . . this is a
>   real person?
> WITNESS: A real person.
> THE COURT: And this is a part of the . . .
> WITNESS: . . . of the services.
> THE COURT: . . . the services

WITNESS: And he would do this. And this was his
job to make sure I got good service. So finally
after about a year of this periodic phone calls
and me pretending "Everything is fine. Bye."
And he says "call me if you need me," and I
said", "there was one time that I really needed
you and I called you and you were not there".

And he told me that he had tried and
OSA INT told him that they had it under
control . . .

MR. WEINBERG: Objection, hearsay, Your
Honor.

WITNESS: . . . and for him to stay out of it.

THE COURT: The objection is overruled.

MR. WEINBERG: Because it is not hearsay?

THE COURT: Because I overruled it.

MR. WEINBERG: I know, but for the record . . .

THE COURT: Because I don't have to tell you
why. I overruled it, Counselor.

A: He told me that he was told to stay out of it but then he
never called me again after that conversation.

BY MR. DANDAR:

Q: Did anyone ever offer you the Introspection Rundown?

A: At one point, I actually packed my bags because I thought
I was going to go, you know to have a formal baby watch.

Q: Is that what they call an Introspection Rundown, a baby
watch?

A: Well, a baby watch would be kind of part of it.

Q: Okay.

A: Yes that would be the step for somebody who is
hallucinating. You now, you don't do the other steps.

Q: What is involved in the baby watch?

MR. WEINBERGER: Personal knowledge, our
honor? Is she . . .

THE COURT: It's about as personal as it gets, I assume. She was there.

MR. WEINBERG: No, She said she wasn't on one.

THE WITNESS: Only a light one, a muzzled one. It wasn't a formal baby watch, no.

BY MR. DANDAR:

Q: Within your 20 years and the highest on the bridge that you can go, do you know what a baby watch is?

A: A baby watch is when . . .

(Loud sound.)

THE COURT: Who threw that?

MR. WEINBERG: I just put it on the desk.

THE COURT: Well, I hope it wasn't thrown, Mr. Weinberg . . .

The remainder of the morning session covered several other topics. These were things that had happened between me, Greg Bashaw, and Jeannine, which are covered elsewhere in this book. There was a point about Greg Bashaw's family that I wanted to say but was not allowed.

We took a break for lunch. I was still pretty wired and did not eat very much. During our morning session, I had made it a point to look at the Scientology lawyers in their side of the courtroom, both to show I had no fear and that I acknowledged that they existed and were part of this process. After lunch, the hearing continued with Mr. Dandar still asking me questions. He only had a few more things to ask me and then it was Mr. Weinberg's turn to examine me. I will not deny I was a bit nervous at this time.

As it turned out, I really didn't need to be. Mr. Weinberg kept trying to say that my speaking with Arnie Lerma and Kim Baker and others on the Suppressive Persons List would prevent me from getting any help from the church and could have contributed to my going crazy.

Arnie Lerma and Kim Baker had nothing to do with my confusion. In fact, as stated clearly in the morning session, I was confused by my work for RTC and OSA and going back and forth between those diametrically opposed ideas. Also, the honesty I got from Gary Klinger in letting me know that the horrific things the "other side" had been doing had really been done by Scientologists. In other words, the critics of Scientology were not lying. The OSA mantra of "We have changed now, we know that wasn't right, and we just want to fix it all now" continually worked on my hope of things improving.

Mr. Weinberg's attempts that this had been brought down upon myself were ridiculous. Being a Scientologist does not mean one has to be a true believer all the time; it means that when there are doubts, one seeks out help, which I had clearly stated by going to the ethics department at both Celebrity Centre International and the Advanced Organization (AOLA) and then later tried to take up the help offered by both RTC and OSA.

He insinuated that they hadn't helped me once I had gone over the edge and that that was due to my communications to suppressive people like Arnie and Kim Baker. If this was a true statement, it demonstrates a complete and willful neglect when I had come to them in my dire time of pain.

He also erred by asking me one of those questions you shouldn't ask if you don't already know the answer.

> Q: You have never met David Miscavige, have you?
> A: Yes I have.
> Q: What, back in the early '80's?
> A: After the David Miscavige court case was the last time that I met him . . . I mean after the David Mayo court case.
> Q: It was a social . . .
> A: He shook my hand.

I wanted to speak of the other times I had met him, the first being in England when he was fourteen and doing the briefing course. Of course, I knew his brother Ronny a lot better because he married a friend of mine. But there were several instances over the years that David and I had crossed paths. But after not hearing what he expected, Mr. Weinberg quickly turned to asking me about another person.

Ken Dandar questioned me for almost four hours while the Church of Scientology kept me on the stand for an hour and a half. When it was over, I felt that I had maintained my integrity. I had not stooped to Scientology's level, but I had been clear about their true lack of caring for someone in severe mental distress. I had been open about the internal and well-documented policies that were used to intimidate and shudder into silence anyone who spoke out against him or her.

One of the Scientology attorneys or assistants wished me well during the break after my testimony. I was pleasantly taken aback. It was a heartfelt communication, and in that moment, I felt I had reached the humanity that I knew was on the other side. They hadn't all been taken over by Marcabians after all.

July 13, 2002

It is over, at least my part in the hearing is. I was very surprised that the Scientology cross-examined me for so little an amount of time. I don't think they knew that I was a deep-cover agent in intelligence for both the Guardian's Office and the new Office of Special Affairs. The Office of Special Affairs personnel feel very proud that they are not doing the same unscrupulous actions as the old Guardian's Office, but I am one of the few if not the only deep-cover intelligence operative that worked for both. The only difference I experienced was that OSA now gets approval from the lawyers for the special projects and operations whereas the Guardian's Office did not. Maybe they did. I don't know. The entire transcript of my testimony is available on the Internet under my name.

Dee said I got a laugh out of one of the OSA guys; she had never seen him laugh. I had been asked if I thought everyone was a Marcabian and I responded, "No, just the staff at OSA International."

I hope they offer Laura (Greg's widow) a lot of money—a lot of money so she and her son can get on with their lives.

Then she will not need to have to go through court and all that. I do want copies of my transcript; I do want them sent to Laura and Jeanine. I want them to hear how I spoke for them, for us.

July 24

Scientology International has made an appointment for my friend (who is a Hubbard family member) to a marriage and family therapist during her divorce. She said Scientology has special therapists that are approved. It was not surprising to me that Scientology would allow her to see a therapist, but they sue to defend the death of Lisa because Scientology purports to never use a professional in the mental health field. What hypocrites—so there you go—I can't testify about this because it would be considered hearsay even though I know it to be true. So life goes on.

I returned first to college in Vermont and then back home to Los Angeles. My stepson, Corey, was getting married in a couple of months on September 2. Chris and I agreed that we would not tell him I testified until after the wedding. We didn't want to give him anything to worry over before his big day. There were enough things going on with wedding plans.

August 6

Tuesday, we are in Malibu at the Malibu Beach Inn. Taylor came with us this time. I really wanted him to experience the beauty and the calm of the ocean right out the window. The ocean really does come crashing in and out here loudly.

Last night, I had to get up to go to the bathroom. I poked my head out to Taylor's room. It was around 11:00 PM. His room was dark. His TV was off, and he was sitting out on his balcony, gazing out to the ocean. I felt then that he is his own person with a vast internal life of thoughts and feelings. I hope that this trip does for him what it always does for me—allow the dust to settle. Let the water achieve clarity because the sand falls to the bottom. It usually puts things in perspective and allows my center to just arrive—to just be.

I can see him now sleeping on the pullout couch. His arms stretched back behind his head. His eyes are closed and his mouth is soft—his breathing is easy and gentle; like the waves, the breath comes, one falling upon the next. I was thinking "OK, we have to stay till noon 'cause we paid and we can," but then I realized that we could stay till we are done. Until the ocean has worked its way through us, till we are so certain of our centers that we can stand up to the onslaught of the waves of life. There is an unrelenting drive to wear us down, to shift our shapes, to erode us. However, it cannot happen; only our decorations can be eroded.

I would like to wish for many things. Mostly, I would like to wish for more of what I have or for just what I have to continue forever, yes, forever. These are good days. These are good times.

Our family has had drama and adventure and excitement, but also we have had peace, joy, love, and passions.

August 27

I heard from Lisa's attorney. He has added me onto his witness list; they will want to depose me. I am not happy about that—being deposed—but if that is what it takes me to get in front of a jury, then I will. I will get through it.

Chapter 30

Family Turmoil

COREY'S MOM WAS coming out from Tennessee for his wedding. I was looking forward to seeing her again. We had always had a good relationship, and I told her that I always appreciated that. She said that she felt the same; she would tell people how well we got along as mom and stepmom and that this would be a wonderful trip.

Ronnie had been out of Scientology for some time but had gone a different route than I had. Her husband, Randy, became one of the ex-Scientologists who believed there had been a coup within the church and that the deal with the IRS, as struck by David Miscavige, was indicative of a government takeover.

I agreed that it was very strange indeed that the current board of directors of the owners of Scientology copyrights included a person who was a former executive of the IRS, but I did not see the full-blown conspiracy that Randy apparently did.

My testimony arrived on the Internet and Randy read it. He ended up writing some very negative e-mails to both Corey and me.

Corey arrived one morning when I had just read a copy of an e-mail Randy had sent to him. Randy officially disconnected from me and forbade me to communicate to any members of his family. Then he told Corey that I had testified against Scientology. I was hysterical by the time Corey arrived at our house as I didn't want this to interfere or overshadow one of the most important moments of his life.

Corey was calm, just like his father always was in these situations. I told Corey that we were not keeping anything from him but that we decided not to tell him about my testimony until after his honeymoon. He told us that he had already known I had testified and that Bill had called and told him as soon as it happened.

I had written an earlier e-mail to Ronnie and Randy, explaining to them my decision to testify and why I made that decision. At this point, the milk was already spilt, and I wanted Corey to at least hear my reasoning. I gave him a copy of this e-mail and he read it. By now, we were a week away from the wedding and, at this point, Ronnie and Corey's half sister Paige were scheduled to fly out for the wedding. Corey's other half brothers were not able to fly out, but everything was all prepared for Ronnie and Paige.

Ronnie did have some issues. I understood that she was afraid because Corey was still connected to Scientology, and I imagine because I had just testified she thought that somehow made me suspect as well. Los Angeles is a major headquarters for Scientology and therefore there are a lot more opportunities for harassment than in Tennessee, where she and her family lived. She and her husband had already received enough ill treatment from Scientology. The Scientology operations had cost them their jobs a few years back. I'm sure the pain and fear of that was still fresh.

Corey even offered to hire a security guard for her during her time in Los Angeles to put her at ease so she could enjoy his happy day.

Unfortunately and unbelievably, on the day she was to arrive for her son's wedding, she backed out. It is so sad that she missed her son's wedding. I have yet to speak with Ronnie about the actual reasons for not attending. I know that her marriage to Randy and his anger about my testifying against Scientology must have been a factor, but I can also understand her fear.

It was a wonderful wedding. Bill was there for the Catholic service, and we hugged before he took off. I did not see his wife with him, and he did not attend the reception afterward.

Despite all the pre-wedding drama, it was beautiful and we had a great time.

December 18, 2003

I just spoke with Ken Dandar. Scientology is very intent on resolving things—settling—but they are nowhere near the ballpark of numbers that Ken needs and knows he can get from a trial. All is going to come out just fine—I know it and I feel fine with that. If things were settled right now, I would feel incomplete—I would definitely want to communicate more as to what they are doing that can harm people. I have not spoken because I want to save it for a trial if there is one; but if there is not one, then I will want to speak, to say something. I don't know what, but I know the feeling is there and is still there—the need for closure, the need to tie up all my loose ends and to come to a place of peace inside. Perhaps my posttraumatic stress workbook will hold an answer.

March 8, 2004

I'll be graduating college this year. I should have graduated in 1974, so I've taken a thirty-year detour. What did I do during those thirty years? I guess I did live a lot of life, and I put together some adventures.

I can remember when I first joined Scientology and I had an early meeting with a high-ranking member, David Light. He asked if I had any compulsions and I said writing, and he said that Scientology could handle that. I did not write for many years.

I married, had children, bought houses, went to Cub Scout meetings, and made brownies.

May 30, 2004

I found out yesterday morning that Lisa's case was settled. I am torn between two feelings. On the one hand, I have great relief I don't have to testify; I don't have to worry about all my private thoughts coming out. But on the other hand, I feel being let down about the things that won't get exposed in front of a jury and for the public record. A part of me is being let down, hurt, maybe even harmed by this.

July 6, 2004

Corey spoke with Chris the other day and asked him about his feelings about Scientology. I guess Corey is getting ready to move on to the higher levels. Chris said he was amazed nothing has come up about me with Scientology, and Corey said, "No, it had." And Chris asked about me testifying, and Corey said he heard that I was not so bad; in fact, he was told by Bill that I had helped the Scientologists' case in a way! I could not believe it. How could my testifying against them possibly be construed as helpful to them? That has to be a PR spin from Bill; it had to be, and it is really weird and bizarre. Well, I need to go off and do my meditation and then treadmill.

August 6, 2004

The trauma for me was such a huge thing. It shifted and changed me so deeply. So deeply and I fear I can never get myself back. But do I even want that old self back? I have boundaries now; isn't that a good thing? I feel it's an important and good thing. I don't know. I don't have time for the whining. I have things of my own to accomplish. I want to complete some things before I die. I want to have lived a full life.

Sometimes I feel I need to do something active *about Scientology. I cannot have them do what they did and get away with it. It is just not fair—but life is not fair, is it? Things don't always go the way you want them to. I can remember crying and having my father yell "What are you crying about? You want to cry? I'll give you something to cry about!" I think all fathers learn that line; there must be a "father school" for toughening up your kids.*

July 4, 2004

I have books to write, but my creative self has been so damaged. Scientology didn't damage Chris deep inside; they did not get to him, not to his internal self, not to the essence that is his soul.

They got to me. They were deep inside and cracked me apart. The havoc was immense. I need to make things safe for myself. I need to feel safe.

At the end of 2004, I got back in touch with an old friend from the days I had worked in Florida. Chuck Beatty was married at one time to a friend I had worked with in Boston, so the connection goes back over thirty years. He had only recently left Scientology and had only recently begun to speak of it in public and on the Internet.

Chuck had been on the Rehabilitation Project Force for over seven years. Seven years! I find that so difficult to process. I was on for several months and still carry the scars. I cannot digest the thought of doing that rehabilitation program for seven long years. He has communicated that things are better in some ways and worse in others. The food is much better. Apparently, the Sea Org has updated their policies on children and families. It turns out that as soon as you are found to be pregnant, you must make an immediate choice to either abort the child or leave the Sea Organization. Thus, there are no pregnant women within the confines of the Rehabilitation Project Force. On the other hand, it can and does go on for years now. There is no time to be with family or spouses; in fact, many people ask for a divorce when their spouse is assigned to the RPF.

September 8, 2004

I got myself all stressed out about so many things recently. Chuck Beatty's response to Kathryn's story touched me deeply. Arnie Lerma asked for an update on the Kathryn story. Then there was my conversation with Ken Dandar on my availability to testify and/or speak to the press. Chuck Beatty was on the RPF for seven years. I cannot fathom it, I really can't. In addition, he seems so not bitter. I cannot imagine being under guard, behind barbed wire, and unable to even see my husband for over seven years.

October 3

I need to get through the upcoming stressful things I have going on. I don't know. I have changed. I do not have it in me to do the day-to-day fight of a high-pressured job. I used to be up for all the challenges. I was able to push myself beyond normal limits. I could hold in my head many projects and their details at once. I had drive. I no longer have that drive. I find I easily fall off the road. I fall into ditches. I spin my wheels. I am locked into a small box of my own limitations. I no longer am the person I was. I am not that person. I do not have the strength. I have been beaten. I have been changed. I have been outwitted. I have been bested. I am a broken shell of myself. I am no longer who I was. Nancy is still in here someplace. On the one hand, I have to accept the devastation—the shattered battleground that was once a free mind. I have to mourn the loss of the executive me. I have been changed. I do not have the resilience I once had. I do not have the strength I once had. I cannot take the punches I once took. I just can't I have to accept that. I have had that breakdown associated with war. Battle fatigue. I took too many punches. That strong executive me is gone, dead, over.

I have to let go. Sometimes it is important to let things go. Sometimes it is time to let go of the oar and stop pulling, relax and find the deeper inner strength. There is an inner strength that is bigger than all of this, deeper than all of this.

October 5

I have been reading the stories the RPF Insider *posted on the Internet about the Los Angeles RPF. Not only are things in the Rehabilitation Project Force still horrific with people being treated like nonhumans, but also they actually have gotten worse. The story of that poor guy with lung cancer trapped in the RPF. Stuck in a corner with nowhere to go. I think of my friend as I watched her die from lung cancer, and I know how painful it can be. Chris spent so much less of his life involved with Scientology than I did. Some family members feel trapped because of other family members. Chris and I and Carey and Corey as well as Chris's brother, wife, and daughter are so lucky to have gotten out together. So few families make it out intact.*

I do have so much wonderfulness in my life that I am grateful for. I have people who love me, people I love, incredible children (two are now happily married), two great dogs. I finally finished college that was interrupted during my years in Scientology. Life is good. I am good. I am a good person.

November 11

 Veteran's Day is today. Things are so divided here in the country. The Red States, the Blue States.

 The religious right has hijacked the Republican Party. They scare me in the same way that Scientology scares me. The Jesus I understand to have walked the earth and preached I don't think would have approved of all this division and anger.

 I think Scientology is listening on Jeannine's phone calls. If they know she doesn't really want to file suit, she has lost her leverage. I think the phones are tapped. I think they do keep their ears open and use whatever information they find in whatever way they can.

November 12

 I have been thinking about seeing a psychiatrist, and it just freaks me out, triggers me into a flashback. Silences me. I have so much I want to say, but the jumble comes out like a logjam and nothing comes out. Not really pleasant.

 I wish I had a deep faith in someone or something to pray to or to ask direction or counsel. It is missing in my life, and I think I need that. I have a personal focus, and I have things to say and do. Also, "Good/bad, who can tell?" This is a watchword for my life. I had such turmoil in the Sea Org, but I also learned so much and got so much stronger; and those good things have stayed with me. But was the price worth it? It cost me a lot.

 There were times I felt connected, plugged in, energized. Everyday sacred. That's what I want; I want to feel the holy in the smallest of things.

 Funny, I got so upset about going to that party here in LA last night. I remember the party we had in Vermont after graduation in the hotel with Michael and Sandy and Terry. It was late. It was past my bedtime and usually I just want it to be over, but that night, I wanted it to go on and on. I was just enjoying the moment. I enjoyed being with Chris and seeing my friends and their spouses. I have not felt that pleasure in such a long time. That gave me hope and gave me a feeling of goodness and that all my pieces will finally integrate.

Chris pointed out that part of my enjoyment that night was that those people had no Scientology attachment so there was nothing to trigger me. I paid attention to that last night, and I found myself enjoying myself. Meeting new people, speaking about new things—that is good for me.

Sometimes with distance and time, we can see things so much clearer.

November 28

What was it like to be crazy? It was hell—a relentless, relentless hell. A broken mind is the worst. Paranoia—it goes beyond paranoia because you know they are there, not maybe, but for sure.

I need a higher power because this is too much for me, way too much for me. Doesn't matter if it's real; it matters that I can lay my burdens down. I can let up on the control. It's OK to have a higher power.

December 12

I am so happy to have such a good family. With lots and lots of love and care and just enjoyment of the presence of each other. I am reading Thich Nat Hahn No Death, No Fear, and he is making me feel better. Just as the five-year-old in me is different than the fifty-year-old me, so I would be in a new body with a new life, still the same, but different, makes me feel lots better.

December 31

I sent my friend, Annabelle a book and a CD. I read the Web site for her daughter Tori again last night. Once again, I felt the grief of that loss. Tori was born the same year as my son Taylor. The driver that killed Tori ran the red light, so he was clearly at fault. Yet Annabelle was able to forgive. At least she was able to not ruin his life by pressuring the judge to send him to prison. I have been taking my time this week, reflecting and planning and organizing what I want the future to look like for my family and myself. Chris and I are going to break open some champagne. We will do our list of accomplishments for 2004 and plans for 2005, right here in our beautiful master bedroom, in front of the fire in the fireplace. I am happy about so many things this morning, things to look forward to.

I will do my annual pilgrimage to the site where Scientology caused my breakdown and feel stronger and more whole. I would like to connect with a community that I feel I can support and a community that gives me support. I do have support in my life, but I would like to have a community of support.

I need to stop striving so much and start being where we want to be. Accepting the truth of it all. Envisioning myself already there. I need to keep the picture being there, not arriving there; otherwise, I will always be just arriving.

Chapter 31

Integration

THE NEW YEAR of 2005 has given me a renewed feeling of freedom. The cases and the potential cases of Lisa McPherson, Laura Bashaw, and Jeannine have all been resolved. I am no longer facing the possibility of being a witness for them in their cases against Scientology. It is the first time in many years I have not had that worry as part of my life.

The year 2004 also brought many other things to a new level. My stepson, Corey, and his wife, Mayra, had another daughter so I now have two grandchildren, Katelyn and Jocelyn. Corey is doing well enough with his work that he is able to spend a lot of time with his family.

Carey not only graduated from college but also got a full-time job as a teacher at the same Catholic high school he graduated from and has been coaching basketball for the past six years. He has a wonderful girlfriend and is working on his master's degree while saving his money to buy a condo.

Taylor, our youngest, graduated from high school, got his driver's license, and is now exploring his higher-level education and is working on getting himself focused in life.

The fall of 2004 was the first time in many years that Chris and I did not have to think of driving any child to school or other activities like soccer or high school concerts or dances. It has been such a freedom to have a complete day with no thoughts of how a child was going to get someplace. I had no idea how much time that occupied in my life until I no longer had to think of it.

January 5, 2005

I'm going to Hollywood tomorrow to do my annual pilgrimage. It is my yearly anniversary of them locking me in the room and driving me psychotic. I want pictures of that room. I don't want to engage. I just want to comfortably be there with the scene of the trauma. I want to just sit and be present. Just allow my cloudy water to settle. See what comes of that. Just having some peace of mind and taking care to get into the right place for myself. I need to bring my iPod and to have Chris's music he wrote for my journey in it. I need to bring myself fully into the present with all the things I need and want to do, taking it one step at a time. I also need to do some more writing to get this all out.

January 9

I went by Celebrity Centre International in Hollywood first. I sat in the coffee shop across the street and simply meditated and wrote in my journal. I was sitting in a warm place on a comfortable couch, sipping delicious tea, remembering so many of the Thursdays at 2:00 PM, which took place in that building across the street. I noted how hurried and frantic that life was and how my current life is not hurried and frantic at all.

I think I would like to write some memoirs of my time in Scientology for the future. I think I will feel better with them written, whether published or not. I should like to write perhaps for my grandchildren just for some time down the road. There were times working in that celebrity center was peaceful.

I allowed the memories of the years I spent in that building, both good and bad, to wash over me. When I felt I had gathered all I could, I left for the International Headquarters Building on Sunset Boulevard, the place where they drove me psychotic. It still houses the international intelligence department of Scientology.

I brought my camera. I especially want a picture of the room I had been taken to. I knew it was high up and in the back of the building.

I drove around the block and ended up parking in the same lot I had parked in when I was interrogated nine years ago. I took the pictures I wanted and then went to a pizza place directly across the main entrance to the building. I watched people dressed in their signature naval uniforms going in and out of the building. I allowed the present to mingle with my memories. Since my only experience with this particular building was the handling I received, there were no good memories for me. But watching the staff and the camaraderie between them caused other memories to drift up. I saw two women bump into one another. They were happy to see each other even though it seemed they were only passing by and had but a moment to speak. I remember that feeling of connection and community that went deep like a family. I loved people. As a Scientologist, I connected with lots of people. The common ground we had shared was large enough to relax.

January 20
Calmness came over me last night during my drive down San Diego. I am a survivor. I have my angels, my guides, my Catholic upbringing, and a childhood surrounded by nature that fed me so much.

I have come this far upon my journey; this chapter is done. I need to heal a bit more so I can move to the next phase. I have traveled and learned and paid a steep price. What to do with all of this? The words still get tangled, but the words are less frozen. I know I can do things, but now, I am still a bit too uneven or pained to be able to.

The angels, all the angels. I don't speak of them much, but they are with me, guiding me. All is unfolding just as it should.

This is just as it was meant to be. Chris, Taylor, and I were laughing the other day. Taylor should have a T-shirt that says "I survived Opposite Day."

I think all the different Nancys have finally arrived and we are ready to tell our story.

Peace. Silence. I need to take things slowly.

I had a birthday lunch with Jeannine a few months ago. She mentioned that she had read the newspaper articles regarding Jeremy Perkins from Buffalo, New York.

Jeremy was born and raised a Scientologist. A couple of years ago, he developed mental difficulties; and instead of treating him with standard therapy and medications, his Scientology family fed him megadoses of vitamins. He got worse. He eventually attempted to kill himself, and when that didn't work, he was then driven to murder his own mother. He stabbed her seventy-seven times.

We talked of how tragic that was and how both Jeanine and I escaped that route as we traveled through our own insanity. We'd also avoided the path of suicide. Jeanine reminded me of her fascination with knives while she was psychotic. Before she came to stay at our house, she had gone to visit her father with a very large kitchen knife in her purse. She said she had never felt such rage. While she was sitting and talking to him, an image of stabbing him repeatedly in the leg ran through her mind. A part of her realized how over the edge that was and she did not act on the impulse, but that is how close she came to being another Jeremy.

I remembered when I was psychotic I would be driven to do a certain thing like call someone on the phone. If the person didn't answer, my head would be a cacophony of noise and stress until another loud voice would take over and send me in another direction entirely. These little missions or errands would keep me focused and somehow eased the chaos that was my mind. Jeanine felt the same.

We spoke of Greg Bashaw and Lisa McPherson who

didn't make it back from their own psychosis and of all the others Scientology may have driven over a cliff that we don't know of and never will.

I told her of the *20/20* special I watched about Lisa's death. An expert came and explained how the megadoses of vitamins contributed to her deterioration, how none taken alone was toxic, but how the combination created a tremendous imbalance. I knew myself that I only began to get better after I stopped taking all the pills that Scientology had told me to take. Luckily, my mind had taken a weird turn and I was driven to do the opposite of everything Scientology told me to do.

It was difficult for me to think of all this tragedy and mental anguish, knowing that Scientology places itself so arrogantly above reproach. They ignore results like these. Instead, they have increased their attacks to destroy all mental health professionals. In fact, they have recently begun a program where they are assigning each of the 170,000 individual psychiatrists around the world a dedicated team of Scientologists whose purpose is to put every psychiatrist on the planet out of business. They plan to investigate each one till they find enough dirt to get them to shudder them into silence and, if at all possible, uncover crimes so they can be prosecuted, convicted, and sent to jail. Scientology might do well to realize that people in glasshouses should not throw stones.

In early 2005, Chuck Beatty introduced me to a young woman, Maureen, who was leaving Scientology. She had been through a rough time similar to mine. She had been labeled PTS type 3, which is another Scientology label for a psychotic and was then isolated from the group. She actually had her breakdown around the same time I had mine (1997), but unlike me, she was located at the international compound in Hemet, California. This is the home of Scientology's main headquarters and is replete with security cameras, barbed wire, and sensor detectors placed throughout the property. When she had her mental collapse, she was assigned to live in a small shack at the rear of the property. She was not allowed to eat with the staff because she had to be isolated from them. A security guard was assigned to bring her daily meals on a tray although apparently, sometimes he forgot to do so. The thought of being as out there as I was and being cut off and isolated, fenced behind barbed wire, resonated deeply with me.

She had joined Scientology and the Sea Organization when she was a child of fourteen so she had no real education and no way to get herself around in the real world. She needed help. When I first met her, I found that although she was mentally out of Scientology, she was physically still very much entangled with them. She had worked at the highest levels for a long time; she had been David Miscavige's personal videographer for years, so she was someone to be watched by the powers that be. Having noticed that she was having mental troubles, a friend of hers who was being overseen by the same guard once asked what was going to be done with Maureen. The security guard answered that Maureen would never be allowed to leave because she had worked with both L. Ron Hubbard and David Miscavige.

She had eventually been taken off the Hemet base and sent with two handlers to help her. In an effort to help destimulate her, they rented a cabin in Big Bear and were very friendly and nice. She watched videos, took walks, and swam in the lake; and after several months, she was adjudicated safe enough to leave the care of her two Sea Org watchdogs. She had been removed from the Hemet base on the same day the daughter of Scientology attorney Moxon had died in a tragic accident on the base in an electrical generator. It is only natural for a company or group that has suffered a tragedy to look for other potential tragedies to follow. I personally don't believe it was a coincidence that she was removed from the Hemet base the same day Moxon's daughter died.

Instead of being allowed back into the Sea Org, she was offloaded—dismissed from the service of the Sea Org. She had an assigned watcher from the Office of Special Affairs, someone who would check up on her weekly. She was directed to live in a Scientologist's house and work for a Scientologist. She had no safe point from which to grow nor did she know where to begin. She made a plea to Chuck Beatty, and he called us. Chris and I realized we needed to reach out, and we offered to help her on her journey. Maureen initially told Chuck she wasn't ready for that right now, she didnt know us, but perhaps later. Two days later 2 friends of mine came to visit me. They brought with them a woman named Maureen. The four of us talked and laughted for at least an hour before both Maureen and I realized that this was the connection he had wanted to make. A connection between Maureen and myself.

In the spring, Maureen got a new place to stay, a safe non-Scientology place. Charlie, her new landlord, called me as a reference. He asked me questions, but I could tell he had something he did not quite know how to ask. I asked him outright, "What concerns do you have about renting to Maureen?"

"Well, why is she thirty-six years old and have nothing? I mean, did she go through an ugly divorce or is something else going on?"

I answered, "Yes, divorce is probably part of it."

Then he explained that he's been renting the room out for years and that the last guy he rented to was not as he appeared. He checked his references and got a response about his last employer, but it obviously was false because right after he moved in, he lost his job and then lazed about the house. He was also involved in theft from other people in the house. "I used to feel I was a good judge of people, but after that, I don't know and I am just very careful."

"I can understand that, and I can assure you that Maureen is a good person," I said with certainty. But inside, I thought about the job Maureen had held for two years with the Scientologist that she had to leave. Then I realized that she would never become a stay-at-home bum, so I reassured both him and myself that even if for some unseen reason she did lose her job, she would get another one.

"What could have happened that she is thirty-six and has nothing?"

I realized it was better for him to know the truth and asked if he had heard of Scientology.

He said that he had bought a book once but found it so convoluted he couldn't get through it.

We laughed.

I told him that Maureen was in the process of leaving the group and her life was in transition and that there were a lot of not-so-nice things that happened to her during that time.

Thoughts of her escape attempts and her resultant mental instability floated through my mind. I wondered if he, or anyone for that matter, would ever understand the underbelly of Scientology—the secret world that very few experience and that most of those who get out are too traumatized to speak about. *Not so nice*—that's a kind way of putting it.

He answered, "You are joking, right?"

"I wish I was."

He asked what kinds of not-so-nice things, and I told him about the rehabilitation project forces where people who aren't quite with the group are sent to get their thoughts more in line.

"It's kind of a gulag or the thought-reform camps they had/have in China," I said. "I know someone who recently left who was kept in the RPF for seven years!"

I told him that I knew it was hard to believe with all those celebrities and good works they claim they are doing.

"I don't know that Tom Cruise or John Travolta are even aware of what's going on," I said.

"Or maybe they just choose not to know it is going on," he replied.

He rented her the room.

After a few weeks, Chris and I realized Maureen needed more help than we originally thought and she needed it from people who could understand what she had been through. We agreed to take her into our home and help her through her transition from the secluded world of the Sea Org to the real world. She lived with us permanently for over a year, and we became close friends. It is safe for her because we do understand both the mental and physical trauma she experienced in the Sea Org.

June 16, 2005

I was thinking about my scattered selves the other day. Maureen apologized for telling my chiropractor that I was once a Scientologist. I have been going to him as my doctor for over five years and had never mentioned that part of my life.

My friend Marion was present for the conversation I had with Maureen. Marion has been a good friend for over fifteen years. She knew that Chris and I had been Scientologists at one time, but she never knew about the rehabilitation program we endured or the escape Chris and I had made or the trauma I experienced in 1996. She felt so bad for me that even though she had been a part of our lives, she did not know and therefore had not been able to help me.

I explained to her that it was her very not knowing that had most helped me recover. She was never a part of my Scientology life, so she had nothing to trigger me with; I was able to just be myself. The crazy elements were not brought to the fore when I was around her.

The world is so much bigger than the small kingdom of Scientology. It may give the appearance of being large and having lots of power, but the truth is that in the scheme of life, it is not a major factor.

Marion and other friends, by their not knowing of my past, actually helped me gain strength in myself and in the parts of me that had nothing to do with Scientology. The friends who had no knowledge actually helped the most. When I was with them, what I had been through was a distant nightmare and it allowed me the time to get stronger, to be able to look at what happened to me in the small details.

I was able to slowly get stronger over the years and recover from the insanity by not being immersed in it.

My dear friends who felt it was their purpose to fight the fight against Scientology's tyranny were left behind or left out of sections of my life for my own sanity and healing. It was not that they were doing anything I disagreed with or felt was wrong; it was that being near them and that energy would bring that energy and many triggers into my present day life. It could be days before I could get myself back in balance.

As I sit and write this, I can feel the different parts of myself as they bump into each other. The needed integration is occurring, but it is a turbulent ride.

Trauma is not an easy thing to nail down; it slips and slides. Posttraumatic stress syndrome can attack from the lowest levels, making you feel you are not safe you just have to leave; you don't know why, but you just have to leave.

In the early years after my psychosis at the hands of Scientology, Chris would ask me to stop going to the Internet, to stop reading the posts about Scientology. It took me quite a while to realize that I did not read the posts on the Internet to participate. In fact, I hardly ever answered or engaged the participants in any way. Instead, I realized that by checking each day, I could keep track of where Scientology's attention was. Each time I heard of some attack they were fighting in Germany or Switzerland or with a government bureau, I would feel a little bit safer because I would know they were nowhere near myself or family.

I monitored them because I was afraid that they would come back and do more damage to my mind. I monitored them because it made me feel safer to know where their interests lay and to know that they weren't coming after my family or me. I was not consciously aware that this was why I was doing this for several years; I simply knew that I needed to check the Internet every day.

I also developed other fears. I found that I needed a good, stiff drink or something stronger to make it through a long airline flight. That was not too disconcerting in light of 9/11, but then I noticed that same fear seemed to spill over into other parts of my life. I found myself reluctant to go out to social functions where I would feel I would have to stay, and I avoided anything but last-minute appointments or meetings. As soon as I committed to plans in advance, I would begin to feel trapped.

Last year, I signed up for an all-day writing workshop at UCLA on the art of the sentence. I really wanted to do this class. I noticed myself choosing my usual position closest to the door. I did not think much of it because I often felt I needed to use the women's room and did not want to disturb others. About ninety minutes into the class, I was sensing a rising sense of panic, a feeling of being trapped. It did not seem to have any logic behind it. I was in a class I was enjoying, the teacher was interesting, and I could clearly see my exit. As the teacher gave the next writing exercise, I decided to use the time to dig into these feelings and discover their source. As I wrote, I found I was drawn back to that tiny, little room. I was there in one of the top floors of Scientology International—in a small *auditing room with Joan seated so as to block the door. There was a camera in the upper corner of the room, and I could not catch my breath. I felt trapped and in danger. I stayed with all of these feelings and physical sensations as they poured from my heart to the page.*

I wrote,

> Devastation—can't get out, trapped—trapped by doors, guards, and cameras. Stuck in a seat—trash can as a barf bucket—small space. Golden opportunity they had said to me. "This is a golden opportunity." Broken mind, it cracked into shards, and I slipped into hell. I remember the sound, the unforgettable sound of my cracking mind, my freefall.
>
> The shattered shards of myself. I tried to pick the pieces of my mind up the floor. I held them up as prisms to the light, wondering where in the world the Nancy who had been here a few moments ago had gone.
>
> Humpty Dumpty can't put Humpty Dumpty back together again. I looked and acted normally; she knew she did until she engaged in dialogue. She wondered if her audience could see where she was.
>
> She lived in this world from a place far away—she was alone in hell. Stuff fell from the attic of her mind.
>
> She would pause and take a step back to check for reality—did he say that, or was that imagined, real or dream? Could he see the wires connected to his head? Could he feel when they took over or was that just a glimmer of forgotten thought? I could see. I knew when they were present; I knew when they were coming.
>
> Seven years ago?
>
> Get over it.
>
> Get over it.
>
> How could they have that much power? How powerful they are. Connections—who is connected to whom? Ominous quality, the power they have over her and me.
>
> Trapped—I cannot leave, nowhere to go, even if you left, there is nowhere to go. Bridges burned.
>
> Check
>
> Check
>
> Check
>
> Checkmate
>
> They want to destroy me. I need to destroy those parts of myself.

Destroy and go back to where we were. Perhaps I can go deeper now because the levels are better.

Pressure—pressure

Squeeze it all in there . . .

Hammer and hammer

Screaming and screaming . . .

I look around the classroom at the students who have continued the lessons while I was exploring my state of mind.

After the class, when I had time to digest what I'd learned, I looked back over the years since my entrapment. I realized that about ninety minutes is the length of time I can be anywhere. I realized I have not held a full-time job since Scientology caused my breakdown. I had never thought it was because I couldn't. Just the thought of having to show up somewhere and remain there for eight hours, let alone for more days than one in a row, immediately brought up feelings of panic. I have never tried to work for someone else since I had my breakdown; I never realized that I no longer really had that choice.

It is the same with social activities. I may be invited to a party, I may love the people and want to go, but the fear of entrapment begins to rumble. This is further exacerbated if any of the guests are people who used to be members of Scientology. It is not that I do not like ex-members of Scientology; there are many that I love. It is that there is an unknown of what may come up in a conversation. I still have not mined the depths of my trauma. Most experts do not recommend digging too deeply too fast. I have no idea what is a trigger for me. It is not as simple as just saying, "Please do not speak of 'apples' for I find them upsetting." What is upsetting to me is a vast unknown tangle of triggers that I carry with me every day just under the surface. I only discover them when I experience a familiar rising tide of panic. I attempt to notice what occurred just before that so I could learn to avoid it in the future. Over the years, I have found many ways in which I change the subject, change what I was doing, or, if needed, change my location to bring balance back to my spirit.

I am giving myself time to let the trauma surface and untangle as it will. I try to live my life in the here and now. I have friends who joke about my desire to go to sleep at a regular hour every night even though that may disrupt weekend party or late-night activities. How can I tell them that this is for my mental health? How can I communicate that this is part of how I walk the balance beam? When I do attend a party and want to leave earlier than most others do, they would try to make me stay. How do I explain that I have to do this to keep my self in some semblance of balance? How do I explain that the price I pay for messing with my sleep schedule is so unpleasant? I live with the jokes because that is so much easier than telling the truth. Besides, the truth is so entangled; I would not know where to begin.

Chapter 32

Catholics and Other Organized Religions

THE POPE HAS died today. Chris and I are in San Francisco, and we stop at several churches. The first is a cathedral. As soon as I enter, I notice its beauty, but I also see that it is not Catholic. The holy water fonts used by Catholics to bless themselves before entering the church are absent from the doorways. The red candle on the altar is absent. In a Catholic church, the lit red candle represents the ever presence of God. I find some literature that tells me that this is an Episcopal church. From what I remember from my childhood teachings, the Episcopalians are the closest, along with Greek Orthodox, to the Catholics. Young Catholic children were taught that if we were ever caught on a Sunday in some location without a Roman Catholic church, then we would be allowed to attend the Episcopalian. It could serve in an emergency. Episcopalians believed most everything Catholics did, but they found they could not agree to an infallible pope.

I walked into a small chapel at the back of the church that was dedicated to victims of the AIDS epidemic. The church felt very ecumenical with recognition of the many religions that the victims had practiced. One could enter the quiet, sacred corner to light a candle and meditate on the effects of AIDS on our personal lives and on those of our fellow travelers.

I also found two labyrinths: a carpeted one located inside the church itself and a stone labyrinth located outside on a large patio with an incredible view of the city. These two labyrinths were copies of the famous labyrinth of the Chartres Cathedral in France.

There was a time in history when the Episcopalians and the Catholics were one religion. At some point, someone decided to take the parts of what they liked of Catholicism and leave the rest and start their own faction.

I thought how in Scientology these would be called squirrel groups. Scientology has vehemently attacked anyone who has attempted to splinter off from what it considers its mainstream practice. I bet it wasn't much different when the Episcopalians left the mainstream Catholics.

As Chris and I walked across the city, there were things inside several other churches that I recognized as Catholic as soon as I entered: the red light on the altar, the holy water freely available, and the statues of the saints and the Holy Family scattered about the edges. The alcoves contained tiers of candles lit for blessings or special intentions. I placed my candle in the slot that felt right. I looked at all the candles and tried to feel the prayers they represented—people in sickness, people in pain or some, just as I was—lighting them in gratitude for the chance to breathe, the chance to love. I made my prayer of gratitude and saw my candle join the others. I thought how each candle represented a person who entered and knelt here, pausing to reflect and pray. I wished them peace, crossed myself, and moved back to sit in a pew and take on the presence of the building itself and the serenity and calmness of the architecture.

I looked at the stained glass windows above and remembered the days I walked to the church close to my house in Burbank when I was flipped out of my mind. I remembered sitting in a pew, feeling safe in the sanctuary of the stained glass and burning candles. At the time, my mind was wide-open, way too far and wide-open. It felt like a funnel that traveled from the top of my head to the largest stained glass window behind me above the choir loft. Within that funnel was my wide-open mind full of many things happening at once: thoughts, feelings, random musings, unexplainable sights, and sensations. I remembered the feeling of fear bubbling up from deep inside.

I had heard two people talking about me around the edges of my huge mind funnel: a man and a woman discussing the state of my cracked-open head. There was no one present in the church besides me. I couldn't see them, but I could hear them clearly. From the tone of their voices, I felt they didn't understand what was going on with me. My level of fear rose. If these guides, from whatever place they came, had nothing to help me with my cracked mind, then what was to become of me? I felt my fear interrupt their huddled conversation. The male directed his attention to me, and I heard him clearly tell me that all would be well, that my mind was wide-open now, but that it would heal and close up. His voice was accompanied by such a feeling of comfort that I could not help but calm down. He said to enjoy this opening as best I could; it would not last forever.

I had left the church in Burbank that day, still crazy but with an internal feeling of comfort that things would not always be like this. I had been given hope.

Now I sat in a pew in a church in San Francisco. I thought of Pope John Paul who had just died. He was such a great man in some ways. He was a pope of the people with great caring for the downtrodden, outspoken against war and poverty. He was a pope who traveled around the world so that people who could not be with him in Rome could see him. But this was a pope who had his blind sides too. He did not measure up to what I considered a larger truth. He could not open himself or his church to the concept that there might be other correct ways for people to reach God than his one and only apostolic church. He did not see that women were equal to men and could lead flocks of people to the way of the Christ. He also was fixed in the view of celibacy that the church has demanded for centuries even in the face of abuse of children. He refused to allow the use of condoms, even in continents like Africa, which are being devastated by the pandemic of AIDS.

I wonder how different is this church and this leader from the Scientology that I came out of. Scientology also feels that it is the "only way" to spiritual freedom.

I remember when our recent pope went to prison and called his would-be assassin his brother. He spent two and a half hours at his side and spoke of their lives and the things that brought their lives to an intersection. This was not a public relations stunt; this pope truly believed in forgiveness.

I can't imagine David Miscavige ever doing something like that. He and the church that he currently runs do not practice forgiveness. As they have stated many times to the press, they are not a "turn the other cheek" religion. In fact, they *never* apologize even for the most horrendous mistakes they make. I have seen and experienced Scientology not as a "turn the other cheek" religion, but more of a "blame the victim" religion.

The Catholic Church did survive its Inquisition years and seems to be surviving its awful "child abuse" years. So perhaps Scientology can also grow into something more compassionate and kindly. Hope springs eternal in my heart.

I can hope for a new Catholic pope who not only continues the presence and openness of the pope who just passed, but also takes us into an era of respect for all faiths and an end to poverty, AIDS, and unwanted pregnancies. I can also hope for a Scientology that lives up to its promises of a better world.

April 6
Maureen came over for dinner last night. She saw Karen, her therapist, during the day, and she looked like a big weight had lifted off her shoulders. She has a safe place to sleep, and she told me that she realized she had been sleeping late at her other place because her

Scientology roommate would get up early and chat, asking her questions about things like her beer consumption.

Now in her new space, she woke up early and felt refreshed. She had thought she had a sleep problem, but perhaps it was just a safe space problem.

Maureen shared some stories about her life at the international headquarters in Hemet, CA. Apparently, they have instituted a card system. At the beginning of each week, a staff member is given five cards:

1. *A social card allows you to watch a movie on the weekend.*
2. *A bonus card allows you to be paid bonuses.*
3. *A pay card allows you to be paid your weekly allowance of $35-50.*
4. *A berthing card allows you to sleep in your own bed.*
5. *A food card allows you to eat with the crew.*

"What happened if you lose your berthing card?" I asked.

"You would have to sleep in a shack or on the floor or in your office."

"People could just walk up and take away your cards?" Chris asked.

"Well, mostly your senior, but yes, they would just physically take the cards."

"How often did you lose your cards?" I asked.

"Oh, all the time. That's why I have trouble sleeping in a bed because I spent so many years sleeping on the floor in my office."

She said that if they took a food card, the person would still be allowed to eat rice and beans. Unfortunately, she was allergic to rice and beans.

"They would let me have peanut butter."

Chris and I looked at each other. Thank God we both left the Sea Organization before that system got put in. Talk about control, I thought.

Before she left, Maureen and I spoke privately. She told me some of what she talked about with Karen. Maureen told Karen that she had started to feel she was a dangerous person that she shouldn't be hanging out with Chris and I and that she was dangerous and shouldn't be around regular people.

"Karen asked me why I felt I was dangerous, and I just started

crying. It was being kept isolated from the crew and under guard for five years that gave me that feeling. She understood, and I felt better for just getting it out."

It broke my heart to hear this beautiful, fragile woman feeling that she could be dangerous to others. It reminded me of when I had gone psychotic and felt that I was not good. Scientology had taken away my inner feeling of being a good person. It had been such a deep cut; I hadn't been able to talk about it for years. I looked again at Maureen and took in her dangerously low body weight and her lack of self-confidence, and I thought again of what my son Taylor had said to me. Was I in denial? Were the Scientologists truly worse than I could imagine?

I am leaving in the morning for a trip that will take me to Chicago to visit Laura, Greg Brashaw's widow. I have no doubts as to Scientology's hand in his death and in Lisa McPherson's. And here is Maureen right in front of me with the damage done to her, written all over her frail body. Taylor's words came back to me: "Mom, you are more brainwashed than you even know."

Am I? I wondered as I walked Maureen out to her car.

Chapter 33

My East Coast Spring Visit

MY EAST COAST trip finds myself drawn to talk radio as I drive through New England. It's not something I listen to on the West Coast much, but I am drawn to the familiar accents of home; and immediately I am drawn into the hot topic of conversation. Cardinal Law was the Catholic cardinal in New England when the child abuse cases by priests were uncovered. In fact, the *Boston Globe* did the original investigative reporting that uncovered what was to become an international Catholic scandal. Cardinal Law was found to have sent priests known to be pedophiles into new unsuspecting parishes; he sent them in with glowing letters of recommendations even though he knew about their previous activities with children. Catholics and non-Catholics alike were outraged about the lack of accountability that fell onto Cardinal Law. No criminal charges were placed against him. He was replaced as the cardinal of New England and transferred to the Vatican. It was felt he didn't even get a slap on the wrist. Now this week, it has been announced that he will not only vote for the new pope but be possibly considered as a candidate himself. He was also chosen to preside at one of the special memorial masses held in Rome over this next week of mourning.

Callers were incensed. The announcer called Cardinal Law a pimp. One of the callers who responded said that it wasn't right, that it demeaned the Catholic religion and was a bigoted statement. I thought of how many times I had heard any criticism against Scientology being called bigoted, and they responded by attacking the critic instead of a sane review of the issues brought to the forefront.

The announcer was very direct and polite. He stated the facts: Cardinal Law had sent priests whom he knew have been pedophiles into unsuspecting parishes, where they might molest young children again, with glowing letters of recommendation. He said if you would not call him a pimp, then what word would you use? The caller could not come up with an answer and could only continue to rant that the announcer was attacking his religion. The announcer held his ground that he was not attacking the religion but merely pointing out that the actions of one individual were clearly wrong and caused harm to innocent children and their families.

The remainder of the callers supported the talk show host and voiced their disappointment and horror at the cover-up they felt the Vatican was doing. Parishes in New England had to be shut down due to the financial burdens of restitution for the harm done by the pedophile priests. Protests and sit-ins were occurring at several closed parishes in an attempt by the members to maintain their local churches.

I thought of those protesters and how they still attended Mass, how they disagreed with specific faults of individuals and individual practices, yet still felt there were hope and goodness in the whole.

I doubted that these callers or individuals demonstrating at the shut-down parishes had to worry about their phones being tapped or their businesses being harmed or other scare tactics Scientology uses to shudder them into silence.

When I first began to read the book put out by the reporters from *Boston Globe*, which included previously unpublished documents written by Cardinal Law, I found that I had to put it down. I found one letter in particular to one woman to be exactly what I imagine Scientology would have said. A mother wrote to him that two of her sons were abused and the priest in question had also molested two more of her nephews. She was asking for his help, not for any monetary gain, but she only wanted his help so that this would never happen again. Cardinal Law answered back that while these were not good things that had happened, the reputation of the church was foremost and must be protected. He asked that she not speak publicly about this abuse because it would only harm the Mother Church and that superseded all else.

At the time, it sickened me to be reminded of all the negative things that had happened in Scientology that should not be spoken of.

When I saw the words written by Cardinal Law himself, I heard echoes in my head of the same words spoken so many times by senior executives of Scientology and, yes, even spoken by myself, and as my stomach turned over, I closed the book. I was physically unable to read any further. Is this the way of all religions and wannabe religions? Is this the way of all groups? It reminded me of a battered wife or a dysfunctional family keeping the secrets at whatever cost.

Here, the secrets were finally being spoken aloud. Changes were being made, lives being improved. The Catholic Church is, I believe, a much better church in New England now that all the incredibly dirty laundry has been aired.

I know of one ex-senior executive in Scientology who had knowledge that was possibly relevant in the death of Lisa McPherson. She so feared for her safety that she refused to come forward without a million dollars in protection and money to cover business losses.

I remember the magazine article entitled "Shudder into Silence" detailing how effective Scientology has been at silencing its critics.

Yet here we were, in Massachusetts, on talk radio where free speech is still alive and it is making a better Catholic church, a better group.

No Catholic today would say that the Inquisition was a good thing. Pope John Paul has apologized to the Jews for the centuries of persecution. It seems that the group has gotten larger and stronger by the public admission and recognition of wrong choices made or wrong turns taken and with subsequent shifts in policy and behavior.

I've always told my children that one of the largest parts of learning something new was failing at something. It was not the mistakes that were so all important; it was what one learned from them. It was acknowledging the truth and struggling to improve oneself.

May 22

I'm in Chicago now. I noticed the FBI building was near my hotel. I thought about somehow getting them to listen about the Rehabilitation Project Force and to go see it for themselves. Then I realized that most of the members, while still in the cocoon of the Scientology group, would say they were there of their own freewill. After all, Congressman Ryan went down to the Jim Jones camp, and only a very small percentage of the people took him up on his offer of a ride back home.

Yesterday I met with Laura Bashaw. I knew this would be emotional and cathartic. She is much as I expected—petite, beautiful, fair-skinned—but her hair, her hair hangs down her body to the bottom of her butt. I was impressed. I used to have long hair but had never been able to grow it that long.

She brought me some beautiful daffodils from her garden. It was so special, finally meeting her after many years of telephone talks, so much pain, and so many tears.

"Remember the clicking phones?" I asked.

"Oh, yes, every time we would talk, as if we had the bonus listeners."

"You know, after I settled with Scientology, they went away. But just recently, they have started up again."

"How recently?" I asked.

"This past week, especially around this weekend."

I took a pause to wonder about the paranoia of that. The thought that I could still be under someone's watchful eye and devoid of privacy is not a comfortable one.

I flashed to the odd person following my car at my Dad's home in Massachusetts just a few days ago. He would pull over and wait for me to pass him, and then he would follow a bit more only to pass me again and pull over to watch as I passed him. I shrugged it off as odd; it was an area filled with elderly drivers after all. Now hearing the sounds of her clicks had increased; its significance shifted, ever so slightly, in my still-unstable mind.

Chapter 34

Scientology Celebrities

R ECENTLY, TOM CRUISE has been speaking vocally and forthrightly to the press and anyone else who will listen about Scientology. Today, I read where he credited it with an improvement of his IQ and with his newfound ability to know that he can learn just about anything he sets his mind to and wants to learn.

Last month, I became concerned about Oprah. She had a run on Scientology celebrities coming into her life with gifts and friendships and, I am sure, a lot of personal chatting.

Years ago, I used to run the Celebrity Centre International first from the level of international management and then from the position of president of the Celebrity Centre International. Even after my tenure as president, I remained connected as a volunteer.

Hubbard saw early on the value of a celebrity, and I have read references dating as far back as the '50s to the desire to cater to and include celebrities. Celebrities sway public opinion and are therefore considered a significant factor in the growth of the movement.

During the '90s, I was a volunteer for them and would work with celebrities who were interested in Scientology services. I had one woman in particular, which, while not famous, was well connected to big-name celebrities. Somehow, her name found its way onto the International List. The International List was a weekly report of the status of these special people who were either targeted for membership or were already members.

When I first saw Tom Cruise on the *Oprah* show, I could tell that not only was he in love with Katie Holmes, but that this woman must also share his devotion to Scientology. Recently, press has written about Katie's many visits to Scientology centers and her participations in courses and counseling sessions. Her close friends have complained that they now cannot get through to her, and those friends who do not share her excitement for Scientology are being dropped from her life. Tom took Katie's parents on a tour of the Celebrity Centre International in Los Angeles.

I am glad he has found something that he feels has helped him. I'm actually happy he now has a love in his life that seems to share that belief system. However, I am concerned that Tom is receiving and promoting a very different Scientology than the audience listening to him would receive.

Today, I received an e-mail from a person who had read my Kathryn's story of how auditing had driven me to the depths of insanity. It also included how lucky I felt to have been able to claw my way back to a sense of normalcy. She said that listening to Tom and John Travolta made her feel that auditing was awesome. She was wondering if I knew where she could get it more cheaply, perhaps from some other location.

I am very aware of the salesmanship and manipulative abilities taught and used in Scientology. While I don't know Tom Cruise personally nor do I know exactly how he is taken care of, I have had plenty of experiences with the care and handling of other Scientology celebrities to know that they are monitored and catered to. They have special course rooms, specially trained staff, and they are kept in a bubble.

Their bubble operates a bit like the film *The Truman Story*. Most of the celebrities are not aware that the offers of assistance and help come with a price. If a celebrity is having difficulty with a personal assistant, the offer of help in finding an effective replacement is seen as some welcome aid. In this way, the celebrity gradually commingles more and more of his personal life with these special services offered by the Scientologists.

I've been told by someone who was part of it, that when Tom Cruise was given a tour at the base at Hemet, it was all set up for him. Staff was stationed at various places with walkie-talkies alerting his next stop on the tour of his imminent arrival, and the staff was to be at their places ready to do their "scenes." They had practiced this for several days prior to his actual tour. I wonder if Tom knows of the abuse, the rehabilitation project forces, or the screaming and sometimes physical abuse the staff is reportedly subjected to. It is very possible he doesn't have a clue. Most celebrities are given Scientology in a well-controlled, perfect bubble.

All Scientologists are given a policy early on about writing knowledge reports on each other. It is expected that all "good" Scientologists will write reports on any perceived or suspected behavior that is not in keeping with the standards of Scientology. In this way, the Scientologists can be kept in line or at least be guided ever so gently and ever so subtly to stay with the mainline membership.

People who bring the celebrity any negativity about Scientology will find a hard time getting through to him or her. If they do make it into the inner circle, handlings will be arranged to get this person out of the celebrity's life.

There are people within the Scientology celebrity network whose job is to do nothing but run interference and slowly create the dedication that would lead a celebrity, like Tom Cruise, to risk everything to forward the group that he believes in so strongly.

Celebrities are specifically named and targeted so that they are introduced to Scientology radiantly and are handfed with the appropriate information and assistance till they reach a point of becoming a fully committed member.

I remember when Tom Cruise was first involved in Scientology and I was one of the few who knew. Someone leaked that information to a tabloid reporter. The amount of pressure and interrogation that was undertaken to find who had leaked the information was enormous. The pressure to locate the culprit came from David Miscavige himself. It has been a long road from Tom being quiet in his pursuit of Scientology to the Tom Cruise who now is so vocal and focused. I may not know all the ins and outs, but I'm sure that many man-hours of Scientology Sea Org staff went into the planning and hand-holding that created that end result.

Chapter 35

Scientology and Me Today

IN EARLY JULY 2005, I e-mailed Laura, Greg Bashaw's widow, and asked if she would be willing to speak out, if she felt she were ready. She referred me to Greg's sister, also named Laura. Greg's sister and I got in touch and spent time catching up on each other and talked about Laura's vulnerability and the struggle she has had to go through.

During our conversation, my phone started clicking again so much so that Laura mentioned it. She said that that used to happen all the time with Laura's phone when she was working on legal actions against Scientology.

It gave me pause. I too had noticed incessant clicking of late. Are they tapping my calls? Do they have a private investigator with one of those long-distance machines able to listen to my conversations in the privacy of my home? It is easy to get paranoid, and of course, there is an immediate adrenaline rush of fear. However, as I take my time to analyze it, I find that it is a flimsy field of energy. I have nothing to hide. They know who I am. I have given them numerous opportunities to communicate with me like normal people.

I am not out to destroy them or to shut them down. I simply want them to be truthful and to stop mentally harming people and degrading them in work camps they call the Rehabilitation Project Force.

I have two areas in which I feel a need to speak out and do what I can to help, those held in the RPF, and I need to do whatever I can to prevent any more people from entering the type 3 zone of Scientology, psychosis, and to help those that do fall off that cliff. I have many things I want to do with the rest of my life that have nothing to do with Scientology.

In August, I went to the Immaculate Heart Retreat Center in Montecito. I had heard of this place over the years as an excellent place for a spiritual retreat. Montecito is a breath south of Santa Barbara and has the same cool ocean breezes. I didn't know much about the sisters of the Immaculate Heart, but I do know that a developer recently offered them 50 million dollars for their property and they refused. It is their home and sanctuary for the many thousands of souls who come there to rest, rejuvenate, and recover their spiritual center.

The nuns who built this retreat center originally broke away from the archdiocese after a difficult time in the early '70s. They opened up their community to men and opened up this retreat house to people of all faiths. They found that Catholicism was true for them, but they did not have to bow down to the patriarchal control that had always been there. They splintered, yet held on to what was most true for them, to what was at the core.

In my small room, I had a statue of the female goddess of Buddhism. The room was decorated with several crosses and the beautiful art of Sister Corita, who lived her life as an artist and nun within these walls. I went there to work on the writing of this book. I find that in its openness, it helps lead to so many roads of the spiritual and it touches that same self that was moved during those conversations with Abigail way back in 1986. My spiritual journey continues, but I am now comfortable with the paradox. I am comfortable that my relationship with

God and the universe is so personal that it may never fit inside one structured group of believers. I find I can now hold many of the beliefs of different religions all at the same time.

Personally, I always felt Scientology was more of a business, and I learned a tremendous amount how to run businesses as a result. When I joined, we were not called churches, but simply Orgs, Scientologese for organizations.

Early on, in one's involvement with Scientology, a person was (and I think still is) offered an FSM (field staff member) course for free. It trained him how to bring his friends and family into the group and established that the Org would pay a 10 or 15 percent monetary commission for every dollar that these new prospects paid into Scientology. There were many times during the course of Dianetics and Scientology where people could, did, and still do make a very good living off simply disseminating Scientology and Dianetics and collecting their commissions.

During the course of this book, I interviewed many people including sociologists who specialize in new religious movements. My key question was this: Could you name me one religion that took all newcomers, trained and drilled them as salesmen to bring even more new members in, and then actually pay them 10-15 percent of all income generated by that new person? The answer was a resounding *no*. I asked if they knew of *any* religion at all that trained their registrars, salesmen, or proselytizers utilizing a high-powered textbook on sales? I have yet to hear a positive answer to that question.

I remain befuddled by the term "Fixed Donation". This oxymoron came into use after Scientology won its final battle with the IRS. Tithing—donating 10% of your income has always been a part of a lot of religions. But it is considered a true donation, the services you receive as a member of that community do not change simply because your 10% happens to be higher or lower than another member. Scientology has a menu of services with prices attached, no matter what dollar amount your tithe is, you will not receive that service until your donations have met the price charged for the service.

I personally feel that Scientology could be a religion. It has a spiritual base of help and self-help that it could construe as a religion and act like one. I also feel it could just as easily be a business where commissions and bonuses are paid on a regular basis on income earned for services delivered. The services could easily have fixed prices for certain self-betterment and counseling.

It is not considered a religion in all the countries of the world at this time. I think it will be interesting to watch how it shifts and grows over the coming years. I simply want to watch from the balcony.

Chapter 36

The Visitor

IN SEPTEMBER OF 2005, my husband answered a knock at the door. After hearing a bit of the conversation, I joined Chris on the porch of our house. Eugene Ingram was visiting us on behalf of Scientology's lead attorney, Elliot Abelson. Eugene has been the mainstay of Scientology's private investigation team since 1982. He said that they were doing an investigation into a friend of ours, Tory. It was a prelitigation investigation prior to filing libel and slander charges against her. Tory had recently been speaking out to the press.

My husband had been answering him in quick and simple monosyllables—yes or no. I realized that Chris had no idea who was standing on our porch or who the referenced attorney was. This was not some simple $40 an hour private investigator. This was their head investigator, the very one that had been working with them to gather information to destroy potential witnesses for years. Chris also didn't know the meaning of the attorney's name upon whose behalf he was on our front porch.

I knew not only because of my readings on the Internet, but also because of my days as a deep-cover spy for Scientology. Eugene Ingram may have never known of me as deep-cover agent's identities were very protected; but I knew of him, and I knew the actions that private investigators were taking on behalf of Scientology back in the '80s.

Eugene said that they were investigating Tory to see if they could find out who was funding her. "By the way you have a nice house here," he added.

We couldn't help but laugh out loud at that. As far as we knew, Tory worked very hard for her money and didn't get help from anywhere. I told him truthfully that I had been out of town most of the past summer and Tory and I had not been in touch, but he could tell me what kinds of things they were exploring.

"For example," he said, "if Tory was working with reporters and she publicly said Scientology had asked her to do illegal things and they hadn't, that would be libel."

"But if Tory *had* been asked to do illegal things that wouldn't be libel, then would it?" I rebutted.

We danced around that for a little bit.

"No, it wouldn't," he finally admitted.

I assumed he had already been fully briefed about me and my background long before he came out to our house; that briefing is usually included when they do one of these "stir up the bushes" activities. But maybe, he hadn't.

I told him Tory and I had known each other from mutual friends. I told him that after she left Scientology, we reconnected. I let him know that I had been an undercover agent for the Guardian's Office in the '70s and then more recently for RTC and OSA International. In fact, I had been one during the '80s when he was just beginning his time working for them. I wanted him to know that I did know of some of the illegal and immoral things he and others had been involved with.

"If we wanted to serve you guys for deposition, where would we do that?"

We told him they could serve us right here. We work at home and our phone is in the book. We shook hands before he left.

When Maureen heard who it was at the door, she said, "Oh, if I had known it was him, I would have come out and joined you. He is well respected in the hierarchy of Scientology. He's gotten awards and medals for all the suppressives he has helped destroy. And he would know me too; we sat next to each other at a couple of events."

I found out he paid one other visit that day to another friend of Tory. He threatened her business (she works with high-profile celebrities), and she slammed the door in his face. Both this friend and I had spent many years in the Sea Org, working with celebrities; perhaps that was why we were singled out.

The visit threw me back into a mental quagmire for a while. The timing was especially critical because I had just spent the previous weekend fleshing out the first chapter of this memoir: "The most awful day of my life." I had just written about things I had never really allowed myself to view in their totality; there were some parts of that day that had never been shared with anyone.

I was very proud of myself. It took me only four days after Ingram's visit to feel that I had rebalanced myself back to my center. The pieces of my self are finally coming together, and I stand tall and certain in the belief that I will be whole and all the stronger for it.

Chapter 37

Where Are They Now?

Lisa McPherson

HER CASE WAS settled with Scientology for an undisclosed amount of money. She is resting in peace.

Laura and Greg Bashaw

Greg Bashaw did not make it and also is resting in peace.

Laura had a very difficult time of it for quite some time. She settled with Scientology for an undisclosed amount of money. She has taken back her incredible artistic talents. She has pieces hanging in some prestigious buildings in Chicago. She has recently remarried and is starting a new chapter of her life.

Maureen

Maureen is now recovering from both the emotional and the physical situations she left the Sea Org with. She is now enrolled in college, seeking a degree in finance.

Jeannine

Jeannine has almost gotten past her physical and emotional difficulties, and she is pursuing a new career.

Myself

I continue to heal and am very happy with my life and family. We live in a large Tudor house behind a black wrought iron gate with a basketball hoop in the front yard. I finished my bachelor's degree that was interrupted by Scientology. I am pursuing a career in writing.

Appendix

Why I Remained
High Control Groups And Cults
The Social Dynamics

IN RECENT YEARS I have been finding and learning of studies in the social sciences in an attempt to understand how an organization could get someone like me to commit some of the unethical and/or immoral things I did. In her book "Opening Skinner's BoxL Great Psychological Experiments of the Twentieth Century" Lauren Slater summarizes and compiles in one volume some of the most groundbreaking experiments in social psychology. These experiments, in many cases, have caused us to re-think human behavior. I found I could relate in some way to almost all of these experiments, yet it was the "Stanford Prison Experiment" I felt directly related to my experience as a member of a high control group.

The "Stanford Prison Experiment" was a social experiment done in the early '70s. It was meant to be a two-week study but was forced to end within 6 days. This exercise was conducted on 12 average college students. They had all undergone psychological testing and were found to be normal. At random, the originating sociologist, Philip Zimbardo, chose six people to be prisoners and 6 to be guards. He had the Stanford Police "arrest" the prisoners and enter the system as any other prisoner would. The end results, forcing the early termination, were astounding.

I had studied the "The Stanford Experiment" before, but this new book by Phil Zimbardo, "The Lucifer Effect: Understanding How Good People Turn Evil" added enormous detail. The Guards took on their roles seriously and within 5 days were involved in a degrading treatment of Prisoners. Five of the kids chosen to be prisoners experienced emotional breakdowns. It could clearly be seen that institutions have a lot of power to change human behavior. What I did not know until Zimbardo wrote his recent book was that he was not the one that stopped the experiment. His fiance' and now current wife came to visit him on the fifth night, saw what was going on and said "What are you doing?" Zimbardo could not see the brutality himself because he was already too deep into his chosen role of Warden and lost his exterior view of his sociological "experiment". He could not see clearly what was happening.

More recently, Zimbardo has acted as a consultant to one of the arrested soldiers in the recent Abu Ghraib prison torture. He never denied the culpability of the individuals involved but was certain to bring up the lack of oversight and structure. In his recent book he states "Aberrant, illegal or immoral behaviour by individuals in service professions, such as policemen, corrections officers, and soldiers, are typically labeled the misdeeds of "a few bad apples". The implication is that they are a rare exception and must be set on one side of the the impermeable line between evil and good, with the majority of good apples set on the other side. But who is making the distinction? Usually it is the guardians of the system, who want to isolate the problem in order to deflect attention and blame away from those at the top who may be responsible for creating untenable working conditions or for a lack of oversight or supervision. Again the bad-apple dispositional view ignores the apple barrel and its potentially corrupting situational impact on those within it. "A systems analysis focuses on the barrel makers, on those with the power to design the barrel."

Zimbardo isolated 7 social processes that grease the slippery slope of evil. I found myself in all of these seven steps, to a greater or lesser degree. They are:

1) Mindlessly taking the first step.
2) Dehumanization of others.
3) De-individualization of self (anonymity).
4) Diffusion of personal responsibility.
5) Blind obedience to authority.
6) Uncritical conformity to the group's norms.
7) Passive tolerance of evil, through inaction, or indifference.

In hindsight, I can see each one of these points were present in the apple barrel of Scientology that I lived through.

Acknowledgments

THERE ARE NUMEROUS people I would like to acknowledge for their support and encouragement during the very difficult task of going back to some dark places in my past to get this book written. They do no want their names used, but they know who they are, and my appreciation is deep and well known to them. I would like to thank Jeferson Hawkins for both his Cover designs and other help along this road. I want to acknowledge Bernice Mennis, Ben Bashore for their personal help over the years. There is much I can say about Vermont College, but the simplest is that they gave me the environment, freedom and courage to study what I needed to write my story. I would like to give Chuck Beatty a special thanks because it was his fearlessness in speaking out and encouraging others to get their stories out, that made speaking out begin to feel safe.

The majority of names in this book have been changed at the request of the individuals, but the events are all true and supported by my memory, documents, notes, medical records as well as conversations with other people who had been present at the time.

Sometimes memory is not exactly the same as fact, but I do want to be clear that the events I write occurred and are the truth as I have seen, experienced, been part of, or done myself. My thoughts are those I had at the time the experiences were occurring. Future events, circumstances, or more knowledge may have changed those opinions, but I have written the truth to the best of my ability as it unfolded.

I am very thankful to Greg's widow, Laura Bashaw, to Jeannine, and to Maureen who have been most open with me and have allowed me to use their real names. I never knew Lisa McPherson personally, but since my breakdown occurred weeks after her death, I cannot help but acknowledge that while our care after our breakdowns were similar in some ways, different in others. My care allowed me to live and to now speak for myself and all the others who have suffered mental turmoil while members of this group.

Suggested Further Information/Assistance

Windhorse Assistance:

AS DESCRIBED IN this remarkable story, the Windhorse Therapy process is a comprehensive approach for people with complex life and mental health recovery needs. While helping people live in as ordinary a way as possible, an individually tailored recovery environment is created for each client, addressing their needs in whole person manner. A key element of potency in this approach, both in it's view and in the experience of the clinicians and program graduates, is that no matter how severely confused a mind has become, recovery is possible. If you are interested in learning more about the Windhorse approach, please see the following resources:

Windhorse Books:

"Recovering Sanity", Edward Podvoll,
Shambhala Publications, 2003
"Brilliant Sanity": Buddhist Approaches to Psychotherapy,
Francis Kaklauskas, Susan Nimanheminda, Louis Hoffman,
MacAndrew Jack, Rocky Mountain Press, 2008

Windhorse Services:

Windhorse Community Services, Inc. Boulder, Colorado
www.windhorsecommunityservices.com

Windhorse Associates, Inc. Northampton, Massachusetts
www.windhorseassociates.com

Thesis:

"Compassionate Perspectives on Psychosis", Ben Bashore, 2000
Copies available directly from Ben at *BENBSOL@hotmail.com*

Books Regarding Sociological Studies:

"The Lucifer Effect: Understanding How Good People Turn
Evil", Philip Zimbardo, Random House, 2007

http://www.Prisonexp.org—The Stanford Prinson Experiment

"Opening Skinners Box: Great Psychological Experiments
of the Twentieth Century", Lauren Skinner, WW Norton &
Company, 2004

Web Sites of Interest

www.mybillionyearcontract.com
www.Scientology-cult.com
www.xenu.net
www.forum.exscn.net
www.exseaorg.com
www.LeavingScientology.WordPress.com
www.TampaBay.com—Search for recent exposee "Truth Revealed"
http://Forums.whyweprotest.net
www.lermanet.com
www.cs.cmu.edu/~dst/secrets

Official Scientology Web Site: *www.Scientology.org*

For Someone Safe to talk to: 1-866-XSEAORG